TEXT✗ET

Studies in comparative literature 9

Series Editors
C.C. Barfoot and Theo D'haen

CONRAD
Intertexts & Appropriations

Essays in Memory
of Yves Hervouet

Edited by Gene M. Moore
Owen Knowles and J.H. Stape

Rodopi

Amsterdam - Atlanta, GA
1997

This volume has been produced with assistance from
The Yves Hervouet Research Fund at Lancaster University
for Anglo-French Relations.

The paper on which this book is printed meets the requirements
of 'ISO 9706:1994, Information and documentation
- Paper for documents - Requirements for permanence'.

ISBN: 90-420-0218-2

Contents

Notes on Contributors

HUGH EPSTEIN is a teacher in London and the Secretary of the Joseph Conrad Society (U.K.). His essays on Conrad have appeared in *The Conradian*, *Conradiana*, and *Conrad's Cities*.

AMY HOUSTON, a graduate of Edinburgh University, completed an M.A. in Performance and Drama with a stage adaptation of *Lord Jim* and is currently studying law.

SUSAN JONES completed a D.Phil. thesis on the novels of Marguerite Poradowska. Her essays have appeared in numerous Conrad volumes, including *The Conradian*, of which she is currently Reviews Editor.

PAUL KIRSCHNER, the author of *Conrad: The Psychologist as Artist* (1968) and of numerous Conrad essays, has also edited *Typhoon and Other Stories* and *Under Western Eyes* for Penguin Books. With Owen Knowles, he helped to prepare *The French Face of Joseph Conrad* for publication after the death of Yves Hervouet.

OWEN KNOWLES is Senior Lecturer in English at the University of Hull and the author of *A Conrad Chronology* (1989) and *An Annotated Critical Bibliography of Joseph Conrad* (1992). A former editor of *The Conradian* and co-editor of *A Portrait in Letters: Correspondence to and about Conrad* (1996), he is currently co-authoring a *Joseph Conrad* volume in the Oxford Author Companions Series. With Paul Kirschner, he helped to prepare Yves Hervouet's book for posthumous publication.

HANS VAN MARLE is a Contributing Editor to the Cambridge Edition of the Works of Joseph Conrad, for which he is currently co-editing *Suspense*. He has also co-edited *An Outcast of the Islands* for Oxford's World Classics, and is currently assisting with *The Collected Letters of Joseph Conrad* and with the *Joseph Conrad* volume in the Oxford Author Companions Series.

GENE M. MOORE is Lecturer in English at the University of Amsterdam. The author of *Proust and Musil: The Novel as Research Instrument* (1985) and editor of *Conrad's Cities* (1992) and *Conrad on Film* (1997), he is currently co-editing *Suspense* for the Cambridge Edition of the Works of Joseph Conrad and co-authoring the *Joseph Conrad* volume in the Oxford Author Companions Series.

J. H. STAPE, currently Visiting Professor of English at Kyoto University, Japan, has taught in Canada, France, and Singapore. He is editor of *The Cambridge Companion to Conrad* and co-editor of *A Portrait in Letters: Correspondence to and about Conrad* (both 1996), and has co-edited *An Outcast of the Islands* and *The Rover* for Oxford's World's Classics. His other publications include *Angus Wilson: A Bibliography, 1947-87* (1988), *An E. M. Forster Chronology* (1993), and an edition of Virginia Woolf's *Night and Day* (1994).

A Bibliography of Works by Yves Hervouet

French Linguistic and Literary Influences on Joseph Conrad, Ph.D. thesis, University of Leeds, 1970.

'Conrad and Anatole France,' *Ariel* 1 (1970), 84-99.

'Joseph Conrad and the French Language, Part One,' *Conradiana* 11:3 (1979), 229-51.

'Conrad's Relationship with Anatole France,' *Conradiana* 12:3 (1980), 195-225.

'Joseph Conrad and the French Language, Part Two,' *Conradiana* 14:1 (1982), 23-49.

'Conrad and Maupassant: An Investigation into Conrad's Creative Process,' *Conradiana* 14:2 (1982), 83-111.

'Conrad's Debt to French Authors in *Under Western Eyes*,' *Conradiana* 14:2 (1982), 113-25.

'Aspects of Flaubertian Influence on Conrad's Fiction, Part One,' *Revue de littérature comparée* 57:1 (1983), 5-24.

'Aspects of Flaubertian Influence on Conrad's Fiction, Part Two,' *Revue de littérature comparée* 57:2 (1983), 185-207.

'Why Did Conrad Borrow So Extensively?' *The Conradian* 9:2 (1984), 53-68.

The French Face of Joseph Conrad (Cambridge: Cambridge University Press, 1990).

The Legacy of Yves Hervouet: An Introduction

Paul Kirschner
London

> Le devoir et la tâche d'un écrivain sont ceux d'un traducteur.
> —*Proust*

I have just been re-reading a letter I received from Yves Hervouet some twenty-six years ago. Its origin was chance. I had read an article in the journal *Ariel* identifying many translated passages from Anatole France woven by Conrad into his own work. Some of them I had recently pointed out in my book, of which the author of the article seemed unaware. Since *Ariel*'s editor had also co-edited the series in which my book had appeared, I wrote to him about the coincidence, and he passed on my letter to Yves, from whom I presently received an earnest and friendly reply, giving the history of his research on the French influences on Conrad, which as a Frenchman he had found 'fascinating and rewarding.' After reading my letter, he had hastened to read my book, and it seemed to him that at times we had been 'covering the same ground.' He wound up flatteringly: 'In the light of your own major contribution to French influences on Conrad I hope that one day you would be interested to read my findings.'

Naturally I said I would (little guessing how that would come about). I also assured him that our aims were different. I had been trying to give a coherent picture of Conrad's ideas on human nature, and although I did wish to fit them into a continental literary tradition I had had no time to pursue an exhaustive study of French influences for their own sake.

Yves found the time, despite a teaching burden probably inconceivable to his counterparts in France. Over the years I read his articles in *Conradiana,* but we did not correspond. Then, in 1984, I met him, for the first and last time, at a conference of the Joseph Conrad Society at the Polish Cultural Centre in London. Yves gave a paper entitled 'Why Did Conrad Borrow So Extensively?' throwing a very human light, I thought, on Conrad's predicament writing in a third language.[1] He was clear, too, in the way the French used to be clear. Unfortunately, during his talk he used the word 'plagiarism,' provoking an angry reply from a refreshingly unacademic Polish woman who took it as a slur on Conrad's honour. Yves

---

[1] This paper was published in *The Conradian* 9:2 (November 1984), 53-68.

was baffled: nothing had been further from his intention. I recall trying to smooth things over by saying idiotically that the word 'plagiarism' was less pejorative in French than in English, but I succeeded only in eliciting the Polish woman's grateful outburst: 'Thank you for defending Conrad.'

In fact, the dreaded word had long proved a stumbling-block to understanding Conrad's literary method. I had carefully avoided using it in my book, only to have so eminent a critic as Ian Watt ascribe it to me ten years later, prompting my reply that I considered the term 'plagiarism,' implying an intention to deceive, too harsh to describe Conrad's creative use of passages from Maupassant and Flaubert.[2] To hear Yves similarly misunderstood cemented the bond I had already begun to feel with him. He impressed me as being no career-minded academic frantically seeking the right buttons to push for promotion, but a disinterested truth-seeker with a passion for ideas. He looked fit and youthful, and I was shocked later to learn that he was being treated for a spinal tumour. He died within a year.

Before then, however, we grew closer. He sent me the typescript of his nearly completed book for comment. I liked both its style and content, and made some sixteen pages of notes which I duly forwarded. Yves answered ecstatically: no one, he said, had read him as I had. Some of my suggestions he staunchly rejected; others he adopted, always trying to be objective and placing the quality of his book first, in the knowledge that it would soon be all that remained of him on this earth.

We spoke by phone a couple of times; I remember trying to persuade him to come to Charing Cross Hospital, but he resolutely stuck to Lancaster. Then came a letter saying he was going downhill fast but still working. His last phone call was unforgettable. He began by telling me to pay no attention if he began to weep (he didn't), since it was a side-effect of his medication. He then asked me to keep and 'look after' his typescript, adding that he regarded me as an 'elder brother' (thus becoming my only sibling). I suspect, though, that I was not the only one to whom Yves appealed on behalf of his book.

The appeal was irresistible. At the next Joseph Conrad Society conference in London, soon after Yves's death, some of us gathered to decide what to do with the surviving typescript of well over 500 pages. A reader for Cambridge University Press had made editorial suggestions, but asked who would do all the work, prudently adding, 'Not me.' Ultimately Owen Knowles and I shared the task.

---

[2] Paul Kirschner, 'Some Notes on *Conrad in the Nineteenth Century*,' *Conradiana* 17:1 (1985), 33.

I found it absorbing, but stressful. Cambridge wanted the text cut by 30%; Dr Lindsay Newman, Yves's long-time assistant and literary executrix, loyally defended every word she thought he would have wanted left in. I felt caught in the middle. There were also internal stresses in the book itself (though Yves never thought so). On the one hand there was a dragnet for every Conradian phrase of possible French origin—and in leaving no stone unturned, Yves had inevitably turned up a good many pebbles. On the other hand, there was the more discriminating aim of underpinning the 'appropriations' (to use Yves's term) by æsthetic theory, expounded in a monumental chapter on Flaubert. These related but distinct projects, as well as its copious quotation of corroborating criticism, gave the book, for me, a rudderless feeling. It was only at the end that, leaving other critics aside, Hervouet delivered in his own right a lucid reply to the troubling questions raised by the crushing weight of his evidence.

To me this was the most interesting part of his book. It stressed that 'originality can only be relative,' that 'there can be no influence without ... kinship in psychological and intellectual make-up'; and that 'an artist chooses his influence,' guided by what Valéry happily called 'ce qui veut croître en nous.'[3] Conrad's mimetic powers derived from his linguistic situation and his concept of fiction, which involved 'aping' native speakers and writers:

> Thanks to his amazingly retentive memory, Conrad must have gleaned a vast pool of phrases and sentences from his immense English reading, and this habit may also explain many of his borrowings from, and allusions to, French writers.   (*H* 225)

As Thomas McFarland wrote of Coleridge, for Conrad another writer's exact wording was 'some sort of talisman that allayed his anxieties' (*H* 223). More importantly, Conrad's own reference to the historical part of *Nostromo* as 'an achievement in mosaic' gives the key to understanding his imagination 'as an integrating faculty, ... the shaping and unifying power' (*H* 232), working with literary materials the way a mosaicist works with gems and precious metals. Summing up Conrad's method as 'autonomy in terms of the general design of the work, with heavy reliance on countless models in its crafting' (*H* 230), Hervouet dismissed the irrelevant charge of plagiarism ('the one issue of real interest is not so much the material the

---

[3] Yves Hervouet, *The French Face of Joseph Conrad* (Cambridge: Cambridge University Press, 1990), 228-29. Future page references will be found in the text, preceded by *H*.

author has used as what he has done with it' [*H* 229]) and invoked T. S. Eliot's definition of poetic originality as 'largely an original way of assembling the most disparate and unlikely material to make a new whole' (*H* 232).

These conclusions make his book appear retrospectively not as a chaos of clear ideas (that famous definition of the French mind) but as four interwoven achievements:

1) the accumulation of all previously published material, clearly attributed, concerning Conrad's use of French writers. This unique thesaurus not only strengthens the case but provides a chronological guide to the slow academic recognition of how Conrad worked, vindicating findings at first ignored or dismissed. I owe Yves a personal debt here. When in 1968 I published extensive material on Conrad's 'borrowings,' Rayner Heppenstall, reviewing my book in *The New Statesman*, breezily made clear that he hadn't bothered to read it, saying I had 'spread myself' on French sources such as Victor Hugo, to whom I had made a single passing reference, while remaining mute about the fifty-odd pages I had devoted to Flaubert, Maupassant, and Anatole France.[4] Ten years later, Ian Watt downplayed the significance of the French material, saying that Conrad 'forgot that he was remembering' yet paradoxically adding that he was 'perhaps too proud to own up to what he owed'—a good example of critical embarrassment at the subject.[5]

2) the unearthing of new evidence far exceeding what I and others (notably Owen Knowles) had discovered. For instance, I had pointed out Conrad's use of several passages from Maupassant's *Fort comme la mort* to describe the Heyst-Lena relationship in *Victory*.[6] Hervouet went to the manuscript of *Victory* and found that Conrad had at first used Maupassant far more extensively, translating almost verbatim a whole paragraph of the analysis of Olivier Bertin's love for the Countess de Guilleroy, nearly all of it omitted from the printed text (*H* 126). This not only showed conclusively that Conrad had deliberately used Maupassant's text as a scaffolding to construct his own, but suggested that he had afterwards as it were dismantled the scaffolding, inadvertently leaving a few pieces behind. I had speculated that Conrad might at times have had Maupassant

---

[4] Rayner Heppenstall, 'Eena Major Minor Mo,' *The New Statesman*, 20 December 1968.

[5] Ian Watt, *Conrad in the Nineteenth Century* (Berkeley: University of California Press, 1980), 50.

[6] Paul Kirschner, *Conrad: The Psychologist as Artist* (Edinburgh: Oliver & Boyd, 1968), 193-98. Future page references will be found in the text, preceded by *CPA*.

on his desk (*CPA* 204, 227); Hervouet showed Conrad's practice to have been systematic beyond anything I had imagined.

3) the underpinning of this practice by a detailed study of Flaubertian æsthetics, portraying Conrad as one of the main literary links between turn-of-the-century France and England. Yves also explored Conrad's affinity with the scepticism of Anatole France, and provided a directory of intellectual relations between Conrad and a whole range of French writers, thereby anchoring him much more firmly in Europe than anyone had done before.

4) the removal of the taboo of plagiarism that had so long prevented understanding of the true nature of Conrad's originality, thus paving the way for a methodology to reveal new layers of meaning in Conrad's texts. For as Hervouet points out, Conrad did not usually try to dissimulate his sources; sometimes, indeed, he invited awareness of them (as in the ironic counterpoint between *Crime and Punishment* and *Under Western Eyes*), while at other times he may have 'appropriated' unconsciously. Five levels of 'appropriation' may be distinguished:

a) the probably unconscious taking of French phrases having no relationship to a deeper theme, e.g., the phrase 'shudders testifying to the most atrocious sufferings' used to describe Nostromo's death, appropriated from Maupassant's story 'Hautot père et fils' (*H* 94);

b) the probably conscious use of a phrase to express or describe emotion from a different but similarly emotional situation, e.g., Natalia's 'It is impossible to be more unhappy' from Mme de Renal's parting from Julien in *Le Rouge et le noir* (*H* 107), or Decoud's being reminded by all his sisters' girl friends of Antonia 'by some faint resemblance or by the great force of contrast' from the description of Madame Arnoud's effect on Frédéric Moreau in *L'Éducation sentimentale* (*CPA* 188-89; *H* 89);

c) the conscious elaboration of a thematically related scene by appropriated details not intended to be identified by the reader, yet, when known, illuminating, e.g., James Wait's death, where the source—the dying Duroy's terror at the priest's visit in *Bel-Ami* (*CPA* 200-4, 107-8; *H* 39-41)—helps to make clear what galvanizes Jimmy into going on deck and precipitating a near-mutiny, thereby implying a parallel between Podmore's religious fanaticism and Donkin's seditious agitation as twin dangers to human survival;[7]

---

[7] The implication is supported by Conrad's remark to Edward Garnett in 1914 apropos of Tolstoy: '... the base from which he [Tolstoy] starts—Christianity—is distasteful to me. I am not blind to its services but the absurd oriental fable from which it starts irritates me. Great, improving, softening, compassionate it may be but

d) conscious adaptation of material throughout a story to a different design that becomes still clearer when we know the source, e.g., the combination, in a moral framework, of Maupassant's 'Les Sœurs Rondoli' with autobiography in 'A Smile of Fortune' (*CPA* 220-29; *H* 112-17);

e) consciously intended intertextuality, inviting recognition by *cognoscenti* of the source, e.g., the interviews between Mikulin and Razumov, imitating those between Porfiry and Raskolnikov.

As Goethe observed, to understand the poet we must go to 'poets' country'; and Conrad needs to be read as we read a poet. This implies 'spotting' other writers in his texts, either from coincidental prior reading or from reading that is inspired by Conrad's own non-fictional writings, letters, or biography, which broadens our historical, linguistic, and political horizons beyond cultural or academic insularities. In this sense, Conrad is not only a '*puissant rêveur*'[8] but a *formidable éducateur*.

The following essays are in themselves perhaps the best way of paying tribute to Yves and his book.

---

it has lent itself with amazing facility to cruel distortion and is the only religion which, with its impossible standards, has brought an infinity of anguish to innumerable souls—on this earth' (*CL*5, 358).

[8] From Gustave Kahn's review of a French translation of 'Karain,' cited by Conrad in *A Personal Record* (London: Dent, 1946), 111.

Conrad's Debt to Marguerite Poradowska

Susan Jones
St Hilda's College, Oxford

Most critics of Conrad associate Marguerite Poradowska with the role of providing moral support for the apprentice author. The widow of a distant Polish cousin, Poradowska indeed provided Conrad with friendly encouragement in the early stages of his career as a writer, but she has occupied a peripheral place in accounts of Conrad's literary life because she has been identified solely with an emotional and financial contribution and not with any creative input. Conrad's fellowship with distinguished writers and men of letters like Stephen Crane, Ford Madox Ford, John Galsworthy, Edward Garnett, R. B. Cunninghame Graham, Henry James, and later André Gide, has thus been privileged in comparison. The critical emphasis on these 'literary' relationships with men has contributed to the endurance of Conrad's strongly masculinist image.

Yet his close relationship with Poradowska, herself a writer of fiction, with whom he corresponded frequently during the period of his transition from sailor to author, offers evidence of one of the strongest female influences on his career. Conrad's letters to Marguerite Poradowska reveal a depth and intimacy that dispel any doubts about his empathy with women. But while Poradowska's personal encouragement of Conrad is well documented, her creative influence has gone unrecognized.[1] In drawing attention to the French influences on Conrad's work, critics have engaged in a canonization of sources, emphasizing the importance of his borrowings from famous male writers such as Gustave Flaubert, Anatole France, and Guy de Maupassant. They have overlooked the possibility that a less highly rated female author of French romance fiction (which Conrad is known to have read) might also have offered him creative inspiration. Yves Hervouet, for example, in his otherwise exhaustive catalogue of Conrad's allusions to French literature, occasionally cites the correspondence with Poradowska,

---

[1] Although he does not specifically suggest a literary influence, Gene M. Moore has written on the significance of Poradowska's novel *Yaga* from a historical point of view. See his 'The Colonial Context of Anti-Semitism: Poradowska's *Yaga* and the Thys Libel Case,' *The Conradian* 18 (Autumn 1993), 25-36.

but mentions none of her fiction, referring to her as a close friend rather
than as a literary figure in Conrad's life.[2] Likewise, in *A Preface to
Conrad*, Cedric Watts includes a section entitled 'Short Biographies,'
specifically citing the literary influences of Flaubert, France, and Maupassant. The entry under Marguerite Poradowska refers to her simply as a
'prize-winning writer of tales and novels' who 'doubtless encouraged him
to persevere with *Almayer's Folly*.'[3]

Yet throughout his career, Conrad drew on a variety of sources, constantly responding to the methods of both popular and 'highbrow' fiction.
And while Conrad was disparaging about other contemporary women
writers such as Sarah Grand, Margaret Louisa Woods, and Marie Corelli,
he constantly praised Poradowska's romances, even after the period of their
most intimate correspondence.[4] Her work dealt, however superficially,
with the struggles of religious and political factions in rural communities
of partitioned Poland, subjects of personal interest to the displaced Conrad.
Her novels stimulated his interest in the plots and situations of romance,
beginning with *Almayer's Folly*, and provide evidence of a considerable
creative impact that extends also to Conrad's later fiction, when he turned
more frequently to the genre of romance.

Poradowska was already a well-established author when Conrad first
met her. Her romances drew on her experiences in Galicia, in the Austrian
part of Poland, where she had lived during the early months of her marriage to Aleksander Poradowski. She published fiction in the internationally
respected journal *Revue des Deux Mondes* in Paris, as well as French translations of Polish writers, including Henryk Sienkiewicz, in Paris and
Brussels. She was the only living writer known to Conrad as he worked on
his first draft of *Almayer's Folly*, which he had begun in 1889. Shortly
after their first meeting, Conrad took his manuscript and a copy of
Poradowska's novel *Yaga* (1887) with him on a visit to Poland.[5]

---

[2] *The French Face of Joseph Conrad* (Cambridge: Cambridge University Press,
1990), 10-11, 220-21, 237-38.
[3] *A Preface to Conrad* (1982; rev. edn. London: Longman, 1993), 204.
[4] See Frederick R. Karl and Laurence Davies, eds., *The Collected Letters of Joseph
Conrad* (Cambridge: Cambridge University Press, 1983-), vol. 1, 185; vol. 2, 137; and
vol. 5, 213. This eight-volume project, of which five volumes have appeared to date,
will henceforth be abbreviated *CL*.
[5] See letter to Poradowska, 14 February 1890, *CL*1, 39. *Yaga: esquisses de mœurs
ruthènes*, was serialized in the *Revue des Deux Mondes* 82 (1 and 15 August 1887) and
published in book form by Ollendorff (Paris) in 1888.

After Poradowski's death, Marguerite and Conrad corresponded frequently in French, meeting occasionally in Brussels or in Paris, where in 1891 Poradowska took an apartment at 84, rue de Passy. They shared both personal and professional confidences until 1895, after which no letters are known to exist before 1900, when the tone of their renewed correspondence loses its emotional intensity. By this time Conrad had married and settled in England, and Edward Garnett had become his main correspondent about literary matters. While critics have made much of a possible romance between Conrad and Poradowska, they do not always acknowledge the importance of the intellectual aspects of the relationship, and tend to overlook the fact that his first *literary* friendship was with a woman.

Conrad's intimacy with Poradowska developed rapidly through the correspondence conducted during his trip to Africa in 1890. She had helped Conrad to secure the post in the Congo that would inspire *Heart of Darkness*,[6] and in April of that year he acknowledged her assistance as a gesture that 'touches me more than I can express' (*CL*1, 48). In his letters to her from Africa he surmised that an imaginary 'other' self, a 'secret sharer' remained behind with Poradowska. In mid-May, for example, he wrote: 'Heureusement il y a un autre moi qui rôde de par l'Europe. Qui est en ce moment avec Vous' (*CL*1, 50). His former apathy about his destiny had been replaced by an interest in her: 'ça me fait oublier les petites misères de mon chemin a moi' (*CL*1, 54).

His sense of a strong feminine presence accompanying him to the Congo creates a vivid contrast with Marlow's presentation of the European women of *Heart of Darkness*, who are categorically 'out of it.' Unlike the Intended, who hovers on the novella's periphery, and from whom Marlow withholds knowledge of Kurtz's experiences in Africa, Poradowska received, in Europe, a detailed account of Conrad's journey. In late September he appealed to her in confidence: 'Je Vous charge par tous les dieux de me garder le secret de ma santé devant *tout le monde*' (*CL*1, 61). Far from representing the passive, ineffectual white women of *Heart of Darkness*, Poradowska was acknowledged by Conrad as a successful writer who lived at the centre of European culture. In the same letter from Kinshasa he refers to her prize-winning novel, *Demoiselle Micia*: 'J'apprends avec joie Votre succès a l'academie dont—du reste—je n'ai jamais douté' (*CL*1, 59).[7] Cedric Watts's claim that Poradowska's chief

---

[6] For an account of Poradowska's intervention with Albert Thys in Brussels on Conrad's behalf, see Frederick R. Karl, *Joseph Conrad: The Three Lives* (New York: Farrar, Straus & Giroux, 1979), 282.

[7] *Demoiselle Micia: mœurs galliciennes* was first published in the *Revue des Deux*

influence on Conrad was that 'she was evidently a model for the Intended'
(204) seems inadequate in the context of Conrad's response to her in his
letters from Africa.

The earliest letters show an instant rapport, yet are characterized by
a greater formality than the modern reader might expect. Translation cannot
adequately render the idiosyncrasies of Conrad's French: 'J'étais avec Vous
de pensée et de cœur hier partageant, qoique loin de Vous, Votre douleur
comme du reste je n'ai cessé de le faire depuis que je Vous ai quitté' (*CL*1,
36).[8] The letters contain frequent grammatical and spelling errors, like
'qoique,' but often convey an expressive overflow of feeling that belies the
almost ritualistic formality of their mode of address. Throughout the period
of their most prolific correspondence, Conrad continued to write to Poradowska as 'Tante,' a gesture not only of respect, but one that positioned
him in a specifically unthreatening relation to her: that of a younger, less
experienced family member.

Conrad's emotional involvement with Poradowska during his change
of career was complex. The tone of the letters is intimate, but often tinged
with awe for the accomplished woman who was ten years his senior, show-
ing the admiration of the novice for the successful professional. We must
remember that Poradowska was the first person to whom Conrad proposed
a joint authorship. In late July 1894, he tentatively suggested the possibility
to his 'chère Maitre': 'nous aurions pu peut-être faire paraître Almayer pas
comme traduction mais comme collaboration' (*CL*1, 164). Later, in August
of the same year, before hearing that Fisher Unwin had accepted his first
manuscript,[9] Conrad again pursued the idea, this time asking her to translate *Almayer's Folly*, but offering her full acknowledgement as author and
proposing to reduce his own identity on the title page to the letter 'K'
(*CL*1, 169).[10] The letter confirms Conrad's profound lack of confidence
in his position before he secured Unwin as his publisher, but may also
indicate his indebtedness to Poradowska for her creative inspiration as he
persevered with his first novel.

Mondes 90-91 (1 and 15 December 1888; 1 January 1889) and in book form by
Hachette, 1889.

   [8] For an extended discussion of Conrad's French, see René Rapin's essay 'Le
Français de Joseph Conrad' in *Lettres de Joseph Conrad à Marguerite Poradowska*
(Geneva: Droz, 1966), 15-53.

   [9] See the letters of 4 October 1894 to T. Fisher Unwin and to Poradowska, *CL*1,
176-78.

   [10] Conrad wrote that 'K' represented the Malay word *kamudi*, meaning 'rudder,'
but it might also suggest his family name, Korzeniowski.

The early letters offer an intriguing opportunity to observe some of Conrad's earliest epistolary 'rehearsals' of later fictional themes. At the most profound level of exchange Conrad encouraged Poradowska to explore an inward vision, the growth of knowledge through the spiritual adventure that occupied the lives of his male protagonists: 'Elle est si humaine, Votre lettre, dans cette douleur de tous les commencements. ... C'est l'hesitation du seuil, de degout des choses neuves, l'incertitude du noir ou on tatonne du pied avec effroi' (22 October 1891; *CL*1, 99). Again, in a letter of early November 1893, we recognize the isolation of consciousness perceived by the individual who is projected into the darkness of insecure psychological states: 'Il me semble que je n'ai rien vu, que je ne vois rien, que je ne verrai jamais rien' (*CL*1, 130). We might think of the painful encounters with the abyss expressed by Marlow in his journey to the 'heart of darkness,' of Jim in his fateful leap from the *Patna*, or Razumov's confession to Natalia Haldin in *Under Western Eyes*. We are most familiar with Conrad's 'rehearsals' of his fiction from much-quoted letters to Garnett and Cunninghame Graham; but he also wrote to Poradowska of moments in which 'l'âme sans guide roule dans un âbîme' (23 March 1890; *CL*1, 42). In early November 1893 he expressed his own sense of isolation: 'Je jurerais qu'il n'y a rien que le vide en dehors des murs de la chambre ou j'ecris ces lignes' (*CL*1, 130). Three years earlier, in mid-May 1890, Conrad had summed up a view of life that recurs in the experiences of Almayer and Willems, the protagonists created during the years of his most intimate correspondence with Poradowska: 'Un peu d'illusion, beaucoup des rêves, un rare eclair de bonheur puis le desillusionement, un peu de colère et beaucoup de souffrance et puis la fin' (*CL*1, 50).[11]

These letters point to a paradox in Conrad's work. As he fixed the energy engendered by this kind of emotional conflict in his male protagonists, he initially found an attentive response to his own sense of moral and psychological despair in a woman. (Not until the creation of *Chance* [1913] did he place an isolated female protagonist at the centre of the

---

[11] Edward Said has suggested that Schopenhauer's influence on Conrad's evocation of the 'abyss' may have come through the work of Ferdinand Brunetière, in particular 'La Philosophie de Schopenhauer et les conséquences du pessimisme' in the 1892 collection *Essais sur la littérature contemporaine* (see *Joseph Conrad and the Fiction of Autobiography* [Cambridge, MA: Harvard University Press, 1966], 102). This was not necessarily Conrad's first encounter with Schopenhauer, but it is of interest here since Poradowska sent Conrad copies of the *Revue des Deux Mondes*, of which Brunetière was editor, and in which he published his work.

narrative.) Yet the tone and content of these letters is by no means uniformly philosophical. Conrad's voice expressed cross-currents of emotional honesty, gentlemanly decorum, and playful didacticism tempered occasionally with an astonishing departure from traditional nineteenth-century attitudes to women, such as his petulant objection, on one occasion, to Poradowska's excessively dutiful behaviour towards an elderly aunt. In early March 1892, he reprimanded her severely for her self-effacing actions, suggesting that her position bordered on the 'dangerous' rather than the worthy: 'l'abnegation poussée dans ses lointaines limites ... devient non pas une faute mais un crime ... cette tendence dormante de l'humanité vers l'hypocrisie dans l'être ... bienveillant' (*CL*1, 106). Here Conrad's voice shifts from that of the decorous male admirer—'Je Vous dis tout cela car je Vous aime beaucoup, Vous admire immensement'— towards a more radical form of address in which he entered into a dialogue of impassioned and rigorous frankness.

Conrad's formal voice leaves us with the sense of a private and intensely intimate ritual being enacted within these letters, a voice that partially conceals a dialogue of equal integrity. Perhaps the formality of the letters created a medium for handling a developing intimacy with an older woman. Whatever Conrad's intention, it failed to mask the sense of reciprocity that had been quickly established at the relationship's outset. Marguerite's immediate acceptance of his friendship after her husband's death had provided a lifeline for the displaced Conrad as it had for her. She represented for him the only living link (albeit by marriage) to his family outside Poland. With first-hand experience, she could accept both his Polishness and his status as an *émigré*, while he also understood her sense of isolation and could share her grief for the departed. At the same time, Poradowska provided the initial and fundamental link to the literary world that Conrad now entered.

Critics have been reluctant to associate Poradowska's fiction with Conrad's work, since her somewhat florid prose now seems dated and over-written. The first editors of Conrad's letters to Poradowska, for example, were baffled by Conrad's enthusiasm for her work.[12] Yet, as Conrad continued to work on his first novel, his relationship with Poradowska flourished with a frequent exchange of ideas and discussion of her novels, moving towards a serious professional correspondence. With a formal gesture, Conrad sent her the first page of the manuscript of

[12] John A. Gee and Paul J. Sturm, eds. and trs., *Letters of Joseph Conrad to Marguerite Poradowska 1890-1920* (New Haven: Yale University Press, 1940), xvi.

Almayer's Folly in late March or early April 1894, accompanied by the decorous comment, in reference to the manuscript of her novel *Marylka*: 'Cela Vous est du puisque j'ai vu le Votre.—J'aime a me conformer a l'etiquette, moi' (*CL1*, 151).

He paid minute attention to Poradowska's fiction, reading and re-reading *Yaga* not twice but at least three times, and later recommending the novel to literary friends.[13] On his voyage to Australia in the *Torrens* he urged her to send him her most recently published work: 'Joujou' or *Popes et popadias*.[14] He seemed most favourably impressed by Poradowska's descriptive abilities, claiming in early April 1892 that 'Vous possedez le coup d'œil de l'auteur—qui voit les traits qui echappent a la vue de gens dont le metier n'est pas d'observer leur semblables' (*CL1*, 109). In February 1893, he wrote that *Popes et popadias* was 'rempli des traits charmants—d'observations fines,' praising her particularly for the 'atmosphère' she had created for her characters and the 'paysages que Vous avez peints' (*CL1*, 123). He complimented her by suggesting that 'Dans la ... saisissante simplicité de vos descriptions Vous me rappelez un peu Flaubert' (*CL1*, 109).

On the rare occasions on which Conrad used Polish themes in his fiction, we can hear echoes of the style in which Poradowska describes the expansiveness and the extreme contrast in the physical landscapes of rural Galicia, Podolia, or the Ukraine, which form the backdrop to most of her narratives. Discussing her novel *Marylka*, Conrad wrote in February 1895: 'il y a l'espace, le souffle du vent dans Votre description des champs ukrainiens. C'est etonnant! Vous n'avez jamais été la?' (*CL1*, 201). Her romantic style conveys a sweeping panorama of the winter plains at night:

> Novembre! Il gèle à vingt-cinq degrés Réaumur ... Sur la steppe infinie, blanche comme un linceul, s'étend un ciel d'un bleu métallique criblé d'étoiles cristallines ... le vent siffle, le vent se déchaîne, ce vent terrifiant qui vient de Sibérie.[15]

---

[13] Conrad is probably referring to Garnett in his letter to Poradowska of [14 or 21 November] 1894: 'L'autre samedi j'ai passé la soirée avec un de mes amis. Nous avons causé de tout un peu—et nous avons causé de Yaga. Il connait le livre mieux que moi. Nous nous sommes rappelés des scènes qui nous ont empoignés nous avons querrellé la dessus—et nous avons en maint endroit admiré avec une touchante unanimité' (*CL1*, 187). He also recommended *Yaga* to Ford in May 1900 (*CL2*, 267).

[14] 'Joujou' appeared in the *Figaro illustré* of 29 July 1893 (*CL1*, 119n3, 120); *Popes et popadias* was published in the *Revue des Deux Mondes* 114 (15 November and 1 December 1892), and in book form by Hachette (Paris) in 1893.

[15] *Marylka*, in *Revue des Deux Mondes* 127-28 (15 February, 1 and 15 March 1895), 128: 160.

Conrad may echo this juxtaposition of images of mortality and cosmic infinity in his setting for the French army camp in 'The Warrior's Soul': 'the boisterous north wind had dropped as quickly as it had sprung up, and the great winter stillness lay on the land from the Baltic to the Black Sea. One could almost feel its cold, lifeless immensity reaching up to the stars.'[16] In fact we might speculate that Poradowska was a model for Tomasov's French lover in this story. A cultured woman of 'sheer beauty' (8) and 'imagination' (10), she is 'not a woman in her first youth. A widow, maybe' (8), who 'was a secret delight and a secret trouble' (9) to the younger man. In this late tale, Conrad may have parodied the precariousness of his own feelings of devotion as a younger man towards his beautiful and sophisticated 'aunt.'

Conrad was by no means unreservedly enthusiastic about Poradowska's work, and we can detect a hint of occasional frustration at the limitations of her fiction. In February 1895 he expressed severe disappointment at the published version of *Marylka*—'Vous avez massacré ce pauvre livre!' (*CL1*, 201)—although he was careful to blame Ferdinand Brunetière, the editor, rather than Poradowska herself, for being an 'imbecile' in cutting the original manuscript. But on the whole he expressed genuine admiration for her novels, and his own work benefited from his acquaintance with her narrative methods. Poradowska's ability to manipulate pace and create anticipation is evident from her structuring of conventional plot devices and situations. As Conrad struggled with the manuscript of *Almayer's Folly*, his letters suggest that he was alert to her skills, often taking the smallest hint from her methodology and recasting it to great advantage in his early Malay fiction.

One notable example concerns Conrad's extension of the father-daughter role in *Almayer's Folly*. He had read and discussed with Poradowska the early versions of *Marylka* when he began to revise *Almayer's Folly* in April 1894 (*CL1*, 154-55). In early March he referred to a proposed visit to her, and Frederick R. Karl and Laurence Davies surmise that he probably took the first ten chapters of *Almayer's Folly* with him to Brussels later that month (*CL1*, 149n2). On that visit the two writers also discussed *Marylka* (*CL1*, 151n1). In late April Conrad wrote to Poradowska that he was rewriting the first four chapters of *Almayer*, and on 2 May he again mentioned 'le travail de remaniement de mes 3 premiers chapitres' (*CL1*,

---

[16] In *Tales of Hearsay and Last Essays* (London: Dent, 1955), 17. Unless otherwise stated, all references to the works of Joseph Conrad are to Dent's Collected Edition (London: Dent, 1946-55), and page numbers will be quoted in the text.

155). The editors of the Cambridge Edition of *Almayer's Folly* have noted that these particular revisions refer to an intervening stage between manuscript and typescript, recorded in a text that is now lost. However, they have been able to deduce from the extant evidence that in this intermediate document 'the most important revisions' of the novel were achieved, and that one of Conrad's most fundamental changes occurred in the extension of the relationship between Almayer and Nina: 'The major addition, two pages of dialogue between them near the end of Chapter 1, refocuses the misunderstandings of each other.'[17] This dialogue takes place in the domestic situation, at Almayer's evening meal, during which Almayer shares with his daughter Nina his dreams of escaping with her to live in Amsterdam, while the narrator implies Nina's love for Dain Maroola and her quite contrary intentions.

According to John Dozier Gordan, neither of these themes was suggested in the manuscript of *Almayer*, but they both appear in the typescript completed well after Conrad's visit to Poradowska.[18] His letters to her, and their professional relationship at this time, also suggests that their discussion of *Almayer* and of *Marylka* prompted Conrad to develop the conflict between Almayer and Nina after seeking Poradowska's advice. In February 1895, after reading the final version of *Marylka* in the *Revue*, Conrad wrote, 'Je ne me trompe pas si je pense que la scène: Père et fille, a été abregée?' (*CL1*, 201). He had obviously been impressed with the possibilities of the father-daughter relationship of Poradowska's earlier version of the novel, which, along with his problems with *Almayer*, they had presumably discussed during his visit in March 1894. What remains of the scene between father and daughter in *Marylka* (an altercation between them takes place at the dinner table) suggests that Conrad may well have realized the dramatic potential of presenting the conflict of interests in this relationship during a ritual associated with domestic harmony. Poradowska's scene consists of the daughter's petulant verbal display of resistance to patriarchal authority. Conrad's methods are far more subtle: Almayer voices his hopes and intentions, while Nina's restlessness is revealed in Almayer's responses to her, suggested by the narrator's oblique hints.

---

[17] Floyd Eugene Eddleman and David Leon Higdon, 'The Texts: An Essay,' in Joseph Conrad, *Almayers's Folly*, eds. Eddleman and Higdon (Cambridge: Cambridge University Press, 1994), 167.

[18] *Joseph Conrad: The Making of a Novelist* (Cambridge, MA: Harvard University Press, 1940), 125-27.

Poradowska may have inspired Conrad to extend not simply the father-daughter relationship, but the exterior and interior presentation of Nina's character during these first three chapters, which were revised after his visit. Poradowska's heroines always enter theatrically—'à ce moment la porte s'ouvrit, et dans le cadre lumineux apparurent les figures éffarées' (*Micia*, 90: 523)—and Nina enters the novel, in the final version, 'through the curtained doorway,' accompanied by the dramatic lighting effects and contrasts in colour and texture of a Northern oil painting: 'Nina stood there all in white ... her low but broad forehead crowned with a shining mass of long black hair that fell in heavy tresses over her shoulders, and made her pale olive complexion look paler still by the contrast of its coal black hue' (Cambridge Edition, 15). But Conrad develops much further the statuesque quality of Poradowska's female portraits. Using an omniscient narrator who negotiates between the still, iconographic poses of the silent Nina, he also achieves in these first three chapters a subtle indication of Nina's self-possession, and the reticence developed through the experience of a divided cultural identity. Split between the influence of her native mother and Europhile father, the narrator suggests the inner tensions of her existence, claiming that 'Nina's life for all her outward composure—for all the seeming detachment from the things and people surrounding her, was far from quiet' (30-31).

If Poradowska had advised him and contributed towards Conrad's first major thematic revisions to *Almayer*, then his offer to acknowledge her as principal author of a French translation of the work makes more sense, particularly given his insecurity at this time (*CL*1, 164, 169). It is much easier for us to see the gulf between Poradowska's two-dimensional romance and the level of sophistication that Conrad had already attained with his first novel. In fact, the father-daughter scene demonstrates the way in which Conrad, from the very outset of his writing career, developed a creative opportunism, learning to incorporate the smallest suggestions into his individualized narrative strategies.

Only once did Conrad attempt something closer to Poradowska's actual style and tone, although this was in a novel he never completed. Conrad began *The Sisters* late in 1895, during a period of his life in which we know little of his personal affairs. He was unsure what direction his fiction would take after the Malay novels. However, Ford Madox Ford sheds some light on the professional dilemma Conrad experienced at this time. In his introduction to the remaining fragment, published posthumously in 1928, Ford emphasized that the theme of this story failed to fit the market to which Conrad was addressing his early work:

> Conrad still faced un-shaped destinies. ... Henley, who had just published *The Nigger of the 'Narcissus'* in *The New Review* impressed upon Conrad that his only chance of making a living lay in writing about the sea ... Readers might be found for books about the sea; it was unthinkable that they would support Slav introspections passing in Paris. So, as I have said, the manuscript and the very thought of 'The Sisters' was as it were put away in a locked drawer.[19]

At the same time, Poradowska's role of literary mentor to Conrad was being replaced by others. Following the publication of *Almayer's Folly*, no more was said about collaboration with her. But in *The Sisters* Conrad explored a domestic subject in something like the manner of her own romances; and while Conrad abandoned the novel at the time, it nevertheless constituted an important experiment. He would later return to domestic plots in *The Secret Agent* and in sections of *Nostromo* and *Under Western Eyes*, in *Chance*, parts of *The Arrow of Gold*, and *Suspense*. The later fiction can help us to evaluate more closely the place of this fragment in the context of Conrad's whole career.

The Sisters was set in Europe and written in an over-romantic and mannered style which, as Zdzisław Najder has remarked, translates surprisingly well into Polish.[20] The early descriptive passages are also closely reminiscent of Poradowska, and we have to remember that she frequently translated from Polish to French, and that her romances aimed to suggest a Polish style. It is possible that at the time of the break in correspondence with Poradowska in 1895 Conrad had been contemplating a novel that would in some way reinforce his association with her as a writer, if only to reach the market she had found for her romances in the *Revue* (cf. *CL*1, 204).

The lengthy description of Stephen's homeland in *The Sisters* has some remarkable correspondences with Poradowska's landscapes. Conrad borrowed from her the expansiveness of her sketch of the plains, as well as the heaviness of her sometimes over-written prose: 'Stephen, unwinking, looked on—smiling at Immensity.' From his mother's arms he saw the trees stirring 'in the gentle and powerful breath of the indolent steppe.' Over a hill 'the wide plains would open out again ... the uniform level of ripe wheat stretched out into unbounded distances, immensely great, filled by the hum of invisible life of the infinitely little' (28). In *Marylka*,

---

[19] *The Sisters* (New York: Crosby Gaige, 1928), 4-5.
[20] See Zdzisław Najder, *Conrad's Polish Background: Letters to and from Polish Friends* (London: Oxford University Press, 1964), 48-49; and also Karl, *Three Lives*, 170.

Poradowska had provided a model for this luxuriant, sensuous description (suggestive of the Symbolists), comparing the vast scale of the landscape to the 'infinitely little' inhabiting it: 'Au loin, la moire mouvante des blés verts ondule, bercée par le vent, cette âme mystérieuse de la steppe, qui mêle, en l'endormant, sa plainte amoureuse aux mille susurremen[t]s des insectes' (*Marylka* 128: 453-54). The light imagery characteristic of Poradowska—'le soleil descendait, dorant l'émeraude transparente des feuilles'[21]—translates in *The Sisters* into a somewhat starker Conradian perspective: 'far off ... another village showed above the monotony of yellow corn, the green path of its few trees, and lay lone, minute and brilliant, like an emerald negligently dropped on the sands of a limitless and deserted shore' (28).

There is another, even closer association with Poradowska. In his introduction, Ford does not comment on the obviously autobiographical element of *The Sisters* associated with 'Slav introspections passing in Paris.' Stephen, the restless Ukrainian artist of Conrad's unfinished novel, travelling through Europe to Paris, could easily be identified with Conrad himself. Conrad locates Stephen in Marguerite Poradowska's Paris—and even in Passy, where she was living in 1895, at the time of the break in their correspondence. The omniscient narrator of Conrad's story tells us that Stephen 'had found on the outskirts of Passy an almost ideal retreat' (*Sisters*, 46). The narrative then shifts to the concerns of the Ortega family and the sisters Rita and Thérèse, presumably precursors of characters in *The Arrow of Gold*. Perhaps for this reason, most critics have felt that the antecedents of *The Sisters* are to be found chiefly in Mediterranean experiences that occurred much earlier in Conrad's life.

About a year before embarking on *The Sisters*, Conrad began discussing the progress of Poradowska's *Pour Noémi*. Although this novel did not appear in the *Revue* until 1899, he wrote to her as early as October 1894, responding favourably to her outline for its story. In December, he remarked: 'Le devellopement de l'action me semble sans faute absolument. Je vois un tas des situations dramatiques' (*CL*1, 190). Conrad obviously did exploit the dramatic situation of Poradowska's opening in *The Sisters*, since *Pour Noémi* also tells of an artist who leaves his Ukranian homeland and works for some time in Paris, where he fails to conform to the style of the academic salons, preferring to follow his individual creative instincts. The conflict between father and son occurs in both novels, the father resisting

---

[21] *Pour Noémi*, in *Revue des Deux Mondes* 154-55 (15 August, 1 and 15 September, 1 October 1899), 154: 723.

the son's choice of profession. André's father in *Pour Noémi* complains of his son's reputation in Paris as 'L'Impressioniste, l'Estétique moderne' (154: 727), mocking him for his choice of subject and style: 'à quoi sert la peinture, je vous prie, si ce n'est à exalter ou à réveiller dans nos cœurs ce qu'il y a de plus noble' (154: 729). Like André, Conrad's artist Stephen 'would look to no one as teacher. He stood aloof from the world' (22), while his father 'could not understand the ambition of the youth ... Paint! Why paint? Paint what? Where? What's the good of it?' (31).

In Conrad's novel, Stephen refuses his brother's invitation to return home after their father's death, while in Poradowska's the artist André returns to the Ukraine. But this is not the end of the correspondence between the two works. Najder has suggested that there is no evidence to support Ford's claim that Conrad intended to write about incest in *The Sisters*, and that 'The pensive Slav painter was to have married the older sister and then to have had an incestuous child by the other' (*Sisters*, 5). Conrad abandoned the story before the painter meets either of the Ortega sisters; but Ford's testimony recalls the principal plot of *Pour Noémi*, which tells of André's love for two sisters, Noémi and Malva, and of his inability to face life without either. Poradowska's nineteenth-century decorum never allowed her to write literally of the consummation of love affairs in her fiction, but the sensuous and voyeuristic descriptions of André's painting of their portraits serves as a sufficiently transparent metaphor for the painter's physical possession of the sisters.

The evidence also suggests that *The Sisters* represented, in part, Conrad's gesture of thanks to Poradowska for their professional exchanges. Initially she had drawn inspiration from Conrad. She reproduced her understanding of his national inheritance in *Pour Noémi*, in the artist's struggles of conscience, his frustration with his homeland, and his worries about leaving it. As André contemplates a return to his nomadic life away from Poland, he reflects on his sense that 'l'homme n'a pas le droit de déserter sa patrie,' but that 'si je reste ici, mon talent s'atrophiera' (155: 76). Perhaps Conrad wished to reciprocate by developing a Poradowskan plot for *The Sisters*, acknowledging that much of his own early inspiration to persevere with his writing had come from suburban Paris.

The direction of Conrad's work, as Ford rightly remarked, took him away from the subject of *The Sisters* for many years. When he returned to the genre of popular romance with the serialization of *Chance* in 1912, he once again found occasion to draw on his relationship with Poradowska. Her version of romance had already awakened in Conrad a striking response to the inadequacies of conventional representations of women in fiction. The revisions of *Almayer's Folly* show how he may have learned from Poradowska's example while developing, in his presentation of Nina Almayer, his own methods. But the way in which Conrad and Poradowska had interacted as correspondents also provides an important insight into Conrad's rather problematic presentations of female identity, especially in his later works. We have already seen how his letters to Poradowska are distinguished by a range of tones, oscillating from idealization ('Vous doutez sans le savoir de l'Etincelle Divine qui est en Vous'; *CL*1, 100) and empathy ('Je Vous comprends parfaitement'; *CL*1, 99) to a decorous, affectionate, but sometimes patronizing voice ('Vous êtez un tout, tout petit peu "impraticable" ma tante'; *CL*1, 79) combined with an occasionally unguarded openness: 'Je ne puis pas imaginer sur quelle fondation ethique Vous basez Votre conduite envers Mme Votre Tante' (*CL*1, 105).

The rhetorical jousting of Marlow and his interlocutor in *Chance* may suggest that in this novel Conrad ironized the shifts in tone which he himself had used to address a woman he admired and respected.[22] In this novel, Conrad ironizes the male narrators' attempts to fix the identity of Flora de Barral, presenting a variety of perspectives which they impose upon her. Conrad himself had idealized, cajoled, and sympathized with Poradowska, while the narrators of *Chance* adopt positions ranging from irritation to empathy, in which the heroine is variously categorized as a 'minx' (53), the 'damsel' of the title page for Part I, or a 'victim' of the governess's cruelty (119). Yet these potential definitions are unstable, constantly undermined by a contradictory perspective. Just as Conrad's voice struggled to settle on a consistent register through which to correspond with Poradowska, so the narratorial structures of *Chance* suggest a comparable uneasiness in dealing with its unfathomable heroine. It is as if Poradowska had early on provided the inexperienced sailor-turned-writer with a medium through which to experiment with his writing voice on the subject of women. Whether self-consciously or not, he may have parodied the tones expressed in his earlier letters to his most intimate woman friend.

At the same time, Conrad was equally indebted to Poradowska's fiction when it came to the presentation of his romance-heroine in *Chance*. With the marketing of this novel for a female readership of romance in 1912, Conrad faced the question of how to address women readers without resorting to the methods of popular writers whom he despised, such as

---

[22] Conrad first thought of this narrative at a time close to the 'Poradowskan' period: in 1898-99 he was thinking of a story about 'a captain's wife' (*CL*2, 62, 169). See my article, 'The Three Texts of *Chance*,' *The Conradian* 21:1 (Spring 1996), 57-78.

Grant Allen or Marie Corelli. While critics may now regard Poradowska's novels with equal scorn, the evidence of the letters shows that Conrad had always been generous and attentive to her work, and was not above borrowing from her conventional stories of the quest for a husband that lay beneath the surface narratives of rural Polish politics. Since *Chance* initially appeared in *The New York Herald* in the fiction-slot represented by such items as 'Her Little Young Ladyship,' an unsophisticated adventure of the heart,[23] Conrad's intimate knowledge of Poradowska's novels may well have furnished him with some readily available and highly suitable raw materials for his own later romance.

Critics have recognized Conrad's allusions to Dickens and James in *Chance*, and Yves Hervouet has identified the borrowings from Anatole France,[24] but in the context of Conrad's critique of romance conventions, the initial impact of Poradowska's fiction on the writer during his formative years has been overlooked. Bearing in mind that *Chance* originated as an idea for a short story as far back as 1898 (*CL2*, 62), we might remember that even earlier, in 1890, while in the Congo, Conrad had congratulated Poradowska on her prize-winning early novel, *Demoiselle Micia*.[25] A close reading of this novel reveals how, much later in his career, Conrad appropriated aspects of its narrative to provide the basis for his sceptical presentation of domestic structures in *Chance*.

Although Poradowska's *Demoiselle Micia*, a novel of romance and intrigue set in a mining community in rural Ruthenia, could hardly have been located further from the setting of *Chance* (in the English countryside, in London, and aboard ship), there are some striking parallels between certain plot elements of the two works. Like *Chance*, *Demoiselle Micia* is about a young girl whose father is a financier and whose mother dies young.[26] In both novels the child is left in the care of an unsympathetic

---

[23] Myra Kelly, 'Her Little Young Ladyship,' *The New York Herald* Sunday Magazine, 18 June 1911, 3.

[24] On *Chance* and Dickens, see Jeremy Hawthorn, *Joseph Conrad: Narrative Technique and Ideological Commitment* (London: Edward Arnold, 1990), ch. 4. On *Chance* and James, see Ian Watt, 'Conrad, James, and *Chance*,' in Maynard Mack and Ian Gregor, eds., *Imagined Worlds: Essays on Some English Novels and Novelists in Honour of John Butt* (London: Methuen, 1968), 301-22. Hervouet cites a few passages from France's *Le Jardin d'Épicure* as evidence that 'France contributed to a few of the observations about women sprinkled throughout [*Chance*]' (119).

[25] *Demoiselle Micia* was one of six works receiving French Academy prizes of 500 francs, announced in *Le Temps* for 31 May 1890.

[26] The romantic hero of Poradowska's is actually called Conrad, although this probably refers to Konrad Wallenrod, the hero of Adam Mickiewicz's poem.

governess. In *Micia*, the governess dominates the early part, and in both novels the reader is encouraged (by an omniscient narrator in *Micia*, by a dramatized one—Marlow—in *Chance*) to empathize with the plight of the innocent heroine, particularly in her sense of entrapment in the hands of the governess. In *Micia*, however, a secondary protagonist, Helen, is also the daughter of a wealthy man who wasted the family fortune, and subsequently she marries for money. Thus the combined fates of Micia and Helen are mirrored, to some extent, in Flora de Barral, and those of both their fathers in de Barral himself. Moreover, the ending of Poradowska's novel somewhat undermines the harmony of an otherwise neatly symmetrical, rather conventional romance plot. In *Micia* the survival of the hero is left uncertain, and at the end a bohemian character, Tarasia, declares: 'La vie des créatures est entre les mains de Dieu' (91: 141), presenting a lack of closure that may have appealed to Conrad.

While corresponding elements of both novels may be familiar enough to readers of nineteenth-century fiction—the banker with a young daughter left motherless in the care of a harsh governess, or the woman beset by economic difficulties, marrying out of necessity on account of paternal neglect—one specific incident in *Chance* suggests an even more direct borrowing from *Micia*. An almost identical scene occurs in both narratives—in the description of the banker's grief after the death of the heroine's mother. In *Micia* the narrator tells us that immediately after the funeral the father was inseparable from the child: 'il l'entoura d'une solicitude presque maternelle.' However, the banker soon emerges from his mourning: 'Il éprouva comme un irrésistible besoin de revoir ses anciennes connaisances, retourna à son club, fréquenta quelques salons' (90: 528). Likewise, in *Chance*, Marlow tells us how de Barral 'was extremely cut up, and holding the child tightly by the hand wept bitterly at the side of the grave' (73). He 'clung to the child like a drowning man' (73); yet, like Micia's father, 'He managed, though, to catch the half-past five fast train ... bolted back to his suite of rooms in the hotel' (73). Again, like Micia's father, de Barral rapidly returns to business, abandoning Flora to an uncaring governess.

This, however, is as far as the correspondence goes between the two fathers. The banker in *Micia* remains a fairly innocuous figure throughout. In *Chance*, Conrad takes the possessive element of the pose at the graveside and uses it as a portent of de Barral's recurrent behaviour, destructive and selfish to a degree, when he is released from jail. Conrad's sharper characterization of the egotistical de Barral again typifies his refinement of the narrative elements to be found in Poradowska's novels.

Many of Conrad's characters in *Chance* suggest a specifically contemporary type, like Mrs Fyne the feminist, or the de Barral financial
fraud, which give the novel its topicality in the context of *The New York
Herald*.[27] But we can see from the example of *Demoiselle Micia* that
Conrad also exploited the generic possibilities of nineteenth-century
romance fiction, a move that gives *Chance* its melodramatic tone. Yet
Conrad's oblique presentation of an elusive female figure hardly conforms
to Poradowska's somewhat flat, formulaic romance heroine, described by
her omniscient narrator as 'la personnification idéale' (90: 805-6). Flora de
Barral is presented from a number of different perspectives that draw
attention instead to the inaccessibility of the woman and to her indeterminate identity. Marlow is struck by the elusiveness of her expression
(215); Captain Anthony sees her only as 'a possible woman' (217). Her
actuality, her presence, is always in question, she seems always 'about to
become' (or about to die) rather than 'being.' Except for a few brief
moments of self-dramatization, knowledge of Flora is always mediated,
filtered a number of times through a hermeneutic web. In spite of its
echoes of nineteenth-century romance, Flora's absence from the centre of
the text suggests the novel's modernism.

Conrad's narratorial complexities and his manipulation of conventional romance forms in *Chance* did not prevent him from borrowing directly
from Poradowska's outward description of the tragic heroine. A repetitive
reference to Flora's suicide pose, for example, provides another intriguing
appropriation from her work. Conrad registers Marlow's unreliability
through his narrator's changing perspectives of the heroine as he struggles
to understand her motives for a suicide attempt. As Marlow becomes more
familiar with the details of Flora's history, he recollects her seemingly rash
act with increasing empathy, remembering with greater insight his initial
view of the frail young girl perched on the cliffside ready to leap. The pose
suggests a number of allusions—a parody of nineteenth-century presentations of fallen women, Dickens's figure of the 'pure young girl,' or Henry
James's Milly Theale hovering on a precipice in *The Wings of the Dove*.
Yet Conrad's image also bears a striking resemblance to Poradowska's
treatment of the suicide pose in another novel, *Popes et popadias*, to which
he refers on several occasions in his letters (*CL1*, 124, 127, 220n1).

---

[27] Cedric Watts cites other models for de Barral: 'Jabez Balfour, founder of the
Liberator Permanent Benefit society, who had been jailed in 1895, or Whitaker Wright,
of the London and Globe Empire, who had committed suicide after being sentenced
to prison for fraud in 1904' (*Joseph Conrad: A Literary Life* [Basingstoke and London:
Macmillan, 1989], 118).

Poradowska's reference is of particular interest in relation to Conrad because it is one that she undoubtedly drew from the Polish Romantic tradition and its presentation of female self-sacrifice.[28] (She frequently quoted Mickiewicz and Słowacki in her work.) In Polish literature this version of the suicidal romantic heroine is far from passive, suggesting instead a specifically heroic image in which the protagonist dies for her country or some specific cause. (Adam Mickiewicz's *Grażyna* [1823] provides the most familiar model.) Poradowska reproduces the type in her novel *Popes et popadias*, where the female protagonist, Binia, is fascinated with the history of a Polish monarch, Wanda. Binia reads that Wanda 's'est jetée dans la Vistule' (114: 261) instead of losing her virginity to a German knight who has invaded the homeland. Like *Grażyna*, Wanda represents the trope of the female knight: 'elle s'élance elle-même au combat ... elle lève la visière de son casque' (260). When Binia later finds herself disappointed in love, she contemplates following Wanda's example. She hesitates for a moment on the edge of the river, in which 'son ombre fit ... une tache indécise' (510). Like Flora de Barral ('a creature struggling under a net' [140]) hovering on the cliff-top, Binia is presented as a wraith-like figure, 'pâle et impénétrable,' trapped by her situation: 'ce qu'elle voulait, c'était fuir, échapper au sort qui la menaçait, trouver un refuge. Mais où, comment? elle le savait à peine' (511).

Poradowska's heroine represents a somewhat sentimentalized version of a Polish literary trope, while Conrad's version is highly ironic, since he employs a male voyeur (Marlow) who finds the pose of the suicide victim 'attractive.' Yet it is more than likely that Conrad took note of the Polish resonances in Poradowska's story, and particularly its evocation of active sacrifice in the face of isolation and despair. He had certainly emphasized the importance of female heroism in a Polish story in his letters to Poradowska (*CL1*, 191). The possibility that Conrad was echoing *Popes et popadias* in *Chance* helps us to understand his use of chivalry in the novel, where he deliberately ironizes the conventional gender roles of romance. Flora's role as her father's champion when he emerges from prison is closer to the Polish representation of the activity of the female knight than to that of the 'pale and passive vessel' elsewhere described by Marlow. Indeed, Conrad would again allude to the Polish tradition in his presentation of Lena's heroic death in *Victory* (which again resembles the self-sacrifice of Mickiewicz's heroine, *Grażyna*) and in the sacrifice of Adèle de Montevesso, the heroine of *Suspense*, who agrees to a loveless marriage

[28] See my article 'Conrad's Women and the Polish Romantic Tradition' in *Conrad and Poland*, ed. Alex S. Kurczaba (Boulder: East European Monographs, 1996).

in order to achieve economic security for her parents, exiles of the French Revolution.

Conrad's presentation of the heroine in *Suspense* derives chiefly from the model provided by the Comtesse de Boigne,[29] but it also echoes Poradowska's work in other significant ways. Ford, in his introduction to *The Sisters*, had noted the link between *The Sisters* and *Suspense*.[30] If we accept the influence of Poradowska's *Pour Noémi* on Conrad's earlier unfinished work, we shall see that *Pour Noémi* provides further evidence for a connection between the two. Once again, Conrad borrowed from this novel in his discussions of the relationship between female identity and representation, a theme that emerges as an important subtext in *Suspense*.

One of the most intriguing moments of Conrad's final novel is his presentation of the heroine as a gothic vision. Adèle de Montevesso appears to the hero, Cosmo, as if she had been 'foretold to him in some picture he had seen in Latham Hall ... (mostly of the Italian school).' He imagines the heroine, framed in the costume of a Renaissance martyr, pierced through the heart with a dagger: 'A luminous oval face on the dark background— the noble full-length woman, stepping out of the narrow frame with long draperies held by jewelled clasps and girdle, with pearls on head and bosom' (195-96).[31] Conrad's presentation of Adèle owes much to his appropriation of the devices of the nineteenth-century sensation novel,[32] but he may also have been recalling Poradowska's novel here. She too had

---

[29] See Moore, 'In Defense of *Suspense*,' *Conradiana* 25:2 (Summer 1993), 99-114, and also the essay by van Marle and Moore in this volume.

[30] Ford suggested that both novels were to encompass the issue of incest, but that Conrad lost heart in persevering with this theme in *The Sisters*: 'At the end of his life when he felt his position secure he began upon this task ... to write of the passion between a couple who were, unknowingly, brother and sister. That, in *Suspense*, he was going to risk' (6-7).

[31] The iconography suggests, among other possibilities, the suicide of Lucretia. Conrad may have read an article by M. F. Ponsard, 'La Première Représentation de *Lucrèce*' in the *Revue des Deux Mondes*, 155 (1 September 1899), 168-86, the issue in which the second part of Poradowska's *Marylka* was published. Ponsard, the son of the French playwright François Ponsard, recalled how his father had been inspired to write a drama about Lucretia (1843) by the memory of a painting which had been hanging in the family home, 'sous les yeux depuis son enfance,' which depicted the moment when 'elle enfonce le poignard dans son sein.' The son remarked on the visionary effect it had had on his father's dreams.

[32] In Mary Elizabeth Braddon's *Lady Audley's Secret* (1862) a portrait of the 'heroine' reveals her 'secret' character. See also my D.Phil. Thesis (Oxford), 'Representation and Identity: Women and the Work of Joseph Conrad' (1995), chapter 6, on *Suspense* and the female sensation novel.

used literary portraiture throughout *Pour Noémi*, in the manner of the sensation novel, to suggest hidden identities in the heroine, as well as to imply the hero's fixed assumptions about her role both as idealized woman and as 'victim.' As with Cosmo in *Suspense*, Noémi reminds the artist André of the subject of an Italian Renaissance painting: '[elle] lui était apparue, semblable à certaines figures mystérieuses de la Renaissance italienne' (155: 89). However, André paints her in the costume of a Polish heroine of the Renaissance period, 'la reine Barbe Radziwiłł,' who had been poisoned by her mother-in-law. Like Cosmo's spectral vision of Adèle dressed as a Renaissance martyr, Noémi represents the moment at which the dead woman appears in a vision to the King Sigismond: 'le spectre de sa femme morte' (155: 68). Her costume closely resembles, in its details, that of Conrad's martyred woman:

> la jeune femme ... se laissait vêtir de souple drap ... sa taille gracieuse était enserrée dans une ceinture enrichie de gemmes précieuses, ses lourds cheveux aux chauds reflets s'échappaient en tresses serrées de la caractéristique coiffure royale: un véritable casque de perles qui encadrait divinement son fin visage.   (155: 524)

Conrad, however, undermines in his novel some of Poradowska's implied narratorial strategies. While the protagonist of *Pour Noémi* (who may have been modelled on Conrad himself) sustains his authority as the romantic artist with visionary powers, Cosmo questions the authority of his vision. André's painting memorializes his subject as murder victim, at the same time alluding to his metaphorical possession of her. Cosmo's portrait represents a projection of his own imagination, a subjective reconstruction of his fears rather than an objective insight into the woman's identity. Stepping out of the frame, his vision rejects the self-sacrificial pose with which she has been associated throughout the novel.

As in *Chance*, Conrad's strategy undermines the trope of female self-sacrifice suggested to him by Poradowska's more conventional presentation of the heroine. Yet his echoing of themes from *Pour Noémi* in *Suspense* supports Ford's suggestion of a link between *The Sisters* and this novel. Moreover, Conrad's later allusions to *Pour Noémi* provide further evidence of the surviving influence of Poradowska in his late career. From this perspective, Cosmo's declaration to Adèle in *Suspense* that 'I think that perhaps you could understand me' (92), and her reply, 'That would be because I am so much older,' may contain a sly autobiographical suggestion of Conrad's earlier relationship with a mature woman writer, recording his debt to that experience in his final novel.

Conrad recognized potential in Poradowska's fiction, something of merit that his sophisticated imagination could turn to advantage. His works at times offer an ironic commentary on her methods, and his intimate and influential relationship with her shows that he was far from insensitive to her interiority and emotional isolation. Despite his break in intimacy with her after 1895, his letters to her and the texts of her novels both offer an unexpected source for a deeper understanding of Conrad's early experimentation with romance forms and his earliest rehearsals of the bleaker, more philosophical themes of his middle years. Her specific impact on Conrad then resurfaced in his later years. As he confronted issues of gender and genre in the later fiction, he drew on the intricate interplay of voices in his letters to Poradowska, expressing in these novels the difficulties he had once encountered in addressing a close woman friend whom he admired and respected. At the same time, we cannot neglect the extent to which he also relied on the methods and conventions of her romances to stimulate his own responses to the genre. Rather than dismissing the influence on Conrad of the work of a little-known woman writer, perhaps it is time to recognize that without Poradowska's early emotional support *and* the example of her novels, Conrad may have been reluctant to engage with many of the ensuing issues of his fiction.

A PORTRAIT IN LETTERS
Correspondence to and about
Joseph Conrad

Ed. by J.H. Stape and Owen Knowles

Amsterdam/Atlanta, GA 1996. XXXIII,287 pp.
(The Conradian)
ISBN: 90-5183-962-6   Bound Hfl. 150,-/US-$ 100.-

A Portrait in Letters: Correspondence to and about Joseph Conrad offers an annotated selection of letters to Conrad preserved in widely scattered archives. Augmented by letters about his work and personality, the volume also contains a calendar of all known surviving correspondence addressed to him. An essential supplement to the Cambridge Edition of *The Collected Letters of Joseph Conrad, A Portrait in Letters* presents Conrad in the round, offering glimpses not only of the working writer but of the husband, parent, and friend. The letters offer new information about Conrad's literary circle and fill out numerous details about his career. Brief, authoritative biographies of the correspondents are included, and an introduction, description of editorial principles, and full index to the volume provide the scholarly contextualization and tools necessary for easy access to its contents.

USA/Canada: Editions Rodopi B.V., 2015 South Park Place, Atlanta, GA 30339, Tel. (770) 933-0027, *Call toll-free* (U.S. only) 1-800-225- 3998, Fax (770) 933-9644, *E-mail:* F.van.der.Zee@rodopi.nl
All Other Countries: Editions Rodopi B.V., Keizersgracht 302-304, 1016 EX Amsterdam, The Netherlands. Tel. + + 31 (0)20-622-75-07, Fax + + 31 (0)20-638-09-48, *E-mail:* F.van.der.Zee@rodopi.nl

Conrad and Alfred Russel Wallace

Amy Houston
University of London

Alfred Russel Wallace (1823-1913) is less famous today than his contemporary and friend Charles Darwin, although his independent formulation of the theories of variation and natural selection effectively forced Darwin to publish his own findings. His energy and output were tremendous: he composed scientific papers from the depths of the jungle, wrote two substantial travel narratives, both of which Conrad owned—*A Narrative of Travels on the Amazon and Rio Negro* (1853) and *The Malay Archipelago: The Land of the Orang-utan, and the Bird of Paradise* (1869) —and campaigned vigorously for socialism until late in life. *The Malay Archipelago* is an entertaining and occasionally gripping account of his eight-year long exploration of the Netherlands East Indies on behalf of the Royal Geographical Society. Darwin, to whom the book was dedicated, described Wallace's 'perseverance in the cause of science' as 'heroic'; and it is fascinating to read Wallace's description of venturing alone into uncharted territories, his life ever at risk from treacherous sea journeys and tropical illnesses, all modestly subsumed under his prevailing eagerness as a naturalist.[1] Henry Forbes, also a naturalist and traveller, described *The Malay Archipelago* as one of 'the greatest narratives of travel ... few travellers have possessed Wallace's powers of exposition, his lucidity and charm of style ... of the peoples of the Malay Archipelago he has given us a most interesting narrative, detailing their bodily and mental characteristics' (Marchant II, 230). *The Malay Archipelago* not only broke new ground in natural science (including the formulation of 'Wallace's line' dividing the Asian and the Australian faunal regions of the Archipelago), but as Forbes shows, it is also one of the earliest studies in anthropology. In addition, Wallace argues about the efficacy of colonial government, and the global need for social and economic justice, both topics in which Conrad maintained a keen interest.

Darwin's influence upon Conrad has been traced, most notably by Allan Hunter and Redmond O'Hanlon; but although Wallace's book *The*

---

[1] Letter from Darwin to Wallace, 22 March 1869, in *Alfred Russel Wallace: Letters and Reminiscences*, ed. James Marchant (London: Cassell, 1916), I, 237-39.

Malay Archipelago was described by Richard Curle as Conrad's 'favourite bedside book,' its influence upon Conrad's work and thinking has been relatively neglected.[2] Florence Clemens investigated Conrad's appropriation of characters, descriptions, and anecdotes from Wallace's work in her unpublished doctoral dissertation (Ohio State University, 1937) and in two short articles; Norman Sherry supplemented these 'sketchy' findings in his study of *Conrad's Eastern World*;[3] and Hans van Marle cites Wallace frequently in his notes to the Oxford World's Classics edition of *An Outcast of the Islands*. Conrad defended the authenticity of his Malay settings by invoking his 'undoubted sources—dull, wise books.'[4] Although Conrad's personal copy of the 1890 edition of *The Malay Archipelago* shows no sign of annotation, and he never referred to the work in his letters or prefaces, it is evident that he borrowed from Wallace's account of his travels in order to authenticate his own depictions of the region. But *The Malay Archipelago* is more than a travel book; it is a serious scientific investigation with revolutionary implications, and it stimulated Conrad on an intellectual level as he wrote, as much as bringing his mind back to re-explore regions he had left behind.

Norman Sherry and others have revealed that Conrad's personal experience of the Malay Archipelago was limited. He spent only 'a few months' in the East, as a sailor, not as an explorer; and a mere total of twelve days in Berau, the settlement that reputedly forms the basis for the Sambir of *Almayer's Folly* and *An Outcast of the Islands*, and possibly also the Patusan of *Lord Jim*.[5] Yet one contemporary reviewer of *Almayer's Folly* claimed that it was 'written with manifest knowledge of the life which it portrays'; while another assumed that *An Outcast of the Islands* contained 'not a single literary allusion, not a single evidence of his indebtedness to any other author. It is a perfectly genuine piece of work, the outcome of extensive experience and close observation.'[6]

---

[2] Hunter, *Joseph Conrad and the Ethics of Darwin* (London: Croom Helm, 1983); O'Hanlon, *Joseph Conrad and Darwin* (Edinburgh: Salamander Press, 1984). Curle, 'Joseph Conrad: Ten Years After,' *Virginia Quarterly Review*, 10 (1934), 431.

[3] Sherry, *Conrad's Eastern World* (Cambridge University Press, 1966), 142.

[4] Letter to William Blackwood, 13 December 1898, in *The Collected Letters of Joseph Conrad*, ed. Frederick R. Karl and Laurence Davies (Cambridge: Cambridge University Press, 1986), vol. 2, 130.

[5] Hans van Marle and Pierre Lefranc have argued that the site of *Lord Jim* is in Sumatra, not Borneo; see 'Ashore and Afloat: New Perspectives on Topography and Geography in *Lord Jim*,' *Conradiana* 20:2 (Summer 1988), 109-35.

[6] Cited in John Dozier Gordan, *Joseph Conrad: The Making of a Novelist* (Cambridge, MA: Harvard University Press, 1941), 272-73; and in *Joseph Conrad:*

Without doubting Conrad's personal powers of observation, there is compelling evidence that he supplemented his own experience by reading Wallace and other travel writers such as McNair. Research into the source material of Conrad's novels consistently indicates that his experiences in life and his experiences in reading were hardly distinguished when transmuted into fiction. Yves Hervouet believed that 'the reality of the outside world and the reality of books ... constituted, on equal terms, a vast quarry of raw material from which he could draw at will.'[7] Conrad's works contain a variety of appropriations from *The Malay Archipelago*: descriptions of Malay appearance, character, or society; the natural environment and animal life; and also more anecdotal incidents, all assimilated into the fictional text.

Wallace's primary objective in exploring the Malay Archipelago was to investigate its natural history, and a number of allusions to his work can be found in Conrad's descriptions of nature and geography. The mysterious 'Shore of Refuge' in *The Rescue* appears to be founded on Wallace's descriptions. 'It has no specific name on the charts, and geography manuals don't mention it at all,' claims Conrad (63), while Wallace himself wrote to a friend from the island of Waigiou (now Waigeo, in the North Moluccas): 'I defy all the members of the Royal Geographical Society in full conclave to tell you where is the place from which I date this letter.'[8] 'Its approaches are extremely difficult for a stranger,' writes Conrad. 'The innumerable islets fringing ... the mainland, merge into a background that presents not a single landmark to point the way through the intricate channels.' In *The Malay Archipelago*, Wallace describes a very similar experience of the difficulty of entering Waigeo:

> the entrance to the strait was really in the bay we had examined, but ... was not to be seen except when close in-shore ... the strait was often very narrow, and wound among lakes and rocks and islands ... it took us all day to reach the entrance to the channel, which resembled a small river, and was concealed by a projecting point ...[9]

Critical Assessments, ed. Keith Carabine (Mountfield: Helm Information, 1992), I, 252.

[7] Yves Hervouet, *The French Face of Joseph Conrad* (Cambridge University Press, 1990), 218.

[8] Letter to George Silk, Bessir, 1 September 1860, in Alfred Russel Wallace, *My Life: A Record of Events and Opinions* (London: Chapman & Hall, 1905), 2 vols., I, 371.

[9] Alfred Russel Wallace, *The Malay Archipelago* (Oxford University Press, 1986), 525. Future page references in the text are to this edition.

An examination of the manuscript of 'The Rescuer,' the first version
of *The Rescue* which Conrad began in 1896, reveals that Conrad's use of
Wallace to establish the geographical environment of *The Rescue* was
closer than is apparent in the final version published twenty-four years
later. Conrad describes 'a break in the low coast line, the mouth of some
river' while Carter says, 'What they suppose to be the mouth of a river is
only the salt water channel to the north.'[10] Attempts to free the stranded
yacht resulted in 'the loss of two anchors and nearly all the chain cable'
(59-60; Dent 32); Wallace's disastrous voyage from Waigeo went through
four anchors (544-45), and Conrad himself lost an anchor in Australia. But
whatever the evidence that Conrad used Wallace's experiences around
Waigeo to delineate his presentation of the Shore of Refuge, it is impossible to pinpoint the exact location of this fictional area. The yacht in *The
Rescue* goes ashore 'upon some outlying shoals off the coast of Borneo'
nearly one thousand miles from the island of Waigeo (32). This discrep-
ancy indicates the flexibility of Conrad's appropriation of his sources.
While he uses Wallace to increase the atmospheric authenticity of his
descriptions, he is not writing a travel narrative. Moreover, Conrad steadfastly opposed attempts to demystify his fictional locations; Richard Curle
recalled that 'when he told me the actual name of the island in "Youth"
where the crew of the burned Judea land ... he made me promise never to
reveal it, because ... to pin the story down to facts would rob it of its
glamour' (425).

Conrad was creative with his raw material; as Zdzisław Najder puts
it, he cared for its authenticity, but 'subordinated' it to 'artistic trans-
formations.'[11] Conrad explained to his friend Jean-Aubry shortly before
his death in 1924, 'As you know, I do not write history, but fiction, and
I am therefore entitled to choose as I please what is most suitable in regard
to characters and particulars to help me in the general impression I wish to
produce.'[12]

Florence Clemens was the first to suggest that Dain Maroola's
description of his home country in *Almayer's Folly* may have been based
on Wallace's descriptions of Bali. Wallace was enthusiastic about the

---

[10] British Library, Ashley MS 4787, pp. 59 and 62, corresponding roughly with pp.
32-33 in the Dent edition of *The Rescue*. Excerpts from *The Rescuer* are printed with
the kind permission of the British Library and the Estate of Joseph Conrad.

[11] *Joseph Conrad: A Chronicle* (New Brunswick, NJ: Rutgers University Press,
1983), 100.

[12] G. Jean-Aubry, *Joseph Conrad: Life and Letters* (Garden City, NY: Doubleday,
Page, 1927), I, 77.

cultivation system of irrigated terraces which he discovered on the islands of Bali and Lombock (now Lombok) at the eastern end of Java: 'Every one of these patches can be flooded or drained at will by means of a system of ditches and small channels, into which are diverted the whole of the streams that descend from the mountains' (161). This is echoed in Dain's own praise of Bali's 'terraced fields, of the murmuring clear rills of sparkling water that flowed down the sides of great mountains, bringing life to the land' (130). Dain also speaks of the 'mountain peak that rising lonely above the belt of trees knew the secrets of the passing clouds and was the dwelling place of the mysterious spirit of his race, of the guardian genius of his house.' Wallace estimates the twin volcanoes of Bali and Lombock at 'about eight thousand feet high' (162); and he retells the Lombock story of 'How the Rajah took the census,' which relies on the mythic existence of a spirit of the 'great fire-mountain' (187). Clemens does not mention Wallace's similar description of the beliefs of a Celebean tribe: 'the burning mountain, the torrent and lake, were the abode of their deities, and certain trees and birds were supposed to have especial influence over men's actions and destiny' (250-51); but Conrad, in constructing his own description, may have drawn inspiration from this reference as well as from those more directly associated with Bali.

The storm that hits the *Patna* in *Lord Jim* may also be based on information provided by *The Malay Archipelago*. During his eventful voyage from Waigeo, Wallace describes an encounter with heavy surf. 'We saw a white line of foam coming on, which rapidly passed us without doing any harm, as our boat rose easily over the wave' (542). Before and after the experience, the sea is 'perfectly smooth.' Compare this with Jim's description of the *Patna*, which 'went over whatever it was as easy as a snake crawling over a stick' (28):

> Suddenly the calm sea, the sky without a cloud, appeared formidably insecure in their immobility ... A faint noise as of thunder ... hardly more than a vibration, passed slowly, and the ship quivered in response ... The sharp hull driving on its way seemed to rise a few inches in succession through its whole length ... as though the ship had steamed across a narrow belt of vibrating water and of humming air.   (26-27)

Conrad deliberately presents the experience and survival of the *Patna* in *Lord Jim* as something mysterious and incomprehensible. Jim cannot explain the irony of the ship's survival, any more than he can explain the fact that he 'jumped' (111). But the entire episode is demystified when placed in context with *The Malay Archipelago*. Wallace hears of a strange

phenomenon of 'very heavy surf' at Ampanam (now Ampenan, on the
West coast of Lombok), at a time when the 'tides were low and the surf
usually at its weakest.' He notes that 'the surf had occurred on the very
night I had felt the earthquake at Labuan Tring, nearly twenty miles off ...
the sudden heavy surfs and high tides that occur occasionally in perfectly
calm weather may be due to slight upheavals of the ocean-bed in this
eminently volcanic region' (172). At the time the incident in *Lord Jim*
occurred, the *Patna* would have been passing through the Gulf which lies
on the 'eminently volcanic' belt between the Indo-Australian and African
plates that leads into the Red Sea. In 'The Rescuer' manuscript, the puzzle
seems to be indubitably solved: Lingard describes storms without 'a breath
of wind so that you could not tell where that swell came from. Some
believed in earthquakes thousands of miles away' (541; Dent 247).

Wallace's descriptions of animal life in the Archipelago also inform
Conrad's fiction. Hans van Marle notes that even minor details in *An
Outcast of the Islands* such as 'fruit-pigeons' can be traced to *The Malay
Archipelago*(369), although he does not mention the similarity between the
'loud booming cry, like the note of a deep gong,' of Conrad's 'big fruit-
pigeon' (237), and the 'loud booming voice, more like the roar of a wild
beast than the note of a bird,' of Wallace's pigeons, observed in Lombok
(169). Stein's butterflies in *Lord Jim* are more precisely drawn from
Wallace's descriptions. Marlow's description of one of Stein's specimens
gives it 'dark bronze wings, seven inches or more across, with exquisite
white veinings and a gorgeous border of yellow spots' (205), remarkably
similar to Wallace's 'fine Ornithoptera': 'The ground color of this superb
insect was a rich shining bronzy black, the lower wings delicately grained
with white, and bordered by a row of large spots of the most brilliant
satiny yellow. The body was marked with shaded spots of white, yellow,
and fiery orange, while the head and thorax were intense black' (225).
Elsewhere he describes 'Three species of Ornithoptera, measuring seven or
eight inches across the wings, and beautifully marked with spots or masses
of satiny yellow on a black ground' (239-40). In *An Outcast of the Islands*,
Mahmat compares Willems to 'our master the tiger when he rushes out of
the jungle at the spears held by men' (363). As Van Marle observes,
Wallace tells the story of how a tiger is hunted down, in Java, after it has
killed a boy:

> They only use spears when in pursuit of a tiger in this way. They
> surround a large tract of country, and draw gradually together till the
> animal is inclosed in a compact ring of armed men. When he sees that

there is no escape he generally makes a spring, and is received on a
dozen spears, and almost instantly stabbed to death.   (118)

Conrad may have been unaware that the tiger was foreign to Borneo
(modern-day Kalimantan). His application of this anecdote is literary: he
does not repeat the story, but adopts it into the common language of his
characters. And with a knowledge of Wallace's narrative, it becomes clear
that the men surrounding the tiger are not simply vindictive, but acting in
self-defence; and this helps to clarify our understanding of Willems's role
in this final part of the story.

Conrad could have relied on personal observation for many of his
references to Malay flora and vegetation. Wallace writes that the swamps
of Borneo are 'principally occupied' with the Nipa palm (69), which
figures in *Almayer's Folly* and *An Outcast of the Islands*, both based in this
area. He also refers to a 'beautiful palm, whose perfectly smooth and
cylindrical stem rises erect to more than a hundred feet high' (276)—the
same 'smooth trunk of a tall palm,' perhaps, against which Dain leans in
Almayer's Folly (49), and which shades Daman in *The Rescue* (289-90).
In *Lord Jim*, the 'sixteen different kinds of bamboo ... all distinguishable
to the learned eye' that Marlow observes in Stein's garden in Samarang
(351) may be prefigured in the 'clumps of bamboos of perhaps fifty different kinds' (121) that Wallace discovers in the Botanical Gardens of
Buitenzorg (now Bogor), also in Java (which are also the gardens in which
Almayer's father was employed as a 'subordinate government official' [*AF*
6]). Hans van Marle has traced more specific appropriations in *An Outcast
of the Islands*, such as the 'slender spikes of pale green orchids,' and the
'crimson blossoms and white star-shaped flowers' which form Aïssa's
tragic headdress (76, 351). Although these descriptions appear to be borrowed from *The Malay Archipelago*, Conrad has made certain changes.
Wallace writes of a 'most extraordinary' orchid, whose 'strange pendent
flower-spikes often hang down so as almost to reach the ground ... varying
in color from orange to red, with deep purple-red spots' (91-92). Aïssa's
flowers appear to originate in Wallace's observation of trees 'covered with
large star-like crimson flowers, which clustered over them like garlands'
(92). Richard Curle claimed that Conrad had the 'discriminating memory
of an artist: he was concerned with a fundamental and not a photographic
reality.'[13] In this sense, although Conrad did not physically refer to *The*

---

[13] Curle, *The Last Twelve Years of Joseph Conrad* (London: Sampson Low,
Marston, 1928), 75.

Malay Archipelago when he wrote of these flowers, they may have served as stimuli for his own memory and imagination.

Conrad's appropriations of Wallace's descriptions of the jungle are more conclusive. In *The Malay Archipelago*, Wallace noted the

> abundance of rattan palms hanging from the trees, and turning and twisting about on the ground, often in *inextricable confusion* ... queer shapes ... caused by the decay and fall of the trees up which they have first climbed, after which they grow along the ground till they meet with another trunk up which to ascend.   (275-76, my italics)

In *Almayer's Folly*, Conrad vividly describes the 'intense work of tropical nature ... plants shooting upward, entwined, interlaced in inextricable confusion, climbing madly and brutally over each other' and 'the big trees of the forest, lashed together with manifold bonds by a mass of tangled creepers ... the merciless creepers clung to the big trunks in cable-like coils, leaped from tree to tree, hung in thorny festoons from the lower boughs' (55, 124). However, the differences between the work of Wallace and of Conrad are equally instructive. Wallace repeatedly asserts that in the Malay jungle 'there was no brilliancy of color, none of those bright flowers and gorgeous masses of blossom, so generally considered to be everywhere present in the tropics' (244), yet in *Almayer's Folly*, Conrad describes 'immense red blossoms' that shower 'great dew-sparkling petals that descended rotating slowly in a continuous and perfumed stream' (55). One cannot doubt that Conrad actually saw these flowers, but they nevertheless demonstrate his creative flexibility: Conrad was writing romantic fiction, not fact, and borrowed selectively from Wallace for that purpose.

It is likely that Conrad observed the Malay human environment in detail for himself. Bamboo houses erected on piles along the river would have been commonplace, although it is possible that Wallace's praise of the 'elasticity' of the bamboo floor in a Dyak house, with mats laid on it for sleeping (87-88), contributed towards the description in *An Outcast of the Islands* of the 'flexible bamboo floor' upon which Lakamba's retainers 'were sleeping on mats' (96), and the 'elastic bamboo floor' of Baba-latchi's hut with its 'few shabby mats' (218-19). In New Guinea, Wallace discovers that 'the posts which support the houses, bridges, and platforms are small crooked sticks, placed without any regularity, and looking as if they were tumbling down' (499). This information may have been the inspiration for Aïssa's house: 'dark, closed, rickety and silent on its crooked posts' (*OI* 251). Wallace's further observation, that 'the walls consist of bits of boards, old boats, rotten mats, attaps, and palm-leaves, stuck in anyhow here and there, and having altogether the most wretched and dilapidated appearance it is possible to conceive' (499), possibly helped Conrad to imagine the 'miserable huts built of rotten mats and bits of decayed canoes' that Lingard encounters in 'a small bay on the coast of New Guinea' (*Rescue* 71).

In the same small bay, Hassim intended 'to buy some bird of paradise skins for the old Sultan of Ternate ... negotiating with the treacherous coast-savages who are the go-betweens in that trade' (69). Wallace was particularly keen to capture specimens of the bird of paradise in his travels, and he records that the people of Muka 'are under the rule of the Sultan of Tidore, and every year have to pay a small tribute of paradise birds, tortoise-shell, or sago. To obtain these, they go in the fine season on a trading voyage to the mainland of New Guinea, and ... make hard bargains with the natives' (533). Natives living on the coast do not 'shoot or prepare birds of paradise' themselves, but obtain them by 'barter' (509). There are cross-references to other trading goods. Dain Maroola assures Almayer that he intended 'collecting trepang on the coral reefs outside the river' and 'seeking for birds' nests on the mainland' (*AF* 45); while Wallace describes how 'the Bugis came in their praus to trade in Aru, and to buy tripang [*sic*] and birds' nests' (473). In *The Rescue*, Jörgenson buys his native wife (probably not, however, an Aru islander) 'by way of exchange for a lot of cotton stuffs and several brass guns' (389), so it is illuminating to read in *The Malay Archipelago* that 'native cloth from Celebes is much esteemed ... as well as white English calico and American unbleached cottons ... gongs, small brass cannon, and elephants' tusks. These three last articles constitute the wealth of the Aru people, with which they pay for their wives' (485).

It is evident that Conrad read and assimilated Wallace's observations of the Malay natural environment. Wallace as anthropologist seems to have had an equivalent influence. In terms of religious practices, Wallace describes how 'the old juragan repeated some prayers' just before one of his more successful voyages (413); on the *Patna* voyage, the leading Arab recites a prayer in similar fashion as they cast off (15). In *The Rescue*, Lingard's dead lascar is 'wrapped up decently in a white sheet, according to Mohammedan usage' (74), in a way highly reminiscent of Wallace's response to the death of one of his Malay men: 'As my men were all Mohammedans, I let them bury him in their own fashion, giving them some new cotton cloth for a shroud' (510). And Wallace's description of the 'cry of lamentation' that greets the news of the death of the Rajah's son in Goram ('a score of women ... set up at once the most dismal shrieks and groans and wailings, which continued at intervals till late at night' [378]) is almost certainly the inspiration for Conrad's description of the mourning over Dain Waris: 'on the instant, with one long shriek, all the women of the household began to wail together; they mourned with shrill cries; the sun was setting' (411-12).

Conrad's descriptions of Malay physical appearance are precise, and while he clearly used his own experience, he rarely departs from the details Wallace observes. Wallace notes that the stature of the average Malay is 'tolerably equal, and is always considerably below that of the average European; the body is robust, the breast well developed' (585). Dain Waris in *Lord Jim* is 'of small stature, but admirably well proportioned' (262), and Hassim of *The Rescue* boasts 'a muscular chest the colour and smoothness of bronze' (65); the Malay 'breast and limbs' being, as Wallace reveals, 'free from hair.' Wallace describes the face of the Malay man as 'nearly destitute of beard ... a little broad, and inclined to be flat ... the eyes black and very slightly oblique; the nose is rather small ... the nostrils broad and slightly exposed ... the lips broad and well cut, but not protruding' (585). While not following such a blueprint systematically, Conrad uses individual elements in his descriptions of different characters. Dain Waris has 'big black eyes' (262); Dain Maroola 'full red lips' (43); Hassim's face is 'hairless, the nose short with mobile nostrils' (65). Tamb' Itam has a 'flat' face, and Belarab's retainers in *The Rescue* are 'broad-faced fellows' (270; 292). Doramin is 'one of the most remarkable men of his race ... His bulk for a Malay was immense ... flat, big, round face ... wide, fierce nostrils, and enclosing a thick-lipped mouth' (*Lord Jim*, 259). In this case Conrad allows his imagination to dictate the characterization; adding an element of the grotesque to received fact in order to convert it to his own. But at the same time Conrad is clearly at pains to indicate that his departure from the norm is conscious, and not merely a result of ignorance; he stresses the unusualness of Doramin's appearance.

Wallace's influence in terms of Malay character is demonstrably more profound. In the manuscript version of *Almayer's Folly*, Conrad has Dain Maroola come from Lombok. But presumably having discovered from Wallace that the ruling classes of Lombok are 'natives of the adjacent island of Bali, and are of the Brahminical religion' (182), Conrad declares him, in the published version, to be 'from Bali, and a Brahmin,' wishing to authenticate his status as one of the 'better class Malays' (45). Wallace maintains that 'the higher classes of Malays are exceedingly polite, and have all the quiet ease and dignity of the best-bred Europeans. Yet this is compatible with a reckless cruelty and contempt of human life, which is the dark side of their character' (586-87). Dain behaves with respect throughout the novel, even to his money-grabbing potential mother-in-law; while his gesture to Nina, 'elevating his joint hands above his head in a sign of respect accorded by Malays only to the great of this earth' is positively deferential (42). Nevertheless, his face is 'full of determination and expressing a reckless good-humour not devoid however of some dignity ... the proud carriage of the head gave the impression of a being half-savage—untamed, perhaps cruel' (43). Recurring verbal signs suggest the closeness of Conrad's reference to Wallace. Dain's potential for cruelty is manifested in his liability to 'run amok' at one point, although otherwise he shows little individuality beyond his role as Malay lover. Perhaps Conrad's desire to be anthropologically accurate in his presentation of Malay character overrides a clear conception of Dain's fictional identity.

Wallace repeatedly refers to the impassivity of the Malay character: 'He is not demonstrative. His feelings of surprise, admiration, or fear, are never openly manifested, and are probably not strongly felt. He is slow and deliberate in speech, and circuitous in introducing the subject he has come expressly to discuss' (586). Conrad incorporates these features into many of his non-Europeans. Dain Waris in *Lord Jim* has a 'silent disposition' (262). It is 'very difficult to make Tamb' Itam talk'; the Malay helmsmen of the *Patna* are 'impassive' and 'thought nothing' (*LJ* 284, 97-98). Marlow confides that it 'was enough to strike awe into the heart' to discover that the Eurasian Jewel 'had a voice at all' (315). Half-Malay Nina 'accepted her position calmly, after the manner of her people,' and she is ever silent, 'as became a Malay girl' (*AF* 18, 50). Babalatchi is talkative but circumlocutory and undemonstrative, 'nothing of him moving but the lips, in the artificially inanimated face'; to which behaviour Lingard resigns himself, having been living with Malays 'so long and so close that the extreme deliberation and deviousness of their mental proceedings had ceased to irritate him much' (*OI* 222-23). Such consistently impassive or indirect behaviour on the part of his Malay characters has left Conrad open to criticism from colonial and feminist critics alike. Although both Hervouet and Clemens compared Conrad's 'raw material' to an inert quarry (Clemens declared that 'Conrad found *The Malay Archipelago* a rich quarry which yielded him much constructive material for the foundations of his own tales'[14]), this is a case in which the nature of the source literature has repercussions for the work into which it has been appropriated. Conrad believed that he was consulting the best authority available on the make-up of Malay character. But as a scientist

---

[14] 'Conrad's Favorite Bedside Book,' *South Atlantic Quarterly*, 38 (1939), 308.

and an anthropologist, Wallace is more concerned, in his work, to note the general characteristics of the peoples he came across, and the elements of appearance and character that distinguish different ethnic groupings, than the characteristics of individual men and women. He speaks of his human beings as he does of his animals, referring to 'specimens of several types' and their 'probable origin' (269). In turn, it is arguable that Conrad's Malay characters are rarely so distinct and memorable as his Europeans. Although Conrad asserts that there is a familiar 'bond between us and that humanity so far away,' he does not seem to treat both strands of humanity in the same way (*AF* 3). Yet Conrad was clearly attracted by this possibility: his one explicit reference to *The Malay Archipelago* occurs in *The Secret Agent*, a novel entirely removed from the Malay scene, in which he posits the 'peculiar resemblance' possible between two men of entirely different race (118).

Wallace's differentiation of races throws light upon the nature of Cornelius in *Lord Jim* and the da Souza family in *An Outcast of the Islands*. The Malacca Portuguese were frequently descendants of native slaves of the early Portuguese settlers, but Wallace believes them to be descendants of the Portuguese themselves; 'a mixed, degraded, and degenerate race' (38). Correspondingly, Conrad describes the da Souza family, who live 'in ruined bamboo houses, surrounded by neglected compounds, on the outskirts of Macassar,' as 'a half-caste, lazy lot ... those degenerate descendants of Portuguese conquerors' (4); Willems's feelings of humiliation are intensified by the fact that they are lowest of the low in racial and in moral terms. Cornelius, 'fundamentally and outwardly abject' (286), is a 'Malacca Portuguese' (220) and a Christian. If Norman Sherry is correct in surmising that Cornelius is based on the Eurasian Charles Olmeijer (also an undisputed source for Almayer), Conrad could have adjusted his racial origins in order to authenticate his despicable character in accordance with Wallace's advice. Wallace reports that the Christians living in the Dutch colony of Amboyna are 'thieves, liars, and drunkards, besides being incorrigibly lazy ... the Christians look upon themselves as nearly the equals of the Europeans, who profess the same religion ... and are therefore prone to despise work ...' (358). Though he is not from Amboyna, Cornelius's scorn of work is responsible for the failure of Stein's trading company in Patusan; he certainly lies repeatedly throughout the novel. He also speaks English in order to verify his pretence to be the equal of a 'white man,' asserting: 'I am an Englishman, too. From Malacca' (368). Conrad composed fictional characters and situations from disparate elements in his reading, just as his fiction as a whole is composed of diverse elements in both his reading and his life.

The character of Stein argues the complexity of Conrad's artistic creation. Stein is not a Malay native; Conrad would have had no need, from a straightforward desire for authenticity, to draw his character from any 'undoubted sources.' But Conrad treated the non-fictional *Malay Archipelago* not merely as a factual, but as a literary source. Stein is a composite of different influences, the majority from *The Malay Archipelago*. Florence Clemens was the first to note the similarities between Conrad's description of Stein and Wallace's description of his friend Mr Mesman. Both live in a 'spacious house' surrounded by large gardens, offices, stables, and cottages for their servants and dependents. Both drive to town every morning in a buggy, where they have an office with Chinese clerks. Norman Sherry suggests additional sources for Stein. His early career may well be drawn from the real-life merchant adventurer William Lingard, who is also the source for Conrad's Tom Lingard. But in other respects, Stein bears features of Charles Allen, Wallace's assistant (both went out to the East with a famous naturalist, and went on to travel on their own before finally staying in the East for good), and of Wallace's briefly mentioned 'German naturalist, Dr Bernstein' (344). Most significantly, as Clemens stresses, the character of Wallace himself contributes towards the creation of Stein. Stein's physical description is similar in some respects to photographs of Wallace, and Conrad's description of Stein's 'intrepidity of spirit and a physical courage that could have been called reckless had it not been ... completely unconscious of itself' (203) could have been a reaction to several of Wallace's own adventures. Furthermore, Stein's emotions upon capturing a rare butterfly are irrefutably based on Wallace's own 'intense excitement' upon securing a similar specimen. Wallace declares: 'opening the glorious wings, my heart began to beat violently, the blood rushed to my head, and I felt more like fainting than I have done when in apprehension of immediate death' (342). Similarly, Stein recalls that when he 'opened these beautiful wings ... my head went round and my legs became so weak with emotion that I had to sit on the ground' (210).

Conrad fictionalized not only the real-life people he heard about in his travels and through reading *The Malay Archipelago*. He also deliberately fictionalized the very author of the book. However 'factual' most of Conrad's appropriations from Wallace may be, he approached the work as a total creative inspiration.

Conrad's descriptions of the households of various Malay chiefs rely on a particularly complex structure of reference. In one village in Celebes (now Sulawesi), Wallace observes the women 'weaving the native cotton into sarongs.' This is done 'in the simplest kind of frame stretched on the

floor ... to form the checked pattern in common use' (229-30). In
Conrad's description of Lakamba's house, the chief's 'womenkind' are
'busy round the looms where they were weaving the checkered pattern of
his gala sarongs' (*OI* 96). Wallace also mentions weaving in his narration
of a visit to the Rajah of Goa (now Gowa).

> Near a window sat the Queen, squatting on a rough wooden arm-chair,
> chewing the everlasting sirih and betel-nut...The Rajah seated himself
> opposite to her in a similar chair ... Several young women, some the
> Rajah's daughters, others slaves, were standing about; a few were
> working at frames making sarongs, but most of them were idle. (226)

As Florence Clemens was the first to point out, Conrad's description of
Doramin's household is also heavily dependent upon this passage.[15] The
chief's wife, who chews betel 'assiduously,' 'would sit in a very roomy
arm-chair, opposite her husband, gazing steadily through a wide opening
in the wall which gave an extensive view of the settlement and the river'
(*LJ* 256). She is surrounded by 'a troop of young women ... her daughters, her servants, her slave-girls. You know how it is in these households:
it's generally impossible to tell the difference.' Whatever the evident
similarities, Conrad's narrative is not transposed in any simple way from
that of Wallace. Doramin bears no direct resemblance to the Rajah, but,
as Norman Sherry has pointed out, is probably based on McNair's description of the Bugis chief Nakhoda Trong.[16] Wallace's overall response
to his visit was that 'every thing had a dingy and faded appearance, very
disagreeable and unroyal to a European eye' (227); yet this sentiment
recurs not in Conrad's description of Doramin's household, but in his
description of the Rajah Allang.

Conrad may also have appropriated Wallace's description of his
'cold reception' at the house of a chief in Lombok:

> we were requested to seat ourselves under an open shed with a raised
> floor of bamboo, a place used to receive visitors and hold audiences ...
> It was however about two hours before ... a small tray was brought,
> containing two saucers of rice, four small fried fish, and a few
> vegetables.   (175)

---

[15] Clemens, 'Conrad's Malaysian Fiction: A New Study in Sources with an
Analysis of Factual Material Involved' (Ph.D. Dissertation, Ohio State University,
1937), 59-61.
[16] *Conrad's Eastern World*, 161.

Compare this with Jim's reception by the Rajah Allang, who when giving audience 'would clamber upon a sort of narrow stage erected in a hall like a ruinous barn with a rotten bamboo floor' (228). Jim discovers that he 'couldn't get anything to eat either, unless I made a row about it, and then it was only a small plate of rice and a fried fish not much bigger than a stickleback' (249). Other elements in *The Malay Archipelago* similarly feed into Conrad's description of the Rajah. Wallace considers the Sultan of Batchian (now Bacan) to be, though friendly, 'an old dirty-faced man with gray hair and a grimy beard' (334), while Marlow finds the more invidious Tunku Allang 'a dirty, little, used-up old man with evil eyes and a weak mouth, who ... in defiance of common decency wore his hair uncovered and falling in wild stringy locks about his wizened grimy face' (228). Imprisoned by the Rajah, Jim is repeatedly bothered by 'amazing interrogatories: "Were the Dutch coming to take the country? Would the white man like to go back down the river? What was the object of coming to such a miserable country? The Rajah wanted to know whether the white man could repair a watch?"' (252). Wallace records a similar experience during negotiations with the Rajah of Lombok:

> A long conversation in the Bali language then took place, and questions were asked about my guns, and what powder I had, and whether I used shot or bullets; also what the birds were for, and how I preserved them, and what was done with them in England ... They were evidently quite puzzled, and did not believe a word we had told them.   (176)

Wallace also says that 'while the Rajah sits no one can stand or sit higher' (180), and illustrates his point with a story: 'So unbending are the rules in this respect, that when an English carriage which the Rajah of Lombock had sent for arrived, it was found impossible to use it because the driver's seat was the highest, and it had to be kept as a show in its coachhouse' (227). This anecdote returns in Conrad, not to supplement his description of the Rajah Allang, but in a brief reference in *An Outcast of the Islands* to the Rajah of Gowa. Willems 'had bribed him with a gilt glass coach, which, rumour said, was used as a hen-coop now' (8).[17] There is no simple correspondence, therefore, between the Rajahs in Wallace and Conrad, although many individual details or descriptions are linked very closely.

---

[17] Norman Sherry has uncovered a newspaper article revealing that the Sultan of Sulu did indeed use his coach for keeping hens; see *Conrad's Eastern World*, 163.

Wallace extended his scientific objectivity to his anthropological observations, but he was nevertheless sensitive to the impact of Western intrusion on the East, and his own role in that process. Wallace was a personal friend of the 'white Rajah' of Sarawak, and it was partly from his account of Sir James Brooke's successful methods of government that Conrad elicited information for *Lord Jim*:

> Brooke found the Dyaks ... cheated by the Malay traders, and robbed by the Malay chiefs ... From the time Sir James obtained possession of the country, all this was stopped ... Was it not natural that they should refuse to believe he was a man? ... They naturally concluded that he was a superior being, come down upon earth to confer blessings on the afflicted ... Was he not as old as the mountains? Could he not bring the dead to life?   (102-3)

Jim's situation in Patusan is very similar. At the time he arrives, 'there wasn't a week without some fight in Patusan' (255), with trade 'the primary cause of faction fights' (256). Yet Jim is not in the country long before 'the legend had gifted him with supernatural powers' (266). Rumour has it that 'the tide had turned two hours before its time to help him on his journey up the river' (242-43), and that 'with a touch of one finger' he 'had thrown down the gate' (270). Such magical powers are also attributed to Wallace himself. 'I was set down as a conjurer,' he notes, faced with the charge of changing the weather for the better (464). Arranging his insects, he is 'surrounded by men, women, and children, lost in amazement at my unaccountable proceedings' (329); all his articles, from penknives to bird-labels, are 'unsolved mysteries to the native mind' (393). Conrad makes use of this theme in the Malay story 'Karain,' in which a Jubilee sixpence is held to be a charm, with ironic imperial implications: the Westerners in the story exploit the credulity of the Malay, ostensibly for his own good. Apparently Wallace, like Jim, was an 'insoluble mystery' 'tinged with wonder and mystery on the lips of whispering men' (306, 272). 'I have no doubt,' writes Wallace with no sign of self-consciousness, that 'I myself shall be transformed into a magician or a demi-god, a worker of miracles, and a being of supernatural knowledge' (473).

Wallace is also quite solitary, as 'the only European inhabitant of the vast island of New Guinea' (501); in the Aru Islands, 'few European feet had ever trodden the shores I gazed upon' (419). However, he is more excited than dismayed at the thought of his solitude; even more than Jim, he is 'protected by his isolation, alone of his own superior kind, in close touch with Nature, that keeps faith on such easy terms with her lovers' (*LJ* 176). The isolation of the white man in a foreign environment is perhaps Conrad's single most persistent theme. In *Under Western Eyes*, Razumov finds himself by accident one of a group of traitors he despises; Heyst chooses voluntary exile in *Victory*; and Kurtz is swallowed up by the jungle in *Heart of Darkness*. In the Malay novels, Conrad turns the theme of isolation into something baneful. Jim's status as 'one of us' is emphasized; he can never really be one with the people of Patusan, and this eventually leads to his downfall. Lingard, like Jim, is held to 'cry magic words that make all safe' (*Rescue* 47); but involved in his secret enterprise, he begins to feel 'like an outcast,' hurt by his 'inward loneliness' ('The Rescuer' 171; Dent 97). Ultimately, Conrad's protagonists discover superior status to be no compensation for rejection, and in Willems, the archetypal outcast, the tension is brought to its extreme. In the settlement of Sambir, Willems is disturbed by the effect he has on the Malays:

> indolent men ... looked at him with calm curiosity, the women round the cooking fires would send after him wondering and timid glances, while the children would only look once, and then run away yelling with fright at the horrible appearance of the man with a red and white face ... the very buffaloes snorted with alarm at his sight. (*OI* 66)

Florence Clemens linked Willems's ostracism directly to Wallace's disagreeable experience of a village in Sulawesi: 'wherever I went, dogs barked, children screamed, women ran away, and men stared as though I were some strange and terrible cannibal monster.' Even buffaloes would 'rush away helter-skelter as if a demon were after them' (230). Wallace is disconcerted by this ordeal, but retains a scientific distance; while Willems takes it as yet another confirmation of his own sense of humiliation, and feels 'left outside the scheme of creation in a hopeless immobility filled with tormenting anger and with ever-stinging regret' (65). Jim records a similar reaction: when escaping from the Rajah's stockade, he is 'beplastered with filth out of all semblance to a human being,' leaving men and women 'petrified' and 'screaming' (254-55). The passage is amusing, but it also foreshadows the real danger that Jim poses. The isolated white man is assumed to be morally superior in his solitude, but his difference actually has disastrous consequences for his host community. Western presence inevitably entails a degree of colonization; even Wallace ejects Malay families from their homes so that he can have somewhere to stay.

Despite the evident enthusiasm with which Wallace pursued his scientific investigations, he was consistently aware of broader social issues. His views of colonial government often seem to be directly opposed to the perspective offered by Conrad's fiction. Wallace praised the Dutch system of 'slave debtors' which is 'a great boon to traders,' and more 'sensible' than 'effectually preventing a man from earning anything toward paying his debts by shutting him up in a jail' (412), but Lingard is horror-struck at the idea that 'some of the usurping chiefs had even tried to set up the law of debt slavery' ('The Rescuer' 569-70). By 1868 Multatuli's *Max Havelaar* had been translated into English, and Conrad could have read it. Wallace derided its 'supposed crushing exposure of the iniquities of the Dutch government of Java' (107),[18] although he conceded that the system might not be 'perfectly carried out' in practice. Wallace believed that a colony should be 'to the material advantage of the governing country' (107), but he also insisted that 'paternal despotism' was in the best interests of the colonial natives, just as a certain amount of discipline is good for the wilful child or schoolboy (261-62). The Dutch arrangement of paying local people a small wage to cultivate coffee and sugar, to be sold back to the government, might be contrary to the principles of free trade, but it was 'far less burdensome, and far more beneficial to the people than any tax that could be levied,' for it encouraged 'habits of steady industry and the art of scientific cultivation' (107). Yet the best-laid schemes are not consistently fruitful. The system worked well with the inhabitants of Minahasa (North Sulawesi) on account of their 'natural docility and intelligence,' but the Bantek tribe was 'of a much less tractable disposition' and had 'hitherto resisted all efforts of the Dutch Government to induce them to adopt any systematic cultivation' (263). On Timor, Wallace observed, 'the people retain their independence in a great measure, and both dislike and despise their would-be rulers, whether Portuguese or Dutch' (204-5). Conrad's novels, particularly *The Rescue*, appear to display sympathy with these people of a 'less tractable disposition': Hassim and Belarab feel their freedom endangered by the Dutch who 'grow fat living on our land' (75, 112). The Shore of Refuge, according to Belarab, shelters those who hate 'the new methods of life and happiness forced upon them by superior wisdom and by irresistible strength, all who abhorred restraint, change and a foreign rule' ('The Rescuer' 208; Dent 113-14).

   However, Wallace was also fully aware of the two-sided nature of colonialism. He could be perceived as an aggressive colonist of the world

---

[18] Multatuli, *Max Havelaar, or the coffee auctions of the Dutch Trading Company*, tr. Baron Alphonse Nahuijs (Edinburgh: Edmonston and Douglas, 1868). *The Malay Archipelago* was first published in New York, by Harper, in 1869.

of nature, displaying a relentless enthusiasm for hunting down every rare specimen he saw. Yet he realized that

> should civilized man ever reach these distant lands, and bring moral, intellectual, and physical light into the recesses of these virgin forests, we may be sure that he will so disturb the nicely-balanced relations of organic and inorganic nature as to cause the disappearance, and finally the extinction, of these very beings whose wonderful structure and beauty he alone is fitted to appreciate and enjoy.   (448-49)

His approach to the human inhabitants of the islands he visited was similar. From experience, he considered the Dutch system of colonisation to be morally as well as economically just, but he was fully aware of the inevitable destruction that accompanies 'progress.' He argued that the Malay race 'seems well adapted to survive,' but he had little doubt of the early extinction of the Papuan race: 'A warlike and energetic people, who will not submit to national slavery or to domestic servitude, must disappear before the white man as surely as do the wolf and the tiger' (596).

Like Wallace, Conrad saw destruction as an inevitable by-product of the tension between East and West, with conflicting expectations and patterns of survival. In 'The Rescuer,' his pessimism was particularly evident: 'civilisation stalks from island to island in the old sunshine; and where treads the foot of the greedy sceptre there the song of fierce life dies out, to be replaced by a dreary mutter of laws and statistics' (112; Dent 63). The consolidation of European power jeopardizes traditional patterns of inter-island trade. This ambiguous presentation of the colonial issue is in line with Conrad's approach elsewhere. In *Lord Jim*, Marlow describes how 'light (and even electric light) had been carried' into various parts of the Malay Archipelago 'for the sake of better morality and—and—well—the greater profit, too,' in a typical mockery of philanthropic pretence (219). Similarly, the privileged reader's 'firm conviction in the truth of ideas racially our own, in whose name are established the order, the morality of an ethical progress' (339), caricatures some of Wallace's own sentiments; such as his delight that the inhabitants of Seram 'have the opportunity of acquiring something of European tastes and habits' (359); his advocacy of 'the spread of education and the gradual infusion of European blood' (107).

The Malay Archipelago concludes with Wallace's remarkable observation that 'although we have progressed vastly beyond the savage state in intellectual achievements, we have not advanced equally in morals'

(597). Struck by the magnificence of ancient tombs in the middle of the
Javanese forest, Wallace ponders on 'the strange law of progress, which
looks so like retrogression, and which in so many distant parts of the
world has exterminated or driven out a highly artistic and constructive
race, to make room for one which, as far as we can judge, is very far its
inferior' (114). The survivor is not always the fittest in moral terms, and
civilization may not be far removed from barbarism. This belief lies at the
heart of much of Conrad's work. The message of 'An Outpost of Progress,' as Peter Raby has it, is 'the destruction and despoliation of Africa
by a capitalist Europe, a process which corrupts and destroys the weak of
both continents'; like *Heart of Darkness*, this story lays bare the cankered
nature of European values by displacing them to a foreign environment.[19] The 'old and helpless' Almayer strangely feels 'very much like
those savages round him' (*AF* 24); and when Dain Maroola bribes Mrs
Almayer to gain access to Nina, Conrad notes ironically that 'There are
some situations where the barbarian and the, so-called, civilized man meet
upon the same ground' (67).

Given the complexity of Conrad's appropriations of Wallace, and
the fact that he adapts every borrowing to his own literary purposes, it
would be unfair to charge him with plagiarism. His assimilation of
Wallace's work appears to be both a conscious and a subliminal activity;
he treats *The Malay Archipelago* as a source of factual authority, but also
as a memory-jogger and a more conceptual inspiration. In using Wallace
to such an extent in his work, Conrad is neither seeking support from an
author whose linguistic background is near his own, nor is he borrowing
the voice of literary authority. Rather, Conrad's appropriations of Wallace
demonstrate the absolute intertextuality embedded in his literary creativity.
As Yves Hervouet put it, 'originality can only be relative ... an artist
chooses his influences.'[20] Conrad may have found *The Malay Archipelago* to be wise, but he cannot possibly have thought it dull.

---

[19] *Bright Paradise: Victorian Scientific Travellers* (London: Chatto & Windus
1996), 230.
[20] *The French Face*, 228-29.

Conrad's 'The Idiots' and Maupassant's 'La Mère aux monstres'

Gene M. Moore
Universiteit van Amsterdam

In the 'Author's Note' to *Tales of Unrest* written in 1919 for the Doubleday collected edition of his works, Joseph Conrad declined to comment on his first published story, 'The Idiots' (1896), on the grounds that it was 'such an obviously derivative piece of work that it is impossible for me to say anything about it here.' He added that 'The suggestion of it was not mental but visual: the actual idiots.'[1] Strictly speaking, if the story was not based on a mental suggestion but directly inspired by the sight of actual idiots, then in what sense could it be considered 'derivative'? And why should this 'derivativeness' prevent Conrad from saying more about it? His speechlessness was evidently imposed not by the objects of this visual suggestion, but by his embarrassment at the 'derivative' nature of the artistic treatment to which he had subjected them. The 'actual idiots' were later described by Conrad's widow Jessie, who traced the origin of the story to a remark made by their driver while they were on their honeymoon on Ile Grande, off the coast of Brittany:

> Much of our Ile Grande life is in that short story, for which Conrad had, I think, an unreasonable contempt. The stone-cutters are in it, our landlady is in it, and the feeling of our surroundings, perhaps a little more sombre than the reality. We saw the actual idiots while being driven by our friend, Prijean, from Lannion to Ile Grande. I won't describe the idiots. Conrad has done that; but the story had its origin in Prijean's remark just after we had passed them sprawling in the ditch. 'Four—hein. And all in the same family. That's a little too much. And the priests say it's God's will!'[2]

---

[1] 'Author's Note' to *Tales of Unrest* in *Almayer's Folly: A Story of an Eastern River and Tales of Unrest* (London: Dent's Collected Edition, 1947), vii. Future references to this edition will be included in the text. 'The Idiots' was rejected by both *Cosmopolis* and *Cornhill* magazines before appearing in *The Savoy Magazine* (no. 6, 11-30 October 1906).

[2] Jessie Conrad, *Joseph Conrad As I Knew Him* (London: Heinemann, 1926), 38. A somewhat different account appears in her other memoir, *Joseph Conrad and His Circle* (London: Jarrolds, 1935), 37.

This account may help to explain the satirical treatment of the local priest in 'The Idiots,' but it fails to settle the question of Conrad's contemptuous dismissal of the story as 'derivative.' Writing to Geneviève Séligmann-Lui on 10 August 1910, Conrad spoke disparagingly of all the stories published in *Tales of Unrest* (1898): 'Mais, a parler franchement, le volume de Tales of Unrest est celui de toute mon œuvre que j'aime le moins. Je m'y vois "derivatif" plus que de raison.'[3]

Although Conrad never named a specific author as the source of this 'derivation,' critics have been virtually unanimous in identifying Guy de Maupassant as his primary model. In 1928 Richard Curle asserted that 'The Idiots' was written 'consciously in the Maupassant manner.'[4] The following year, another friend, Edward Garnett, confirmed that 'Conrad's distaste for "The Idiots," in his latter years ... came from the fact that it betrays too openly Maupassant's influence.'[5] In letters to Marguerite Poradowska written in 1894, two years before he wrote 'The Idiots,' Conrad had expressed not only his admiration for Maupassant ('Je lis Maupassant avec delices') but also the anxiety of his influence: 'J'ai peur que je ne sois trop sous l'influence de Maupassant' (*CL*1, 169, 183). René Rapin, the editor of the French originals of Conrad's letters to Poradowska, declared that 'La preuve la plus nette de l'influence exercée par Maupassant sur Conrad est la nouvelle *The Idiots* ... Le cadre, le sujet, les procédés narratifs, le style sont si "maupassantesques" ...'[6]

More recent critics have continued to identify Maupassant as Conrad's primary model, often echoing Conrad's own dislike of the story: Frederick R. Karl has described 'The Idiots' as 'imitative of Maupassant's naturalistic methods at their most simplistic,' while Ian Watt has noted that 'The neat ironic surprise at the end' is 'reminiscent of Maupassant at his most mechanical.'[7] Thanks to the work of Yves Hervouet, renewed

---

[3] Frederick R. Karl and Laurence Davies, eds., *The Collected Letters of Joseph Conrad* (Cambridge: Cambridge University Press, 1983-), vol. 4, 357-58 (cited henceforth as *CL*).

[4] Richard Curle, *The Last Twelve Years of Joseph Conrad* (London: Sampson Low, Marston, 1928), 116.

[5] Cited in George T. Keating, ed., *A Conrad Memorial Library: The Collection of George T. Keating* (Garden City, NY: Doubleday, Doran, 1929), 51.

[6] René Rapin, ed., *Lettres de Joseph Conrad à Marguerite Poradowska* (Genève: Droz, 1966), 146, note 6; this footnote also provides a convenient summary of Conrad's references to Maupassant in the letters to Poradowska.

[7] Frederick R. Karl, *Joseph Conrad: The Three Lives, A Biography* (London: Faber & Faber, 1979), 374; Ian Watt, *Conrad in the Nineteenth Century* (Berkeley and Los Angeles: University of California Press, 1979), 75.

attention has lately been given to the issue of Conrad's 'borrowings' from
French authors, including Maupassant. However, despite the universal
agreement that 'The Idiots' is 'obviously derivative' from Maupassant, and
a good many discussions of thematic and technical similarities between
Maupassant and Conrad (in their descriptions of nature, use of framing
devices, surprise endings, etc.), no one has yet managed to identify any
specific works by Maupassant from which Conrad could have derived 'The
Idiots.'[8] In particular, no one seems ever to have noticed the remarkable
similarities between 'The Idiots' and Maupassant's story 'La Mère aux
monstres,' similarities not only in terms of the explicit content and the
formal structures of the two tales, but also in the themes they address, in
their use of imagery, and in their wider social and ethical implications.[9]
One cannot prove that Conrad was consciously and deliberately 'borrowing' from Maupassant's story, nor can one prove the contrary hypothesis
that Conrad, while writing his own story, never gave Maupassant a passing
thought. Nevertheless, a comparison of these two stories can provide a firm
textual basis for a better understanding of Conrad's repeated assertion that
his own tale was unduly 'derivative.'

Like 'The Idiots,' 'La Mère aux monstres' is the story of a mother
who bears a large number of handicapped children. Both stories are frame-
tales (Maupassant's is doubly framed) narrated by a traveller who recalls
the events which led to his hearing the story of the 'monsters' from a local
informant. The language used in both stories fails to distinguish clearly
between mental and physical deformity, and both kinds of 'monstrosity' are
symbolic of larger marital and social issues.

---

[8] Maupassant's influence has been discussed by Paul Kirschner in *Conrad: The
Psychologist as Artist* (Edinburgh: Oliver and Boyd, 1968), esp. pp. 191-229, and
'Some Notes on *Conrad in the Nineteenth Century*'' *Conradiana* 17:1 (1985), 33-34,
and by Yves Hervouet, 'Conrad and Maupassant: An Investigation into Conrad's
Creative Process,' *Conradiana* 14:2 (1982), 83-111, and *The French Face of Joseph
Conrad* (Cambridge University Press, 1990). Hervouet noted some textual similarities
between descriptions of autumn weather in 'The Idiots' and passages in Maupassant's
Une vie; but comparable descriptions of winter in Normandy can be found throughout
Maupassant's works (for example in 'Première neige,' in which a rain-sodden road is
similarly described as a 'river of mud'). In an earlier essay entitled 'Zola and Conrad's
"The Idiots"' (*Studies in Philology* 52:3 [July 1955], 502-7), Milton Chaikin tried to
argue that 'The Idiots' was influenced chiefly by Zola.
[9] 'La Mère aux monstres' appeared originally in *Gil Blas* on 12 June 1883, thirteen
years before Conrad's honeymoon in Brittany. It was reprinted in the collection *Toine*
(1885).

There are, of course, significant differences between the two stories. 'La Mère aux monstres' is set not in Brittany but in a more generic 'petite ville de province' where the narrator has been visiting a friend. Having exhausted all the local tourist attractions, the friend finally takes the narrator to see 'la mère aux monstres,' the mother of monsters: 'C'est une femme abominable, un vrai démon, un être qui met au jour chaque année, volontairement, des enfants difformes, hideux, effrayants, des monstres enfin, et qui les vend aux montreurs de phénomènes' (842).[10] Unlike the lonely, melodramatic tragedy of Conrad's Susan, whose husband demands an heir 'like other people's children' while she can bring forth only 'idiots,' the mother in Maupassant's tale willingly becomes a demonic machine who places her reproductive prowess at the service of 'affreux industriels' ready to buy her products for display in their freak shows.

The children in Conrad's tale are mentally retarded, while the off-spring of Maupassant's demonic mother are physically deformed; but these differences are minimized in the stories themselves, which not only fail to distinguish clearly between mental and physical monstrosity, but even take each as an image of the other. Conrad's narrator describes the children not as integral beings capable of arousing pity, but as a mixture of dehumanized body parts: at first sight, the idiot child appears not as a 'he,' but a sexless collection of 'its':

> In the long grass bordering the road a face glided past the carriage at the level of the wheels as we drove slowly by. The imbecile face was red, and the bullet head with close-cropped hair seemed to lie alone, its chin in the dust. The body was lost in the bushes growing thick along the bottom of the deep ditch.
> It was a boy's face.   (56-57)

The narrator of Maupassant's tale never actually sees the children, but his friend provides an all too graphic description of the first of the 'monsters' that resulted from the mother's need to hide her pregnancy by compressing her stomach with a specially constructed wooden corset:

> Elle estropia dans ses entrailles le petit être étreint par l'affreuse machine; elle le comprima, le déforma, en fit un monstre. Son crâne pressé s'allongea, jaillit en pointe avec deux gros yeux en dehors tout sortis du front. Les membres opprimés contre le corps poussèrent, tortus

---

[10] Guy de Maupassant, "La Mère aux monstres," in *Contes et nouvelles I*, ed. Louis Forestier (Paris: Bibliothèque de la Pléiade, 1974), 842-47. Future references to this edition will be included in the text.

comme le bois des vignes, s'allongèrent démesurément, terminés par des
doigts pareils à des pattes d'araignée.   (845)

The imagery here is not human, but animal and vegetable: the monstrous
child has a narrow head with froglike eyes, arms twisted like grapevines,
and fingers like spider's legs. The mother is also described in bestial terms:
'C'était une grande personne aux traits durs ... le vrai type de la paysanne
robuste, demi-brute et demi-femme. ... Elle parlait vite, les yeux baissés,
d'un air hypocrite, pareille à une bête féroce qui a peur.' Her body is
described as 'ce grand corps osseux, trop fort, aux angles grossiers, qui
semblait fait pour les gestes véhéments et pour hurler à la façon des loups.'
When the narrator's friend takes him to visit the mother to see her latest
product, she guesses why they have come and indignantly refuses them
access: 'C'est pour ça qu' vous êtes venus, dites? Pour m'insulter, quoi?
Parce que mes enfants sont comme des bêtes, dites? Vous ne le verrez pas,
non, non, vous ne le verrez pas; allez-vous-en, allez-vous-en.' Although
they cannot see the child, the visitors can hear the noises it makes in the
adjoining room: 'Au son brutal de sa voix, une sorte de gémissement ou
plutôt un miaulement, un cri lamentable d'idiot partit de la pièce voisine'
(843-44). And if Maupassant's monster speaks with an idiot's voice, the
idiot children of Conrad's tale are described as creatures with 'misshapen'
brains who inhabit a 'monstrous darkness'; their voices are not human, but
thing-like and mechanical: 'The imperfect thing that lived within them
moved those beings to howl at us from the top of the bank ... The faces
were purple with the strain of yelling; the voices sounded blank and
cracked like a mechanical imitation of old people's voices' (57-58).

    The women in both stories are described literally as 'horrible':
Maupassant opens his story with a reference to 'cette horrible histoire et
cette horrible femme' (842), while at the climax of Conrad's tale Susan is
condemned by her own mother, who tells her: 'You are a horrible woman'
(77). In her final extremity, Susan seeks to justify the murder of her
husband by renouncing her own children: 'Do you think I would defy the
anger of God and have my house full of those things—that are worse than
animals who know the hand that feeds them?' Similarly, the diabolical
mother in Maupassant's tale literally hates her first child with a savage
hatred, 'une haine sauvage,' and when the freak-show impresarios visit her,
she at first refuses to show them 'cette sorte d'animal' (846). In Conrad's
tale, Madame Levaille finally condemns her daughter with the wish that
Susan herself had been born 'simple': 'There are worse misfortunes than
idiot children. I wish you had been born to me simple—like your own'
(77). The mother's hateful wish comes true in the imagery of the final

scene of 'The Idiots,' where the fleeing Susan appears to the seaweed-gatherers not as a person but a 'thing': '"The thing ran out towards the sea. ... Let the accursed thing go to the sea!" ... "Such things ought to be left alone"' (80). Millot describes her with a string of demonic expletives: '"Where the devil did you pass?" ... "Who the devil was she?"' (82-83). She imagines Millot to be the ghost of the husband she has just killed, and tells him "Satan sends you here. I am damned too!" (84).

By contrast, the fathers in both stories are not only exempted from blame, but are scarcely mentioned at all in connection with the children. When Maupassant's narrator inquires about the identity of the father, his host replies: 'On ne sait pas. Il ou ils ont une certaine pudeur. Il ou ils se cachent. Peut-être partagent-ils les bénéfices' (847). The father in Conrad's tale, Jean-Pierre, imagines his son and heir never as a child, but only as an adult reflection and extension of himself: 'A man that would think as he thought, that would feel as he felt; a man who would be part of himself, and yet remain to trample masterfully on that earth when he was gone!' (71). His neglect of paternal responsibility is presented as a traditional form of social monstrosity, 'that indifference which is like a deformity of peasant humanity' (63). Accordingly, his own father, 'the elder Bacadou,' pays no attention to the birth of the first twins: 'Grandsons were all very well, but he wanted his soup at midday. When shown the babies, he stared at them with a fixed gaze, and muttered something like: "It's too much." ... He looked offended—as far as his old wooden face could express anything' (61). The selfish grandfather himself soon becomes childish and senile, and is only dimly aware that his grandchildren are abnormal.

Another point of similarity can be found in the manner in which both stories seek to exculpate the mothers by delivering a moral indictment of the worlds within which they live. If the mothers deserve blame as 'horrible' or 'diabolical' women, both stories strongly imply that they have been rendered 'monstrous' by social and economic constraints beyond their control. The nameless mother of Maupassant's tale becomes in effect an industrial enterprise, a marvel of perverted bio-engineering, with her own special 'machine' for producing monsters and thereby guaranteeing her income: 'pour se faire des rentes comme une bourgeoise' (846). She even becomes monstrously adept at varying the kinds of monsters her body produces:

> Comme elle était féconde, elle réussit à son gré, et elle devint habile, paraît-il, à varier les formes de ses monstres selon les pressions qu'elle leur faisait subir pendant le temps de sa grossesse.

Elle en eut de longs et de courts, les uns pareils à des crabes, les
autres semblables à des lézards. Plusiers moururent; elle fut désolée.
La justice essaya d'intervenir, mais on ne put rien prouver. On la
laissa donc en paix fabriquer des phénomènes.   (846)

Of course the 'monstrosity' and 'horror' of this biological corruption
is fully shared by the buyers who keep her in business by purchasing her
monsters, and by the morbid curiosity of those who keep the buyers in
business by paying to see the monsters in carnivals and *cabinets de curio-
sités*. Maupassant makes this point when the mother, properly angered by
the sanctimonious curiosity of her visitors, finally dismisses them as a 'tas
de mécréants!' (844). In effect, what is miscreant is not only the monsters
themselves, but the social constraints that engender them: the fear of
discovery that led the unmarried mother to create the first one accidentally,
and the commercial incentives that encourage her to continue producing
them like an annual crop.

   This message is writ even larger in the frame surrounding Maupassant's tale, which the narrator begins by announcing that the sight of a
beautiful Parisienne on a beach—'jeune, élégante, charmante, adorée et
respectée de tous'—has reminded him of this 'horrible story.' In the end
the connection is explained when it turns out that the lovely Parisienne is
the mother of three deformed children, all victims of their mother's vanity,
since their deformities were produced by her refusal to stop wearing a
corset: 'Voilà les résultats des tailles restées fines jusqu'au dernier jour.
Ces monstres-là sont fabriqués au corset' (847). A woman who produces
monsters from what she perceives as economic necessity is not to be condemned more than women for whom appearances are more important than
the health of their unborn children. The twist at the end of Maupassant's
tale equates the socialite's behaviour, which has not diminished the respect
she receives from her admirers, with that of the other 'mother of monsters'
who is socially condemned and despised.

   Conrad's narrator also suggests that the children left to wander along
the road are by no means the only 'idiots' in his tale.[11] When Jean-Pierre
and Susan celebrate their wedding with a great dinner that 'was remembered for months,' we are told that 'Farmers of considerable means and
excellent repute were to be found sleeping in ditches, all along the road to
Treguier, even as late as the afternoon of the next day' (60), thus occupy-

---

[11] For a discussion of the 'moral idiocy' that governs the world of 'The Idiots,' see
Daniel R. Schwarz, 'Moral Bankruptcy in Ploumar Parish: A Study of Conrad's "The
Idiots,"' *Conradiana* 1:3 (Summer 1969), 113-17.

ing the same ground in the same postures as the children. Even the tale
itself is described as 'simple': 'it stood at last before me, a tale formidable
and simple, as they always are, those disclosures of obscure trials endured
by ignorant hearts' (58). Both works extend the notion of idiocy and
monstrosity to encompass far more than the pathetic and innocent children
who give both stories their names.

One final but striking bit of evidence to support the connection
between the stories can be found in a remark Susan makes to her mother
just after she has murdered her husband. As she demonstrates, her heart
may be 'ignorant,' but it is not without feeling: "Do you think I have no
heart? Do you think I have never heard people jeering at me, pitying me,
wondering at me? Do you know how some of them were calling me? The
mother of idiots—that was my nickname!" (75). Maupassant's 'mother of
monsters' and Conrad's 'mother of idiots' must bear not only the full
stigma of their reproductive misfortunes, but also the weight of a social and
religious prejudice that condemns them as inhuman or diabolical creatures.

'La Mère aux monstres' is not named in any of Conrad's writings;
but few of Maupassant's stories are thus singled out for direct reference,
although Conrad is known to have read widely in Maupassant and even to
have memorized long passages from his works. In 1903 he helped Elsie
Martindale to select and translate a volume of Maupassant's stories for
publication in Duckworth's 'Evergreen Library,' and the following year he
contributed a preface to a second Duckworth collection of Maupassant
stories translated by Ada Galsworthy.[12] 'The Mother of Monsters' was not
included in either of these volumes. If Conrad were aware of its likeness
to 'The Idiots,' he might well have felt reluctant to call attention to it; and
in any case, this particularly monstrous story was hardly of the sort which
a gentleman could easily recommend to a lady for translation.

It is curious, of course, that Conrad should have written a story like
'The Idiots' while on his honeymoon, and then have asked his wife to type
it for him. He described it to his publisher, T. Fisher Unwin, as 'a story of
Brittany. Peasant life. Not for babies.'[13] Indeed, the qualification 'not for

---

[12] *Stories from De Maupassant*, tr. by E. M. [Elsie Martindale], Preface by Ford
M. Hueffer, Duckworth's Greenback Library (London: Duckworth, 1903); *Yvette and*
Other Stories, tr. by A. G. [Ada Galsworthy], Preface by Joseph Conrad (London:
Duckworth, 1904).

[13] *CL* 1, 279 (22 May 1896). The letters from Ile Grande reveal a fondness for the
story that contrasts sharply with Conrad's later comments. In this letter Conrad added,
'Fancy it, not at all bad.' When it was rejected by *Cosmopolis*, Conrad told Unwin, 'I

babies' can readily be extended to Conrad's *œuvre* in its entirety. Conrad's fictional world is essentially childless. The few infants who do appear in his works are never presented in a positive or life-confirming manner, but are marked instead with some form of fatality: in *The Secret Agent*, for example, a wife murders her husband because he has caused her brother, the 'degenerate' Stevie, to be blown to bits by a terrorist bomb. As Bernard C. Meyer has noted, Yanko Gooral's attempts in 'Amy Foster' to share his cultural birthright with his little son Johnny serve only to highlight the unbridgeable differences between Amy and Yanko, and are soon followed by Yanko's illness and death.[14]

Conrad had two sons, and his letters during the period of their infancy bear witness to his sense of the inconvenience of his role as a father. He described his elder son Borys as an eight-month-old baby in terms that mix sentiment with contempt: 'He is very large and noisy and (they say) intelligent. He has broken ever so many things—a proof of intelligence indubitably. ... He is very precious and very objectionable. I want Ted [Sanderson] to let me know what is the *very* earliest age a boy may be sent to school ...' (*CL* 2, 90, to Helen Sanderson, 31 August 1898).

Maupassant never married, but is believed to have had three illegitimate children by Joséphine Litzelmann, who worked in the thermal baths at Châtelguyon. If Conrad's works are generally 'Not for babies,' this *caveat* applies with equal force to the fictional world of Maupassant, in which children and pregnant women frequently suffer neglect or abuse. For example, 'Le Mal d'André' (from *Les Sœurs Rondoli*) describes how a lover viciously and surreptitiously pinches his mistress's tiny son, to discourage him from coming to his mother's bed. In 'Le Baptême' (from *Monsieur Parent*), a frame-tale set, like 'The Idiots,' in a village in Brittany, a doctor describes the fate of a newborn baby who freezes to death during the drunken celebrations following his baptism. In 'La Confession,' which precedes 'La Mère aux monstres' in the collection *Toine*, a respected provincial bourgeois includes in his last will and testament a letter in which he confesses to having murdered his baby son, the child of his Parisian mistress. Pregnancy is described as a mechanistic and ugly process in many of Maupassant's tales, and this maternal 'deformation' is the main theme

---

am not ashamed of it for all that. Bad or good I cannot be ashamed of what is produced in perfect single mindedness—I cannot be ashamed of those things that are like fragments of my innermost being produced for the public gaze' (*CL* 1, 293 [22 July 1896]).

[14] Bernard C. Meyer, *Joseph Conrad: A Psychoanalytic Biography* (Princeton University Press, 1967), 180-81.

of 'L'Inutile Beauté,' a late story of which Conrad is known to have been especially fond.

In conclusion, both 'La Mère aux monstres' and 'The Idiots' treat a similar subject, both share a common narrative structure as frame-tales told by a first-person narrator, and both develop metaphors and images of monstrosity to suggest that the ultimate 'horror' of these horrible tales lies not with the mothers but in the hypocrisy and bigotry in the name of which they are condemned. Whether or not Conrad was thinking of Maupassant while he was writing 'The Idiots' cannot finally be proven; but if his references to this 'obviously derivative' story imply a specific literary antecedent, then 'La Mère aux monstres' seems the most obviously monstrous literary midwife to Conrad's tale.

'Gaining Conviction':
Conradian Borrowing and the *Patna* Episode in *Lord Jim*

J. H. Stape
Visiting Professor, Kyoto University

In the course of an acute and suggestive discussion of Conrad's lack of religious belief in his introduction to the third volume of the Pléïade translations of Conrad, Sylvère Monod quotes a passage from 'The Life Beyond,' a book review Conrad wrote in July 1910, characterizing the following sentences as 'très belles et émouvantes' (III: xxxiii-iv):

> We moderns have complicated our old perplexities to the point of absurdity; our perplexities older than religion itself. It is not for nothing that for so many centuries the priest, mounting the steps of the altar, murmurs, 'Why art thou sad, my soul, and why dost thou trouble me?' Since the day of Creation two veiled figures, Doubt and Melancholy, are pacing endlessly in the sunshine of the world. What humanity needs is not the promise of scientific immortality, but compassionate pity in this life and infinite mercy on the Day of Judgment.[1]

The words are indeed 'very beautiful and moving' and are no less so for being, aside from the final sentence, Anatole France's from a review entitled 'Pourquoi sommes-nous tristes?' reprinted in his collected essays, *La Vie littéraire*.[2] The case for discussing Conrad's religious views by invoking this passage is none the less justified, for though the words are not in the first instance his, both they and the thought have become so through appropriation.

Such a situation—the direct and unacknowledged borrowing from another writer—has usually caused most literary scholars some, perhaps even considerable, discomfort. Still, just as the æsthetic power of *The Man in the Golden Helmet* or *The Polish Rider* (whatever their considerably altered market value) remains undiminished by their now less certain attribution to Rembrandt, the revelation that Conrad has 'signed' Anatole

This essay first appeared in *Conradiana* 25:3 (1993), and is reprinted here with the kind permission of the editor.

[1] In *Notes on Life and Letters*, 89-90 (cited henceforth as *NLL*).
[2] This borrowing was first pointed out in Stape 1983.

France's work neither lessens the intensity and evocative character of the words themselves nor diminishes the thoughts they embody. 'Problems' posed by such appropriations tend in the end to be more often moral than æsthetic.

Discussions of literary plagiarism are complicated by two factors. The scholar-critic frequently imposes the standards and practice of his own discourse, literary scholarship, upon discourse of another kind. For the literary critic, both customary courtesy and iron-clad rule require the explicit acknowledgement of another writer's words and ideas when these are incorporated into one's own work. The literary artist, on the other hand, remains as free from conventional practice here as, so Oscar Wilde argued, from conventional morality. The other structuring and governing constraint on discussions of plagiarism derives from the metaphoric vocabulary typically used to describe literary production, the keywords of which, the inheritance of the Romantic period of the godlike-artist, are 'creation,' 'inspiration,' and 'originality.' In short, then, considerations of this subject become quickly sidetracked by ethical concerns since, by analogy to other kinds of property rights, 'intellectual property' requires effective means to safeguard it.

Two further examples, suggesting aspects of Conrad's use and re-modelling of other writers' words and ideas, provide a backdrop to larger theoretical issues. These are offered in light of, and in addition to the convincing and copious evidence gathered by a number of scholars during the past twenty-five years and synthesized and abundantly added to by the late Yves Hervouet in his *The French Face of Joseph Conrad*. The sheer quantity of this evidence must put paid once and for all to any arguments for Conrad's 'borrowing' based on pleas for his 'remarkable but erratic memory' (Watt 50).

The first example resembles that cited at the beginning. Conrad has appropriated without acknowledgment an entire paragraph from Anatole France, but in this instance, however, nothing 'very beautiful and moving' is to be found, or, to rephrase this in another way, there is nothing particu-larly memorable in the inflated rhetoric and banal wording that conjoin to make this mere journeyman writing both in France's original text—an essay on Villiers de l'Isle-Adam—and in Conrad's translation of it:

> How better can we take leave of this interesting Vagabond than with the road salutation of passing wayfarers: 'And on you be peace! . . . You have chosen your ideal, and it is a good choice. There's nothing like giving up one's life to an unselfish passion. Let the rich and the power-ful of this globe preach their sound gospel of palpable progress. The part

of the ideal you embrace is the better one, if only in its illusions. No
great passion can be barren. May a world of gracious and poignant
images attend the lofty solitude of your renunciation!' (*NLL* 64-65)

Soyez en paix, Villiers. Vous avez pris la part de l'idéal. La part de
Marie. Et c'est la bonne part. Laissons dire les puissants et les heureux.
Il n'est tel que de vivre pour un grand amour. Vous avez aimé plus que
tout l'art et la pensée, et les sublimes illusions ont été votre juste
récompense. Les grandes passions ne sont jamais stériles. Tout un monde
d'images a peuplé les hautes solitudes de votre âme.   (VII, 127)

Granted, both this and the opening quotation are from minor writings,
hackwork even—reviews for a short-lived weekly column in *The Daily
Mail*—and Conrad's conscience doubtless little bothered him about such
appropriations. But cumulatively, as Paul Kirschner argued in *The Psychologist as Artist* and Yves Hervouet more recently, such things signify with
greater potency when creative work, as opposed to journalism, is at issue.

The second example is of a larger, subtler borrowing involving the
re-shaping of material Conrad had read as a child and that teasingly
stimulated and urged on his imagination during the writing of *Lord Jim*.
The work in question is Louis Garneray's *Voyages, aventures et combats*,
published in Paris in 1853, a book purporting to be Garneray's memoirs of
an adventurous life at sea whilst French-English hostilities were at their
height during the French Revolution and the Napoleonic era.[3] (Conrad
again drew on this volume for a few incidents and for aspects of Peyrol in
The Rover.) Garneray's work is possibly alluded to in *Lord Jim*'s first
chapter, and if not quite 'light holiday literature,' his somewhat windy,
poorly organized, and certainly unauthentic 'memoirs' are precisely the
stuff that Jim calls up in his early vision of heroic exploits: 'He saw
himself saving people from sinking ships ... He confronted savages on
tropical shores, quelled mutinies on the high seas, and in a small boat upon
the ocean kept up the hearts of despairing men' (*LJ* 6). Hervouet identifies
'two striking parallels' (75) with *Lord Jim* and Garneray's *Voyages*—Jim's
warning on the training-ship and the psychology of cowardice as seen
through the French Lieutenant's eyes; but Garneray's so-called memoirs
play a much larger and altogether more significant and sophisticated role
in *Lord Jim* in providing Conrad a model for his treatment of aspects of the

---

[3] On Conrad's reading Garneray as a child, see his letter of 14 May 1923 to G. Jean-
Aubry, *Lettres françaises*, p. 184. Since Garneray's book may not be readily available, my
translation of the episode relevant to *Lord Jim* is appended. I should like to thank Raymond
Gauthier for advice and assistance with the translation.

Patna incident in Chapters 3 to 10. While Norman Sherry's extensive labours on the episode's immediate real-life inspiration, the *Jeddah* affair and enquiry of 1880, remain unchallenged, the atmospherics, structure, and certain thematic ideas and plot motifs can be located in a chapter in Garneray's *Voyages* that dramatically details the sinking of a slaver off the coast of Africa.[4] The identification of this borrowing and remodelling, in addition to bolstering evidence that borrowing constitutes a characteristic compositional method for Conrad, also enriches our understanding of his subtle and multi-layered re-working of typical romance and adventure motifs in the novel. Whereas Garneray offers a straightforwardly chronological narrative, crudely sensationalist in rendering action and replete with stage heroics and self-indulgent posturing, Conrad plays off and transforms these into an impressionistic treatment of event complicated by a network of psychological significances, ironic gestures, stylistic subversions, dramatic tensions, and intense moral enquiry. In the end, what is at issue here is a 'borrowing' so thoroughly transformed as to be dimly recognizable, as a kind of palimpsest, in a generalized similarity of situation.

Garneray's scene opens with the serenity of nature: 'le ciel pur, à peine ridé par quelques nuages légers et blanchâtres, nous présageait une journée superbe; nos voiles, brassées en pointe, attendaient le vent; il n'y avait rien à faire' (171). This description of natural calm and consequent human inactivity obviously sets up a contrast for the tumultuous events to follow, much as Conrad underlines in the opening of *Lord Jim*'s third chapter the deceptive security of both the physical and moral universes: 'A marvellous stillness pervaded the world, and the stars, together with the serenity of their rays, seemed to shed upon the earth the assurance of everlasting security' (17). In both works this serenity proves ironically short-lived as the ship suddenly and unexpectedly becomes imperilled. Garneray registers a gamut of emotions running from shock and surprise to bewilderment with an immediacy consistent with the direct and uncomplicated nature of the average tar of sea fiction: experience is represented virtually unmediated by reflection, and stimulus begets immediate response. The outlines of the adventure hero and the adventure story, as critics have observed, are by contrast subverted in *Lord Jim*, where the protagonist's complications (and Jim is deliberately uncomplicated) prolong each sensation and emotion almost to the point of neurosis, and events take on a significance that extends beyond the momentary and ranges out into the

---

[4] For an extended discussion of the *Jeddah* affair, see Sherry, *Conrad's Eastern World* (Cambridge: Cambridge University Press, 1966), 41-64.

moral and psychological, into realms of innate indeterminacy. This conception is articulated by the intricate narrative technique—the kaleidoscopic perspectives afforded by the shifts in and out of Jim's own narrative—and is furthered by the multiplicity of competing voices, each offering partial interpretations in the face of the comically inadequate organizing conceptions of law and tradition that posit the existence of absolute distinctions and absolute truths.

While Garneray and Jim are so fundamentally different as to make their few similarities and the claims for them appear exaggerated, the case for adducing 'influence' here rests on incident rather than character. First, both protagonists imaginatively envisage the death of all the ship's passengers and crew, and both are passive before imminent death. Secondly, both works vividly contrast their protagonists' heroic conception of duty with that of the captains, who are bent on saving themselves in direct contradiction to the traditions of the sea and of honour. And, lastly, both captains conspire with members of the crew to save themselves without any regard for their human 'cargo.'

While Garneray's account is almost rigorously unpsychological and unreflective, the product of a relatively simple ideology embodied in, and emerging from an appropriate narrative, stylistic, and structural simplicity, one point of confluence with Conrad's conception of Jim can be found in Garneray's initial passivity, almost indifference, in the face of imminent and what appears to be inevitable death. Jim's psychological paralysis is dramatically rendered by his physical immobility:

> He stood still looking at these recumbent bodies ... They *were* dead! Nothing could save them! There were boats enough for half of them perhaps, but there was no time. No time! No time! It did not seem worth while to open his lips, to stir hand or foot. ... he went through it all motionless by the hatchway ... 'It seemed to take all life out of my limbs. I thought I might just as well stand where I was and wait.' (86)

Garneray's apprehension of the climactic moment when he faces death, while not dramatized by physical posture, closely resembles Jim's conception of himself and his situation:

> Une minute, une seule minute, et pas un de nous peut-être ne sera vivant!
> Comme jamais encore je n'avais entendu rapporter l'exemple d'un navire chaviré qui n'eût point coulé immédiatement, je m'attendais à chaque seconde à voir *la Doris* s'abîmer dans les flots. A chaque

secousse qui lui imprimait la mer, je fermais instinctivement les yeux
pour ne point assister au drame terrible dont je devais être la victime; je
regardais ma mort comme une chose tellement inévitable que je ne
songeais même pas à chercher un moyen qui me permît de disputer ma
vie.   (172-73)

While in Conrad violent death remains imagined, projected rather than
actual (following the real-life model of the *Jeddah*, which did not sink), in
Garneray the dramatic possibilities of drowning masses are seized upon and
sensationally rendered, as the ship's crew and human cargo alike fall victim
first to fear and then to the sea. The texts share, however, the central
psychological violence of the protagonist's paralysis of the will to self-
preservation.

The second close thematic parallel is the handling of the crew's
abandonment of their charges, justified to themselves by an underlying
hostility towards their racial 'inferiors'—the pilgrims in *Lord Jim*, the
slaves in Garneray, in the classic alienation of the 'Other.' This 'otherness'
too, as far as both captains are concerned, absolves them from the accusa-
tion of abandoning their duty. An even more important similarity, however,
is the antagonism between Garneray and Captain Liard, which parallels that
of Jim and his fellow crew members, especially the *Patna*'s German
captain. In Garneray's *Voyages*, the conspiracy between M. Liard and his
first officer, M. Boudin, directly parallels that in *Lord Jim*. Setting himself
apart from—and above—his superior officer, Garneray comments:

Un capitaine, on le sait, doit toujours être le dernier à abandonner son
navire: aussi ma première pensée fut-elle, en recueillant M. Liard, qu'il
voulait s'assurer par lui-même de la possibilité de construire un radeau,
et qu'une fois son opinion formée à cet égard, il retournerait à bord.
 Cependant, en considérant son air effrayé, sa pâleur, le tremblement
convulsif qui agite ses membres, je compréhends bientôt que je me suis
trompé et qu'il ne songe qu'à fuir. Je ne doute même plus que cet em-
barquement, en dehors de toutes les lois de l'honneur et du devoir, n'ait
été concerté à l'avance entre M. Liard et son second, M. Boudin. (175)

This alienating moment provides Conrad with some of his most
significant thematic material. While Jim initially hopes to absolve himself
from the rest of the crew's moral contamination, he is gradually forced,
partly by Marlow's questioning and partly by the older man's sympathy,
to see how his own actions, even if unwilled, taint him. Garneray simply
states the contrast: honour and duty isolate him both in *The Doris* and then
in the dinghy, where the hostility between him and the captain openly

breaks out as he accuses the captain of besmirching not only his honour but Garneray's as well. A further link between Garneray and Conrad is that the protagonists of both texts express the desire to swim back to their ships to recuperate their losses. In Garneray's *Voyages* this is mostly a matter of heroic swagger, a dash through shark-infested waters against insuperable odds:

> — Ainsi, vous êtes bien decidé à rester sur *la Doris*?
> — On ne peut plus décidé, capitaine.
> — Soit; mais de quelle façon comptez-vous y retourner?
> Cette question me donna à réfléchir.
> — A la nage, capitaine, lui répondis-je, car vous ne consentirez probablement pas à m'y conduire? . . .   (177)

By contrast to such adventure-tale posturing, Jim's desire to return to the site of the *Patna*'s sinking (for the ship is at that moment believed lost) enacts a poignant longing for a conception of himself and of the universe now irrecoverable: 'It seemed to me that I must jump out of that accursed boat and swim back to see—half a mile—more—any distance—to the very spot . . .' (113).

The most telling lesson in considering the influence of Garneray's memoirs on the *Patna* incident in *Lord Jim* lies in the way such material highlights Conrad's remodelling: the very concept of heroic endeavour in *Lord Jim* is consistently undermined by achronological narrative and insistent and subversive commentary. Where in Garneray the value of 'honour' remains unquestioned, grounded in Latin conceptions of the self and in the traditions of the sea, Conrad's moral universe totters on the indeterminate. It is also signally interesting to watch Conrad in the act of transforming his childhood reading (which may in part have inspired his own desire to go to sea) into the hesitations, qualifications, and outright doubts of a complex adult world in which disillusionment acts as an invigorating and even creative force.

Obviously, such an instance of 'borrowing' (the word is obviously inadequate given the sophistication of the transformation in question) differs from the lifting of sentences or paragraphs. Yet the borrower's condition in both instances differs not in essence but in detail: Conrad's sense of creative isolation lessens in his recourse to other writers with whom he shares his primary identity. Moreover, another defining position can be located in the writer's posture vis-à-vis an audience. Aware of the need to create, and fated to fill up the blank page for an audience ever hungry for novelty, Conrad shares the common condition of the writer of fiction who is pressed by economic necessity: the exigencies of societal role and inner compulsion determine behaviour. Borrowing and transformation tend, moreover, to lend authenticity and even authority to one's words and ideas, and thus to confirm the status of a work (and of a self) that one might question or be uncertain of. In Conradian terms, this becomes the need to find a community of belief sought by all tellers of tales, even if tentatively and hesitatingly, for reasons echoed in the epigraph from Novalis that provides the opening mood of *Lord Jim*: 'It is certain any conviction gains infinitely, the moment another soul will believe in it.' Conrad seeks precisely this confirmation in what might be termed his creative interaction with other writers and prior texts, for there, at least, lies an illusion of security that an anonymous and impersonal readership is by its very nature unable to offer. In this sense, borrowing becomes a means of identity and an affirmation of connectedness. Whatever its ethics, its psychological dimensions are prior and commanding.

WORKS CITED

Conrad, Joseph. 'A Happy Wanderer.' 1910. *Notes on Life and Letters*. London and Toronto: J. M. Dent & Sons, Ltd., 1921. 83-88.

———. 'The Ascending Effort.' 1910. *Notes on Life and Letters*. London: Dent, 1921. 95-100.

———. *Conrad: Œuvres* III. Ed. Sylvère Monod. Paris: Gallimard, 1987.

———. *Lettres françaises*. Ed. G. Jean-Aubry. Paris: Gallimard, [1929].

———. 'The Life Beyond.' 1910. *Notes on Life and Letters*. London: Dent, 1921. 89-94.

———. *Lord Jim*. 1900. Ed. John Batchelor. Oxford: Oxford University Press, 1983.

France, Anatole. 'Villiers de l'Isle-Adam.' *La Vie littéraire*, 3rd series (1891). In *Œuvres complètes illustrées d'Anatole France*, VII. Paris: Calmann-Levy, 1926.

Garneray, Louis. *Voyages, aventures et combats* (1853). Rpt. as *Le Négrier de Zanzibar*. Paris: Phébus, 1985.

Hervouet, Yves. *The French Face of Joseph Conrad*. Cambridge: Cambridge University Press, 1990.

Kirschner, Paul. *Conrad: The Psychologist as Artist*. Edinburgh: Oliver & Boyd, 1968.

Sherry, Norman. *Conrad's Eastern World*. Cambridge: Cambridge University Press, 1966.

Stape, J. H. 'Conrad as Journalist: Further Borrowings from Anatole France.' *The Conradian* 8 (1983): 39-43.

Watt, Ian. *Conrad in the Nineteenth Century*. Berkeley: University of California Press, 1979.

APPENDIX

From Louis Garneray, *Voyages, aventures et combats* (1853)

Naufrage: bonheur providentiel—Catastrophe épouvantable—
Singulière détermination du capitaine—Résignation héroïque de
François Combaleau—*La Doris* abandonnée

Il était alors onze heures du matin: le ciel pur, à peine ridé par
quelques nuages légers et blanchâtres, nous présageait une journée superbe;
nos voiles, brassées en pointe, attendaient le vent; il n'y avait rien à faire.
Le capitaine, fatigué par ses calculs et affaibli par sa blessure, profita de
ce moment d'inaction pour aller prendre un peu de repos dans sa cabine.

Comme dans cette absence de toute manœuvre rien ne nécessitait la
présence de tout l'équipage sur le pont, M. Boudin, le second, homme peu
marin, me pria de descendre dans la cambuse avec quelques-uns de nos
hommes et de nos Noirs fidèles, pour y opérer un rangement devenu indis-
pensable par suite de la consommation d'une partie des provisions. M.
Boudin, après m'avoir donné cette mission, car il n'entendait rien à
l'arrimage, prit le quart à ma place. François Combaleau, qui depuis la
mort ou la disparition du chat avait tout à fait perdu sa gaieté, était alors
à la barre.

J'étais dans la cambuse à peu près depuis vingt minutes, quand une
fraîcheur soudaine et tout à fait inattendue se répandit dans la cale et appela
mon attention. Soudain je sens le navire qui s'incline d'une façon tellement
effrayante que le désarrimage le plus complet s'ensuit! . . . Aussitôt tous
les objets d'armement roulent avec fracas du côté de tribord; l'équipage
pousse des cris d'épouvante et j'entends la voix du second d'abord et celle
du capitaine ensuite qui commandent: 'La barre au vent! . . . Amène les
perroquets, les huniers, le pic! . . . Largue les écoutes du grand hunier!
. . .'

Le doute ne m'est pas possible, quelque grand malheur vient
d'arriver. Je m'élance aussitôt vers la porte de la dunette: un torrent d'eau
me renverse. Je me relève vivement et je parviens à me hisser non sans
peine sur la partie du navire qui n'est pas encore submergée. Combaleau
est le premier matelot que j'aperçois; il a un air hagard, épouvanté, qui me
frappe d'une surprise d'autant plus grande que je connais l'intrépidité et
l'admirable sang-froid dont cet homme est doué.

— Comment cela est-il arrivé?
Car le navire est chaviré!

— Je ne sais, lieutenant! . . . me répond-il avec embarras. On dit que c'est un grain blanc qui nous a assaillis à l'improviste et a fait chavirer le navire devenu rebelle au gouvernail . . . mais c'est pas vrai!

— Comment, ce n'est pas vrai!

— Lieutenant, voyez-vous, me répond à voix basse Combaleau, ce malheur vient de la mort du chat . . . C'était écrit là-haut! . . . nous ne pouvions pas l'éviter.

A présent, comment peindre la consternation de notre équipage et la position dans laquelle nous nous trouvons? Ce n'est pas possible. Nos matelots, accrochés à la mâture et aux points de la carène que la mer n'a pas encore envahis, regardent, immobiles, muets, d'un œil hébété les vagues qui bondissent en les couvrant de leur écume et qui semblent vouloir les saisir!

Une minute, une seule minute, et pas un de nous peut-être ne sera vivant!

Comme jamais encore je n'avais entendu rapporter l'exemple d'un navire chaviré qui n'eut point coulé immédiatement, je m'attendais à chaque seconde à voir *la Doris* s'abîmer dans les flots. A chaque secousse qui lui imprimait la mer, je fermais instinctivement les yeux pour ne point assister au drame terrible dont je devais être la victime; je regardais ma mort comme une chose tellement inévitable que je ne songeais même pas à chercher un moyen qui me permît de disputer ma vie.

Le lecteur croira peut-être que l'homme dans une position aussi affreuse et aussi désespérée que celle dans laquelle je me trouvais doit éprouver un désespoir profond, être en proie à une terreur extrême; il n'en est rien. Soit que l'excès de l'émotion ou de la peur, en paralysant vos facultés, vous conduise à une espèce d'insensibilité, soit que l'instinct de la conservation perde une grande partie de sa force en face d'un mort certaine, assurée: toujours est-il que le sentiment dominant parmi l'équipage de *la Doris*, dans ce moment critique, était celui d'une résignation passive et inintelligente.

Cependant lorsque nous vîmes, après deux ou trois minutes, que notre brick, resté couché sur tribord, ne s'enfonçait pas dans l'abîme, un immense espoir nous vint au cœur et nous commençâmes à reprendre courage.

Plusieurs de nos matelots, passant de leur apathie de brute à une ivresse irraisonnée, se mirent à verser des larmes de joie et à remercier Dieu avec transport.

Celui de nos hommes qui le premier de tous songea à sauver sa vie fut le Bordelais Ducasse, qui se glissa furtivement derrière nous pour s'embarquer dans le canot que *la Doris* traînait à sa remorque depuis

Zanzibar, et dont la bosse s'était par bonheur trouvée attachée au couronnement du bord du vent à l'instant de la catastrophe.

Cette embarcation, celle que nous avions dédoublée, était la seule que
nous possédions, car le lecteur doit se souvenir que nous avions été obligés
d'abandonner les autres à la douane de Zanzibar lors de notre fuite de ce
port. Elle représentait donc notre unique moyen de salut.

On ne s'étonnera pas, en songeant à cela, que tous-les yeux fussent
tournés vers le canot et que dix personnes, au risque de tomber à la mer,
se précipitassent, en abandonnant à la hâte leurs abris, entre l'embarcation
et Ducasse.

— Garneray, me dit alors le capitaine, sautez dans le canot avec
maître Fleury, et allez détacher en toute hâte les espars qui pourront nous
servir à la construction d'un radeau!

Ce mot de radeau avidement recueilli par l'équipage fit battre de joie
tous les cœurs; en effet, avec les brises assez constantes qui règnent dans
ces parrages, et ne nous trouvant qu'à une quarantaine de lieues au plus de
la côte, nous pouvions espérer avec raison arriver à terre.

— Il faut au moins deux hommes pour conduire l'embarcation, tandis
que le troisième détachera les espars, dit Ducasse qui, avant que j'aie eu le
temps de lui répondre, s'est glissé dans le canot entre maître Fleury et moi
et a poussé au large.

Le navire gisait alors, je l'ai déjà dit, sur la côte de tribord, et bien
que la mâture battît la vague à chaque roulis, ce qui rendait notre travail
excessivement difficile et pénible, nous parvînmes cependant à détacher les
basses vergues qui devaient servir de base dans la construction du radeau.
Ce ne fut pas non plus sans danger que nous parvînmes à accomplir cette
tâche, car les nègres dispersés dans le gréement tentaient de s'emparer de
notre canot par la violence et par la surprise, et nous avions toutes les
peines du monde à les repousser.

C'était en vain que nous faisions tous nos efforts pour les calmer et
les convaincre que, dans notre position critique, la bonne entente de tous
pouvait seule nous sauver; qu'au reste, nous ne voulions pas les abandonner, au contraire; que nous allions construire un radeau qui nous
permettrait à tous d'atteindre la terre: dominés par la peur et insensibles à
la voix de la raison, ils n'en continuaient pas moins sur nous leurs dange-
reuses tentatives, nous accablant d'injures et menaçant de nous massacrer.
Leur exaspération finit même par se monter à un tel degré que, dans la
crainte de voir ces misérables envahir notre frêle embarcation, nous fûmes
obligés de gagner le large.

Nous étions désespérés. En effet, la construction de ce radeau qui
était notre seul et unique moyen de salut devint, grâce à la stupide fureur

des Africains, une chose tout à fait impossible. Nous nous tenions station-
naires à quelques brasses de l'arrière de *la Doris* quand M. Liard, se
penchant de notre côté et se faisant une espèce de porte-voix naturel avec
ses deux mains de façon que ses paroles nous arrivassent sans être
entendues par ceux qui se trouvaient à bord, nous héla d'accoster le
couronnement en déguisant notre évolution de façon à donner le change
aux nègres.

Feignant aussitôt de diriger la pirogue sur l'avant du navire où les
Noirs se portent de suite en foule pour s'emparer de notre embarcation, je
fais scier et j'accoste la poupe avant qu'ils puissent se douter de mon
dessein.

Aussitôt M. Liard, M. Boudin et le frère du maître d'équipage Fleury
qui se tenaient sur le couronnement de *la Doris* sautent dans le canot et
nous poussons au large. Un capitaine, on le sait, doit toujours être le
dernier à abandonner son navire: aussi ma première pensée fut-elle, en
recueillant M. Liard, qu'il voulait s'assurer par lui-même de la possibilité
de construire un radeau, et qu'une fois son opinion formée à cet égard, il
retournerait à bord.

Cependant, en considérant son air effrayé, sa pâleur, le tremblement
convulsif qui agite ses membres, je compréhends bientôt que je me suis
trompé et qu'il ne songe qu'à fuir. Je ne doute même plus que cet em-
barquement, en dehors de toutes les lois de l'honneur et du devoir, n'ait été
concerté à l'avance entre M. Liard et son second, M. Boudin.

A peine le canot s'est-il éloigné de quelques mètres de *la Doris* que
les nègres qui nous attendaient sur l'arrière, comprenant qu'on les aban-
donnait, se précipitent en foule à la mer et se mettent à notre poursuite.
Nous prenons chasse devant eux.

Peu à peu le nombre de ces malheureux diminue d'une façon effrayante: les uns sont trahis par leurs forces, les autres deviennent la proie des
requins. A chaque instant, un cri retentit, une malédiction nous est adressée,
et un homme disparaît. C'est à peine si nous osons tourner nos regards vers
la Doris, tant le spectacle que présente notre pauvre brick est affreux!
Chaque lame entraîne dans son ressac des femmes et des enfants que nous
voyons tourbillonner une minute, puis s'enfoncer dans l'abîme. Les
écoutilles ouvertes vomissent les cadavres des infortunés qui au moment de
la catastrophe se trouvaient enfermés dans le faux-pont. Cela ne peut
s'imaginer ni se décrire!

Quelques captifs dans la force de l'âge fendent la mer de leurs larges
poitrines, et, soutenus par un suprême désespoir, parviennent jusqu'à notre
embarcation; mais notre canot, qui n'a que neuf pieds de long et ne

supporte déjà qu'avec peine le poids de six hommes, va couler si un seul d'entre eux parvient à y monter, alors! . . . ma plume se refuse à retracer la sauvage fureur qui s'empare de MM. Liard et Boudin. Pas un seul des nègres ne peut réussir à escalader notre frêle esquif: les avirons, dont le capitaine et son second se sont armés, ruissellent de sang!

Pendant deux heures, deux siècles! nous restons en vue de *la Doris*. Et penser que si les Africains consentaient seulement à se tenir tranquilles, à nous parviendrions peut-être à relever le navire, en tout cas à construire un radeau! Voir la réussite, le salut de tous à notre portée, et ne pouvoir y atteindre! Ah! ce supplice n'est pas le moins cruel de tous!

— Messieurs, nous dit enfin le capitaine après avoir échangé avec M. Boudin un regard d'intelligence que je surprends au passage; que devons-nous faire? A moi, il me semble que dans l'intérêt de tous nous devons gagner au plus vite la haute mer et nous diriger vers la côte. Pour peu que le vent nous protège, nous atteindrons la terre en deux jours et nous pourrons alors revenir au secours de nos pauvres amis.

— Capitaine, lui dis-je, notre honneur n'appartient qu'à vous, et vous êtes certes libre d'en disposer à votre gré; seulement il ne nous est pas permis d'attenter à celui des autres! Or, comme je suis officier et que mon grade m'ordonne de n'abandonner le navire sur lequel je navigue qu'après que le dernier matelot en est parti, je retourne à bord de *la Doris*.

— Êtes-vous fou, Garneray, s'écrie Liard, et réfléchissez-vous bien à ce que vous dites?

— Cela est tellement simple, capitaine, que la réflexion n'a rien à y voir.

— Ainsi, vous êtes bien décidé à rester sur *la Doris*?

— On ne peut plus décidé, capitaine.

— Soit; mais de quelle façon comptez-vous y retourner?

Cette question me donna à réfléchir.

— A la nage, capitaine, lui répondis-je, car vous ne consentirez probablement pas à m'y conduire? . . .

— A la nage? Regardez donc un peu, Garneray, les ailerons noirs des requins qui sillonnnent de tous côtés la mer à l'entour de nous! Croyez-vous que les nègres et ces voraces et impitoyables ennemis vous laisseront accomplir en paix le trajet qui nous sépare du brick? Votre projet, convenez-en, est insensé et ne mérite même pas d'être combattu.

— Mais, capitaine, je suis officier, et comme tel, je dois . . .

— Non, monsieur, vous n'êtes point officier, s'écria le capitaine en m'interrompant. Ne touchant pas d'appointements et ne participant pas aux bénéfices de la traite, votre position à bord de *la Doris* n'a jamais été, et vous-même avez assez souvent pris soin de me le rappeler, que celle d'un simple auxiliaire. Après tout, voilà déjà trop de temps perdu en vaines paroles . . . Si vous tenez absolument à servir de pâture aux requins, libre à vous de vous passer cette fantaisie . . . Quant à moi, comme je suis capitaine et maître ici, je n'ai que faire de votre opposition et de vos remontrances . . .

Cette observation, qui me parut assez juste, jointe à la vue des nombreux requins qui prenaient leurs ébats et se prélassaient dans l'immense curée de notre catastrophe, m'empêcha d'insister. Je me permis toutefois de répondre à M. Liard que peut-être ferions-nous bien de nous rapprocher de *la Doris* pour essayer d'embarquer avec nous ceux des matelots qui ne craindraient pas de nous rejoindre à la nage.

— Votre avis ne vaut rien, me répondit M. Liard, et cela pour plusieurs raisons: la première, c'est qu'il est probable que les requins ne laisseraient arriver que peu de nos amis jusqu'à nous; la seconde, c'est que le poids d'un seul homme en plus serait capable de couler notre canot. Il ne faut donc point songer à cela; néanmoins, je suis d'avis de nous rapprocher de *la Doris* pour tâcher de nous procurer une boussole que l'on pourrait nous jeter . . . Qu'en pensez-vous, mes amis?

Les deux Fleury, Ducasse et surtout M. Boudin, qui pendant ma discussion avec le capitaine n'avaient pas hésité à se ranger du parti de ce dernier, l'approuvèrent.

Un quart d'heure plus tard, nous arrivions, après avoir nagé vigou-reusement, à une encâblure de notre pauvre brick.

Jamais je n'oublierai les supplications et les prières que nous adres-sèrent, pour que nous leur permissions de nous rejoindre, le charpentier Martin, le tonnelier Boubert, le matelot Périn et le lamentable Fignolet. Elles me déchirèrent le cœur, et je crois les entendre encore.

François Combaleau seul, monté sur la partie la plus élevée de la coque du navire, son poing gauche appuyé sur la hanche, sa tête orgueil-leusement rejetée en arrière, n'implora pas notre pitié; loin de là même.

— Mes amis, nous dit-il, le mieux que vous ayez à faire est de décamper au plus vite et d'aller nous chercher des secours. N'écoutez point les jérémiades de tous ces blagueurs, ils ne savent ce qu'ils veulent.

— Mais qu'allez-vous devenir, François? m'écriai-je.

— Merci de votre intérêt, lieutenant, me répondit-il. Je pense qu'avant demain matin tous nos moricauds auront fait le plongeon . . . Alors nous pourrons nous occuper à établir un radeau. Eh bien! lieutenant, trouvez-vous toujours que ce soit une bêtise de croire à l'influence de la mort d'un chat?

Voyant, après quelques pourparlers, qu'il nous serait impossible d'obtenir la boussole que nous désirions et que les hommes restés à bord de *la Doris* eussent été obligés d'aller chercher dans la chambre inondée par la mer, nous adressâmes un dernier adieu à nos malheureux compagnons et nous poussâmes au large.

— Bien du plaisir et de l'agrément, nous cria François, et tâchez de revenir le plus promptement possible . . . Ça ne fait rien, capitaine, sans rancune! . . . mais permettez-moi de vous faire observer, avec infiniment de respect, que vous avez en appareillant de Bourbon un vendredi fait une brioche énorme!

François, fort satisfait d'avoir pu proclamer bien haut, en l'envoyant à l'adresse de qui de droit, cette vérité qui l'étouffait, se mit alors à brailler à tue-tête le couplet de l'opéra-comique du *Déserteur*:

> Mourir n'est rien, c'est notre dernière heure;
> Chaque minute, chaque pas
> Ne mène-t-il pas au trépas?

Forçant alors des rames, nous nous éloignâmes rapidement de *la Doris*. Pendant longtemps la voix de François, mêlée aux imprécations des nègres, arriva distincte, comme un poignant remords, jusqu'à nous. Peu à peu elle se changea en murmures, et cessa bientôt après ...

TRANSLATION

A Sinking: Providential Good Luck—A Horrible Catastrophe—
The Captain's Remarkable Determination—François Combaleau Heroically Accepts his Fate—*The Doris* Abandoned

It was then eleven o'clock in the morning. A clear sky, wrinkled only
by a few light white clouds, promised a superb day; our sails, unfurled,
were awaiting the wind. There was nothing to do. Tired out by his calcu-
lations and weakened by his wound, the captain took advantage of this
moment of inaction to repair to his cabin for a bit of rest.

No manœuvres being required, the entire crew's presence on the
bridge was unnecessary, and Monsieur Boudin, the first officer, not much
of a sailor, asked me to go down into the stores with a few of our men and
some of our loyal blacks to put some order into things, which had become
necessary following the spoilage of a part of our provisions. Monsieur
Boudin, having given me that assignment and because he understood
nothing about stowage, took the watch in my place. François Combaleau,
who since the cat's death or disappearance had lost all his good spirits, was
then at the helm.

I was in the stores for about twenty minutes when a sudden and
altogether unexpected freshness spread in the hold and demanded my
attention. All of a sudden I felt the ship tilt in such a frightening way that
the stores were completely turned about! And at the same moment the
armaments rolled noisily on the starboard side. The crew gave out cries of
terror and I heard first the mate's voice and then the captain's: 'Tiller to
the wind! Haul in the topgallant sail, the topsail, the halyards. Slacken the
main topsail rigging!'

Doubt was no longer possible. Some great horror had just occurred.
I rushed to the poop-deck door: a torrent of water threw me back. I got up
quickly and managed to climb with difficulty to the part of the ship that
remained out of water. Combaleau was the first sailor I saw; he looked
haggard and frightened, which, knowing the man's characteristic bravery
and calm, struck me with surprise.

'How did it happen?'
The ship was capsizing.
Shaken, he answered, 'I don't know, lieutenant. They say a sudden
squall hit us unawares and made the ship capsize because the rudder got
out of control. But that's not true.'
'What do you mean, not true?'

'Lieutenant, you see,' he said under his breath, 'this bad luck comes from the cat's death. It was fated . . . and we couldn't avoid it.'

But how to describe the crew's consternation and the position in which we found ourselves? Our sailors, holding fast to the masts and the points of the keel still above water, were looking, immobile and mute, with a bewildered gaze upon the leaping waves that were covering them with their spume and seemed to want to snatch them!

A minute, a single minute, and not one of us perhaps will be alive!

As I had never heard tell of a ship that capsized and had not gone under immediately, I was waiting at every moment to see *The Doris* swallowed up by the waves. At each jolt the sea gave her, I instinctively shut my eyes in order not to witness the terrible drama of which I was to be the victim; I thought my death so inevitable I didn't even think to look for a means to help me fight for my life.

The reader will perhaps believe that a man in such a terrible and desperate position ought to feel profound despair, ought to be the prey of an extreme terror. That is not so. Whether excess emotion or fear, by paralyzing your faculties, induces a kind of fixed insensitivity, or whether the instinct of self-preservation loses most of its force in the face of certain death, the dominant emotion of *The Doris*'s crew at that critical instant was passive and brute resignation.

But at the end of two or three minutes, when we saw that our brig remained leaning to starboard, but not falling into the abyss, a great hope came to our hearts and we began to regain our courage.

Many of our sailors, passing from brute apathy to irrational happiness, could be witnessed crying tears of joy and rapturously thanking God.

The first of our men to think of saving his own life was Ducasse, from Bordeaux, who slipped furtively behind us to get into the dinghy that *The Doris* had dragged in tow from Zanzibar and whose hump luckily was windward, attached to the taffrail at the moment of the catastrophe.

That small boat, which we had unsheathed, was the only one we had because, as the reader will remember, we had had to abandon the others at the Zanzibar custom-house during our flight from that port. It was therefore our only means of saving ourselves.

It is hardly astonishing that, aware of that, all eyes were turned towards the dinghy and that ten people, at the risk of falling into the sea, rushed towards her, quickly abandoning their refuge between the dinghy and Ducasse.

'Garneray,' the captain then addressed me, 'jump into the dinghy with Fleury and get loose as quickly as possible any spars we can use to build a raft!'

The word 'raft' avidly heard by the crew made all hearts beat with joy; and, indeed, with the steady breezes common to those waters, and being no more than some forty leagues from the coast, we could reasonably hope to reach land.

'At least two men will be needed to guide the dinghy while the third will get the spars loose,' said Ducasse who, before I had time to answer him, slipped into the boat between Fleury and myself and pushed it free.

The boat was lying, as I have already said, to starboard, and although the masts struck the waves at each roll, which made our work extremely difficult and painful, we succeeded none the less in getting loose the lower yards which could serve as the basis for making a raft. Not without risk did we manage to finish this task, because the blacks dispersed about in the rigging tried to get hold of our dinghy by violence and surprise, and we had an awful time keeping them off.

Vain were all our efforts to calm and convince them that in our critical position everyone's good will alone could save us, and that, moreover, we did not want to abandon them but, on the contrary, were building a raft that would let us all reach land. Overwhelmed by fear and insensitive to the voice of reason, they continued their dangerous attempts, calling down oaths upon us and threatening to massacre us. Their exasperation ended by reaching such a pitch that, fearing those wretches would overwhelm our frail dinghy, we were obliged to set out.

We were in desperate straits. In fact, building that raft, which was our only means of saving ourselves, became absolutely impossible, thanks to the stupid fury of those Africans. We were holding ourselves stable at some fathoms off the stern of *The Doris* when Monsieur Liard leaned down on our side and, making a natural speaking-trumpet with his hands so that his words reached us without being heard by those on board, hailed us to come alongside the taffrail and conceal our manœuvre so as to cock a snook at the blacks.

Pretending to direct the boat towards the bow, where the blacks went in a crowd in order to get hold of our dinghy, I managed to reach the poop before they could guess my intention.

On the instant Messrs. Liard, Boudin, and boatswain Fleury's brother, who was on *The Doris*'s taffrail, all jumped into the boat and we pushed off. The captain, as is known, ought always be the last to leave his ship, and my first thought in picking up Monsieur Liard was that he wanted to assure himself about building a raft and that, once sure about this, would return on board.

However, upon seeing his frightened air, his pallor, and the convulsive trembling of his limbs, I quickly understood I was mistaken and that he thought only of fleeing. I no longer doubt that that boarding, beyond all the laws of honour and duty, had been planned in advance between Monsieur Liard and his first officer, Monsieur Boudin.

Hardly had the canoe distanced itself by a few metres from *The Doris* when the blacks who were waiting for us at the stern, understanding that they had been abandoned, rushed in a crowd into the sea and began to pursue us. We took chase before them.

Little by little the number of those wretches diminished in a frightful way. Some gave out exhausted, others became the prey of sharks. At every moment a cry was heard, a curse called down upon us, and a man disappeared. Hardly do we dare to turn our eyes towards *The Doris*, so awful was the spectacle of our poor brig! Each wave took in its undertow women and children, whom we saw whirl about for a minute and then disappear into the abyss. The hatchways vomited forth the bodies of the unfortunates who found themselves locked in the between-decks when the catastrophe struck. Such a sight can neither be imagined nor described!

A few captives young enough to cleave the sea with their broad chests, and sustained by their extreme despair, succeeded in reaching our dinghy. But our boat, only nine feet long and scarcely able to support the weight of six men, would have foundered if even one of them had managed to board. Look here! my pen refuses to limn the savage fury that took hold of Messrs. Liard and Boudin. Not one black succeeded in climbing up into our frail skiff. The oars with which the captain and his mate armed themselves streamed with blood!

During two hours—two centuries rather—we remained in sight of *The Doris*. And to think if only those Africans had consented to remain quiet and let us work, we would have perhaps succeeded in raising the ship, in any case in building a raft! To see success, the safety of everyone at our fingertips and not be able to reach it! Oh, that punishment is not the least cruel of all!

'Gentlemen,' our captain said to us at last after a knowing look had passed between himself and Monsieur Boudin that I caught by chance, 'what ought we to do? As for myself, I think that in the interests of everyone we ought to make for the high seas as quickly as possible and from there direct ourselves to the coast. Providing that the wind is in our favour, we shall make landfall in two days and will then come back to help our poor friends.'

'Captain,' I said to him, 'our honour is in your hands, and you are free to dispose of us according to your will. Only you have no right to mount an attack upon the honour of others! But since I am an officer, my rank compels me not to abandon the ship upon which I sail until after the last sailor has left it, and so I am returning aboard *The Doris*.'

'Are you mad, Garneray,' cried Liard, 'and have you considered what you're saying?'

'It is so simple, captain, that thought has nothing to do with it.'

'Then, you've decided to remain aboard *The Doris*?'

'I couldn't be more decided, captain.'

'So be it. But how do you think of returning to her?'

That question made me think.

'By swimming, captain,' I answered him, 'because you are unlikely to agree to conducting me thither . . . ?'

'By swimming? Look a bit, then, Garneray, at the black shark fins that criss-cross the water all around us! Do you think the blacks and those voracious and pitiless enemies will leave you alone for the distance separating us from the brig? Admit that your project is mad and isn't worth putting into action.'

'But, captain, I am an officer, and as such bound . . .'

'No, sir. You are not an officer,' the captain cried out interrupting me. 'Lacking a monthly salary and the benefit of a contract, your position aboard *The Doris* has never been other than that of a simple auxiliary, as you yourself have reminded me often enough. Now then, too much time has already been lost in useless talk . . . If you are absolutely determined to become shark fodder, you're free to indulge that fantasy . . . As for myself, as captain and master here, I have nothing to do with your opposition and remonstrances . . .'

This observation, which appeared reasonable enough to my eyes, combined with the sight of numerous sharks disporting themselves and taking their ease in the huge scramble of our catastrophe, forbade me to insist. I none the less permitted myself to reply to Monsieur Liard that perhaps we might do well to approach *The Doris* to try to get on board those sailors who wouldn't be afraid to swim over to us.

'Your opinion is worthless,' Monsieur Liard replied, 'and for several reasons. First, it's likely the sharks would let but few of our friends reach us; secondly, the weight of only one man would be enough to sink our canoe. It's out of the question, but none the less I think we ought to approach *The Doris* to try to get the compass, which they could throw to us . . . What do you think, my friends?'

The Fleury brothers, Ducasse, and especially Monsieur Boudin, who during my discussion with the captain had not hesitated to take his part, approved this plan.

After a quarter of an hour of vigorous rowing we arrived at a cable's length from our poor ship.

I shall never forget the prayers and supplications made to join us by Martin the carpenter, Boubert the cooper, Périn the sailor, and the lamentable Fignolet. They rend my heart, and I think I can hear them still. François Combaleau alone, mounted upon the highest part of our hull, his left fist placed on his hip, his head proudly thrown back, did not beg our pity; far from it.

'My friends,' he told us, 'the best you could do is to get out of here as quickly as possible and go look for help. Don't listen to the lamentations of those jokers who don't know what they want.'

'But what is to become of you, François?' I cried.

'Thank you for asking, lieutenant,' he answered me. 'I think that before tomorrow morning all our coons will have made the plunge . . . Then we will be able to get down to making a raft. So, lieutenant, do you still think it stupid to believe in the influence of the death of a cat?'

Realizing after several exchanges that it would be impossible for us to get the compass we wanted, and that the men staying aboard *The Doris* might have had to go look for it in a cabin below water, we addressed our last farewells to our unfortunate companions and set out for the open sea.

'Enjoy yourselves and have a good time,' François cried to us, 'and try to come back as quickly as possible . . . No hard feelings, captain, but allow me to submit with infinite respect that in getting ready to sail from Bourbon on a Friday you made a ghastly mistake!'

Quite satisfied with having been able to proclaim this suffocating truth from on high to whom it might concern, François began braying at the top of his lungs a couplet from the comic opera *The Deserter*:

> To die is nothing. It's our last hour.
> Doesn't every minute, every step
> lead us to our end?

Plying our oars, we rapidly left *The Doris* behind, and for a long while François's voice, mixed with the curses of the blacks, reached us distinctly, like a poignant regret. Little by little, it became a murmur, and, soon after, ceased ...

Conrad, Anatole France,
and the Early French Romantic Tradition: Some Influences

Owen Knowles
University of Hull

The most systematic account so far produced of Conrad's links with
French writers is Paul Kirschner's *Conrad: the Psychologist as Artist*, a
study which rightly emphasizes the influence of Flaubert, Maupassant, and
Anatole France. While the first two are obviously important to Conrad's
entire development, the third writer's influence is more problematic. Why
is Conrad so attracted to France, whose reputation is nowadays not particularly high? Kirschner's conclusion that 'where women and love were
concerned, [Conrad] was willing to take the word of Anatole France' may
be substantially true,[1] yet it hardly seems sufficient to explain Conrad's
life-long interest in France's works and his devoted re-reading of a novel
like *Le Lys rouge* (1894). A more profound source of attraction, I wish to
propose, was France's interest in the early Romantic *désillusioné* and the
dangerous maladies associated with a life-denying scepticism—maladies
which France, with his peculiar combination of indulgent romantic sensibility and philosophic pyrrhonism, may have felt himself to have inherited
from an earlier generation. Here I want to suggest that Conrad was
attracted to France's analyses of particularly debilitating forms of ironic
and sceptical ennui and, in the process, was led to early French Romantic
life and letters—particularly to the spectacle of the damaged and scarred

---

This essay, first published in *Conradiana* 11:1 (1979), is reprinted here in honour and
remembrance of Yves Hervouet. A first draft of the essay was already completed when
I first met Yves at a Conrad conference in Amiens in 1978. On that occasion, we spent
many hours together, discussing our shared interest in Conrad's French literary
inheritance and also considering a possible collaboration. Such did not take place,
although our friendship deepened and prospered over the next few years. Yves's sad
death in 1985 was to occasion a form of collaborative effort, when Paul Kirschner,
Lindsay Newman and I joined forces to prepare for publication the manuscript of
Yves's *The French Face of Joseph Conrad* (Cambridge: Cambridge University Press,
1990). This essay is reprinted here by kind permission of the editor of *Conradiana*.
[1] Paul Kirschner, *Conrad: the Psychologist as Artist* (Edinburgh: Oliver & Boyd,
1968), 235.

sensibility as found in Prosper Mérimée (1803-70) and Benjamin Constant (1767-1830). Their influence, I believe, can be traced in the careers fashioned for Martin Decoud in *Nostromo* and Axel Heyst in *Victory*, two characters alike in their cerebral libertinism and often taken to be very close to Conrad himself.

In *La Vie Littéraire*, a four-volume collection of newspaper articles written during the 1880s and published in book-form between 1888 and 1892, Anatole France concludes a review of a biography of Prosper Mérimée by attempting to summarize the leading qualities in Mérimée's sceptical style of living and unhappy death:

> Depuis longtemps déjà, il avait le spleen et voyait les *blue devils* que n'avait pu conjurer mistress Senior. M. d'Haussonville a recherché la cause de cette mélancolie. Il croit l'avoir trouvée dans 'l'instinct confus d'une vie mal dirigée, livrée à beaucoup d'entraînements, dont le souvenir laissait plus d'amertume que de douceur.' Pour moi, je doute que Mérimée ait jamais eu un sentiment moral de cette nature. De quoi se serait-il repenti? Il ne reconnut jamais pour vertus que les énergies ni pour devoirs que les passions. Sa tristesse n'était-elle pas plutôt celle du sceptique pour qui l'univers n'est qu'une suite d'images incompréhensibles, et qui redoute également la vie et la mort, puisque ni l'une ni l'autre n'ont de sens pour lui? Enfin, n'éprouvait-il pas cette amertume de l'esprit et du cœur, châtiment inévitable de l'audace intellectuelle, et ne goûtait-il pas jusqu'à la lie ce que Marguerite d'Angoulême a si bien nommé l'ennui commun à toute créature bien née.[2]

Conrad clearly found much of this summary to be, in only slightly modified form, a fitting epitaph for the ultra-sceptical Martin Decoud in *Nostromo*:

> Not a living being, not a speck of distant sail, appeared within the range of his vision; and, as if to escape from this solitude, he absorbed himself in his melancholy. The vague consciousness of a misdirected life given up to impulses whose memory left a bitter taste in his mouth was the first moral sentiment of his manhood. But at the same time he felt no remorse. What should he regret? He had recognized no other virtue than intelligence, and had erected passions into duties. ... His sadness was the sadness of a sceptical mind. He beheld the universe as a succession of incomprehensible images.

---

[2] Anatole France, *La Vie Littéraire*, 4 vols. (Paris: Calmann-Lévy, 1888-1892), II, 55. Volumes I and II of this work, to which I shall make reference, are hereafter cited as *VL*I and *VL*II.

> A victim of the disillusioned weariness which is the retribution meted out
> to intellectual audacity, the brilliant Don Martin Decoud, weighted by the
> bars of San Tomé silver, disappeared without a trace ...[3]

While it is disconcerting to find Conrad at such a crucial point drawing so
literally upon an existing diagnosis of the exhausted sceptic, even to the
extent of conflating its contradictory speculations, its presence has a two-
fold interest. In the first place it helps to explain why there is an element
of uncertainty in Conrad's treatment of Decoud's final moments. In this
connection Albert J. Guerard writes illuminatingly of two 'potential'
Decouds and of a 'dramatically invisible Decoud' who at the end of the
novel is belaboured for greater scepticism than he ever shows previously.[4]
To the extent that this borrowing seems to indict Decoud for the sins of
another and to trap Conrad into categorizing him in a way difficult to
square with some of his previous actions, Guerard's judgment appears to
be close to the truth. Is there not something awkward in Conrad's conflation of two directly opposite views of Mérimée—so that Decoud ends
up by being allowed a vague moral disquiet which is neither remorse nor
regret? In view of Decoud's potentiality for commitment together with his
earlier assertion that he is 'too much in love to run away' and wants to live
because there can be 'no love for a dead man' (N 216), does this diagnosis
of the utterly desiccated sceptic capture the spirit of all the previous
dramatic evidence?

The full truth about Decoud's fictional career may include a second
important possibility—that Conrad's borrowing from France represents only
one vestige of a blueprint for the fashionably sceptical Parisian boulevardier and *esprit fort* which he derived from accounts of Mérimée's life.
That Conrad largely succeeds in fashioning from this blueprint a character
of his own imaginative possession is not in doubt. Yet for all this, some
central awkwardness persists in the portrait of Decoud which suggests that
Conrad does not fully reconcile his own intentions for the Frenchman with
the model of the cultivated dandy he seems partially to inherit. Conrad's
debt to accounts of Mérimée's life may have been strengthened by his
knowledge of the Frenchman's stories, which, according to Galsworthy, he

---

[3] *Nostromo*, pp. 498, 501. All page references to Conrad's works are to Dent's
Collected Edition (London: J. M. Dent, 1946-1954), and will normally appear in
parentheses after quotation. Abbreviated titles used in the text are as follows:
Nostromo—N; *Victory—V*.

[4] Albert J. Guerard, *Conrad the Novelist* (Cambridge, MA: Harvard University
Press, 1958), 202.

admired greatly,[5] or through biographies which by the 1890s had made of
Mérimée a living legend. On the evidence of Conrad's interest in France's
portrait, it seems reasonable to assume that such a debt exists and that an
invisible 'parallel' sceptic in the figure of Prosper Mérimée may be of
considerable importance in understanding his intentions for Decoud.

The Mérimée whom Conrad found described by France is a curious
compound of irreverent dandy, public servant, repressed romantic, and a
man so led astray by a pose of sceptical indifference that long before he
died he was to suffer the experience of terminal disillusion and solitude.
Moreover, in suffering the self-betraying conflict between these extremes,
Mérimée is seen to be a typical child of the French Romantic age, a type
of deracinated intellectual libertine whose entire life is a tragic record of
impulses destructively at odds with each other—the romantic and sceptical,
the sentimental and egocentric, emotional timidity and intellectual audacity,
asceticism and cultivated sensualism. Here perhaps lies his attraction for
Conrad, who was always fascinated by the *homo duplex* whose individual
symptoms are also symptomatic of his time, race, and generation. A youth
of tender and expressive sensibility, Mérimée adopted and cultivated a
mask of sceptical indifference which, increasingly becoming a habit of
mind, worked corrosively upon a man who felt himself to have genuine
potentiality for feeling—so corrosively, in fact, that in Wildean fashion he
eventually needed 'a disguise to dare to be himself.'[6] Quoting Mérimée's
biographer, France speaks of

> une de ces natures qui, froissées par le contact de la vie, donnent à leur
> expérience la forme d'un cynisme un peu amer, et qui cachent profondé-
> ment des ardeurs, parfois des convictions, en tout cas des délicatesses
> dont ne se doute même pas la grossière honnêteté de ceux qu'ils
> scandalisent.   (*VL*II, 47-48)

In this awkward, ultimately fatal relationship between a vulnerable romantic and his self-protective mask of 'froideur apparente' (47), one meets a
dilemma very close to that of Conrad's youthful boulevardier. Partly as a
result of inheritance, partly as the acting out of a temperamental weakness,

---

[5] John Galsworthy, 'Reminiscences of Conrad,' in *Castles in Spain* (London:
Heinemann, 1927), 91. Of the biographies on Mérimée to appear in the 1880s and
1890s, the most important are O. d'Haussonville, *Prosper Mérimée* (Paris: Calmann-
Lévy, 1885); A. Filon, *Mérimée et ses amis* (Paris: Hachette, 1894); and A. Filon,
Mérimée (Paris: Hachette, 1898). Several articles on Mérimée by English writers also
appeared during this period, notably by Arthur Symons and Walter Pater.
[6] A. W. Raitt, *Prosper Mérimée* (London: Eyre & Spottiswoode, 1970), 54.

and partly as a pose encouraged by fashionable salon-life, Mérimée chose to adopt an habitual mask, 'brusque et dégagé' (51), under which he suffered cruelly. His was an attitude 'roide et sarcastique' (52); he delighted in shocking and making other people awkward by his extreme cynicism, maintaining to these ends a manner of conscious 'brutalité' (49) and 'sécheresse voulue' (51). One of the ultra-sceptical opinions from the lips of this 'contempteur de la tendresse et de la fidélité' (52) sounds very close to a Decoudian *bon mot*: 'L'amitié, qu'il jugeait tout à fait chimérique entre hommes, ne lui semblait pas absolument impossible d'un homme à une femme' (48). Conrad seems to remember this when he writes: 'It was part of what Decoud would have called his sane materialism that he did not believe in the possibility of friendship between man and woman. ... Friendship was possible between brother and sister, meaning by friendship the frank unreserve, as before another human being, of thoughts and sensations' (*N* 223).

That Mérimée's pose was the deep-seated need of a man intent upon hiding a wound and not merely a symptom of a basically sterile nature, France is in no doubt. In Mérimée, he says, 'ce masque de cynisme et d'insensibilité cachait un visage tendre et sérieux, que le monde n'a jamais vu' (52). Like Decoud in his relations with Antonia, he can be attracted to women whom he loves with 'une amitié spirituelle tout à fait charmante' —in these matters he is 'tendre, affectueux, fidèle et bon' (48). Like Decoud too, he is always most forthcoming in his letters, where the fear of immediate exposure is absent, but is not immune from the habit of giving offence to others and then complaining of being 'mal jugé, injustement condamné par l'opinion' (53). If Conrad does not take over all the symptoms of this *homo duplex*—such as Mérimée's sexual adventurism— he does present in Decoud a suggestive version of its central core of anguish. What may have attracted him in particular was the constantly painful sense of self-betrayal Mérimée suffered in protecting himself from wounding contacts with the world. For all his cultivated irreverence, the latter suffered cruelly under his flippancy and could never really disguise 'une sympathie ardente' beneath his habit of systematic irony (49). Claiming kinship with one of the most Parnassian of French poets, José Maria Herédia, Decoud too adopts a pose of dandyish scepticism which is at odds with, and threatens to take over, his natural spontaneity. He is a product of fashionable Parisian life and emerges as a 'sort of Frenchman— godless—a materialist' (*N* 198). As such, Conrad intends him to be an uneasy combination of earnestness and suppressed passion overlaid by a veneer of cynical indifference which threatens to make him a 'nondescript dilettante' in life: 'He had pushed the habit of universal raillery to a point where it blinded him to the genuine impulses of his own nature' (153). Hence, like Mérimée, who shrinks from involvement even while acknowledging 'la légitimité des passions' (*VLII*, 49), Decoud increasingly feels himself to be a helpless and impotent spectator of an acquired identity which is not truly his. As a 'man with a passion, but without a mission' (246), he has genuine capacity for strong feeling—even faith—but cannot find it in himself to embrace a creed or the habit of instinctive action; hence, as with Mérimée, his growing anguish is indistinguishable from the experience of being surprised by a strength of feeling to which he cannot fully respond—that 'tremendous excitement under its cloak of studied carelessness' (212). From the ineffectual struggle with a compendium of conflicting potential selves stem the paradoxes of Decoud's later life. He can act decisively but without much conviction and even while retaining a 'passive contempt' for men of action (246); his gestures of *non serviam* are made with an intensity of feeling which suggests an underlying romantic attraction for the life of service—to women and society; his very sceptical detachment leaves him accessible, as it does the later Heyst, to outside pressures which his mask is designed to fend off.

   In the light of Conrad's interest in France's portrait other factual parallels between Decoud and Mérimée have an added significance. Both young men have studied law, both are only sons spoiled by adoring families, both claim connections with Spain, and both are remarkably alike in having an appearance which suggests an interweaving of dandyism, Latin passionateness, and pseudo-English hauteur.[7] Moreover the circum-

---

[7] These details of Mérimée's background, including his taste for the then fashionable 'espagnolisme' and Spanish drama, are included in Chapter 1 of Filon's *Mérimée*. Both Mérimée and Decoud seem to depend upon the security provided by the fashionable dandy's external insignia—in Mérimée's case, that of 'une manière de bouffon qui florissait encore sous le second Empire' (Filon, *Mérimée et ses amis*, xv). A. W. Raitt summarizes all previous biographers when he describes Mérimée as a mixture of 'dandyish elegance' and 'pseudo-English impassibility' which constitutes 'a carefully chosen and maintained façade designed to keep the world at a distance.' Thick-set, of medium build, outwardly confident but inwardly much less secure, Mérimée emerges as a combination of detached evasiveness—suggested by the 'ironic curl' of his lips—and youthful vigour as seen in his full, 'sensual' mouth (Raitt, 30). Filon anticipates whole areas of Decoud's character when he says that Mérimée's appearance arouses 'l'idée de la tendresse naturelle étouffé par l'ironie acquise' (*Mérimée*, 9). Conrad captures this same interweaving of suppressed vitality, detached dandyism, and English hauteur in a man who manages to look very much like Mérimée, even to the extent of having a mouth 'rosy, fresh, almost pouting in expression' (*N* 151) and curled lips, 'half-reckless, half-contemptuous' in appearance (213).

stantial ironies in Mérimée's later career can hardly have escaped Conrad when he came to devise a career for his 'exotic dandy of the Parisian boulevard' (*N* 229). Ironically the young dilettantish Mérimée, a fashionable liberal and iconoclast, was lured into the world of official politics which he so affected to despise and which transformed him into a middle-aged conservative. At the age of twenty-eight, the exact age of Decoud when he arrives in Costaguana, Mérimée gained public office and subsequently became Inspector-General of Historic Monuments, Academician, and Senator. In addition, his biographers show him to have been a vitriolic pamphleteer and unofficial historian of the 1848 revolution. Much of the underlying irony of his career consists in the fact that 'dying of boredom and fury' (Raitt, 101), and with a thorough dislike of his fellow-officials, he revealed all the qualities of a good diplomat. The youthful dandy surprises himself by not being able to treat his duties 'with anything other than the utmost seriousness' (Raitt, 100). In the recurring peripeties by which circumstances ordain for Mérimée a public career entirely different from any he had anticipated or even wished for, Conrad may well have found a version of Decoud's fate in Costaguana. He too—as journalist, strategist, and politician—is drawn into playing a part to which he can bring very little conviction but a good deal of seriousness and efficiency: 'Afterwards his sister was surprised at the earnestness and ability he displayed in carrying out his mission, which circumstances made delicate, and his want of special knowledge rendered difficult. She had never seen Martin take so much trouble about anything in his whole life' (*N* 154). Historical events are to make of him, as they did of Mérimée, a public figure of some posthumous note and achievement.

The character of Decoud acquires a sharper focus if he is related to a type of cerebral libertine common in early nineteenth-century French life and letters whose maladjusted sensibility is dramatized in terms of the quarrel between natural, spontaneous personality and corrosive scepticism, the latter conceived as an inherited infection and moral malady which leads to eventual bankruptcy of spirit. The literary heroes of this period are, according to Martin Turnell, submitted to 'a process of gradual corrosion, a paralysis which spreads over their minds and reduces them to complete impotence.'[8] Such a process, treated with greater tragic and ethical realism than in the more comfortably vague *fin de siècle* works of the next generation, also allows their central figures to be used as cautionary

---

[8] Martin Turnell, *The Novel in France* (London: Hamish Hamilton, 1950), 101. For a further interesting account of the characteristics of early ninteenth-century French fiction, see Winifried Engler, *The French Novel* (New York: Ungar, 1969), 3-31.

examples of the dangers of cultivating proud independence without conviction, of being duped by one's own mistrustfulness of life, and of becoming
a victim to an arid lucidity of mind which slowly poisons all spontaneous
impulse.

If Anatole France and other biographers provided Conrad with a suggestive version of such a process in Mérimée's life, they nevertheless left
him with the considerable problem of dramatizing a difficult figure of
many potential selves caught up in Costaguanan politics, undergoing a fatal
ordeal, and confronting death. Now the large problem facing Conrad was
presumably that of distilling into one brief period of Decoud's youthful
career (which occupies a limited area in the novel anyway) something of
the warring complexity of Mérimée's whole life, as well as the general
curve of his fate. In the latter's case the self-defeating pose of ironic
scepticism deepened only gradually into the ingrained melancholy of later
life with the stress of utter isolation—an isolation bringing a death 'as
grisly as one could imagine' (Raitt, 348). Faced with the problem of fore-
shortening large areas of psychological complexity, the ambitious Conrad
also seems to want Decoud to meet such ultimate extremes, and his fate to
carry a repudiation of scepticism similar to that offered by Stendhal to
Mérimée: 'BEWARE OF IRONY' (Raitt, 360). Yet given the self-imposed
limits which Conrad accepts, it is questionable whether he can ever wholly
overcome the central awkwardness which results from his desire to push
the complex man of *his* making with such speed towards the same extreme
fate as Mérimée's. I doubt if the result, in Decoud's case, is anything as
crude as the 'monster' which Eloise Knapp Hay professes to find.[9] But
there is certainly something of the audacious *tour de force* in Conrad's
fabrication and later swift dispatch of Decoud. At a very simple level, he
has little opportunity to give his Frenchman much personal background,
and little time, it turns out, to present his death very fully. Moreover, his
treatment of Decoud's career requires that the latter should be tested and
broken by extreme conditions of isolation and physical distress. But so
extreme are the external pressures brought to bear upon him, and so weak
his resistance, that the reader inclines to one of two reactions: either that
the pressures put upon Decoud are so great that *any* man, even of the most
tenacious faith, would crack under them; or that, despite these pressures,
the Decoud we know would not have collapsed so quickly and spectacu-
larly into impotent despair.

---

[9] Eloise Knapp Hay, *The Political Novels of Joseph Conrad* (Chicago: University
of Chicago Press, 1963), 197.

THE EARLY FRENCH ROMANTIC TRADITION

The technical expedients used to bring about Decoud's disintegration inevitably dictate the kind of character who progressively emerges in the later parts of the novel. Decoud's authenticity as a character depends upon the tact with which Conrad portrays his inner disintegration as a process of inevitable *self*-defeat, the reasons for which are inherent in his character from the beginning. But the test devised for Decoud places so much emphasis upon his extreme isolation, and operates with such ferocity to undermine his total individuality, that virtually all questions of psychological continuity seem an irrelevance. Guerard believes that a collapse is engineered for Decoud because in him Conrad 'attempts to separate out and demolish a facet of himself' (Guerard, 199). A related reason for the awkwardness in Decoud's portrait is likely to be that the suggestions from Mérimée's life initially attractive to Conrad demanded a closeness and concentration of interest which, in the later conduct of the novel, he was not prepared to give. One can go further than this and point not simply to a change in the quality of Conrad's interest in Mérimée but to a change in the *object* of his interest. What looms large in his imagination in the later parts of *Nostromo*, as Conrad's borrowing from France indicates, is the more simple and fixed image of Mérimée the emotionally exhausted dandy who must reap the grim reward for his irreverent apostasy. Hence the dauntingly large test to which Decoud is submitted on the Isabels appears to mark a new desire in Conrad to hasten the progress of the Frenchman towards a 'meeting' with his invisible partner; and it is perhaps a measure of the cost involved that Conrad reaches his destination with a borrowed indictment which applies to the lives of both Decoud and Mérimée.

If the later Decoud gives the impression of being unfairly treated by his maker, it is because Conrad's triumphantly final judgment as well as the entire ordeal devised for the Frenchman seem more like a concerted attack upon a conventional type of trifling dandy than a fair test upon the sensitive individual of Conrad's making. In the first part of *Nostromo* Decoud quickly develops into a character more considerable than the Frenchified dandy to which he is originally compared. He is, of course, shown to have the capacity for breakdown and to be insecure in his iconoclasm. But Conrad never asserts his weakness without some qualifying sense of his potential promise as a man of feeling and action. He is ultra-sceptical but ardent in love, politically detached but a true *hijo del pays*, liable to childish exaggeration but finely perceptive. The test devised at the end of Part Second thrusts Decoud into an isolation so extreme that its effect is to suggest with massive inevitability that his commitment to the world must be a tenuous one. From one point of view Conrad's haste can be seen as the penalty incurred by a narrative method which never allows

him to show the hardening of Decoud's arteries as a gradual and slow
process. From another point of view such haste is symptomatic of a writer
who, in the later parts of the novel, is ready to assume the existence of a
simpler, more typical dandy, the 'Son Decoud,' whose death illustrates the
perils involved in being duped by his own sceptical mistrust of life. The
latter does break quickly, and a grim nemesis is assured. In the process of
securing large situational ironies, however, it is doubtful whether Conrad
sorts out in his own mind the strength of those sides of Decoud's character
which make him a very atypical dandy—his obvious feeling for life,
shrewd wisdom and strong passion. His solution appears to be—and it is
one suggested by the spectacle of the aged Mérimée—that Decoud's mask
of cynicism is, quite simply, not a mask after all: underlying all of his
potential selves there is the utter 'sadness of a sceptical mind' (498).

Conrad seems to have found in Mérimée's life possibilities for
subject-matter which were more attractive in the promise than in the
execution. The early parts of *Nostromo* suggest that he made free use of
hints supplied by France to fashion a basic human type which he then
substantially recreated in the process of bringing Decoud to life. The later
Decoud seems imperceptibly to revert to type with an effect of awkward
technical strain. While the account of Decoud's disintegration and spiritual
agony is a moving piece of impressionism, it does not finally yield the
kind of summary which suggests that Conrad has fully probed Decoud's
spiritual bankruptcy from the inside and in depth. His final willingness to
rest content with France's diagnosis seems, in retrospect, to speak of the
limits within which he is prepared to engage with the later Decoud.
Undoubtedly many chances are memorably taken within these limits. Yet
when measured against the high expectations aroused by the first half of
Nostromo, the portrait of the later Decoud leaves one also with a disappointed sense of chances missed—missed through Conrad's growing
tendency to find in Decoudian energy little more than a warning example
of the spectral 'devils' remorselessly following upon intellectual audacity.

From the evidence of another borrowing from France's *La Vie
Littéraire*, this time from an article on Benjamin Constant, it is interesting
to find that Heyst's lineage in *Victory* can also be traced to roots in early
nineteenth-century French fiction. France describes Constant as follows:

> On peut juger sévèrement cet homme, mais il y a une grandeur
> qu'on ne lui refusera pas: il fut très malheureux et cela n'est point d'une
> âme médiocre.

Il traîna soixante ans sur cette terre de douleurs l'âme la plus lasse et la plus inquiète qu'une civilisation exquise ait jamais façonnée pour le désenchantement et l'ennui. ... Il veut toutes les joies, celles des grands et celles des humbles, celles des fous et celles des sages. (*VLI*, 66, 67)

In *Victory* Conrad writes of Heyst's father as follows:

> Thinker, stylist, and man of the world in his time, the elder Heyst had begun by coveting all the joys, those of the great and those of the humble, those of the fools and those of the sages. For more than sixty years he had dragged on this painful earth of ours the most weary, the most uneasy soul that civilization had ever fashioned to its ends of disillusion and regret. One could not refuse him a measure of greatness, for he was unhappy in a way unknown to mediocre souls.   (91)

This borrowing is helpful for what it provides of a specific source for Heyst Senior's philosophic 'Storm and Dust' (*V* 219) in an age which, according to France, was agitatedly suspended between 'les orages' and pervasive boredom, idealism and scepticism, aspiration and actuality (*VLI*, 72). Like Heyst's father, who grants men the 'right to absolute moral and intellectual liberty of which he no longer believed them worthy' (*V* 91), Constant 'professa la liberté sans y croire' (*VLI*, 72); for both Conrad and France the spirit of an age is caught in a portrait of the pale and attenuated figure of its leading representative—in France's case, a portrait in his possession of Constant with 'cette grande figure pâle et longue, empreinte de tant de tristesse et d'ironie, et dont les traits avaient plus de finesse que ceux de la plupart des hommes' (71).

Even more importantly, France provides a suggestive synopsis of a problematic life and career which, in conjunction with Constant's *Adolphe* (1816), seems to supply an important source for details of Heyst's character, dilemma, and involvement with Lena.[10] As with his interest in Mérimée, Conrad seems fascinated by a man of fragmented sensibility

---

[10] Several other literary parallels and sources for limited parts of *Victory* have, of course, been claimed. Katherine Haynes Gatch examines the influence of Villiers de l'Isle-Adam's Axel in 'Conrad's Axel,' *Studies in Philology* 48 (1951), 98-106; Paul Kirschner draws attention to verbal echoes in *Victory* from Maupassant's *Fort comme la mort* (*Conrad: the Psychologist as Artist*, 193-98); Andrzej Busza has suggested the likely influence upon parts of *Victory* of The History of a Sin by the Polish writer Stefan Żeromski in *Conrad's Polish Literary Background and Some Illustrations of the Influence of Polish Literature on his Work* (Rome: Polish Historical Institute, 1966), 209-23; and David Lodge examines parallels with Shakespeare in 'Conrad's *Victory* and *The Tempest*: An Amplification,' *Modern Language Review* 59 (1964), 195-99.

whose life-history is a record of perpetual inner crisis and who, in suffering the conflict between head and heart in its acutest form, emerges as a distressed child of his age. France provides only the outline of a career which the autobiographical *Adolphe* fictionalizes and expands. Of mixed background, cosmopolitan by habit, and unnaturally transplanted at an early age, Constant lost his mother as a child and thereafter, under the influence of a father 'ironique et timide' (60), was subjected to an unorthodox and lonely education: 'Il fut soumis jusqu'à l'âge de quatorze ans à une éducation sévère qui desséchait son cœur en exaltant son amour-propre' (60). France is largely concerned, however, with the type of life-weary *désillusioné* who emerges in later life. From this early upbringing there develops a man fundamentally mistrustful of life, a despiser of mankind and floating observer who, while he is 'incapable d'aimer que de croire' (63), is subject to an ambiguous impulse of pity which betrays him into fresh ties—'liaisons nouvelles' (65). Like Heyst, Constant is a bewildering compendium of detachment, cold charity, repressed sensuality, world-weariness, and perpetual nervous anxiety which makes him in France's view a prototype of the modern, neurotically self-divided man who is lost because he lacks the simple trust in life to make even the most basic commitment:

> Si l'on pénètre dans le détail des actions, si l'on entre dans l'âme, on découvre des contradictions qui étonnent, des luttes intestines dont la violence effraye, et l'on se dit: Il y avait en cet homme plusieurs hommes qui eussent fait de belles et grandes choses s'ils n'avaient été contraints, par une union intolérable et indissoluble, de s'entre-dévorer.
>
> Il ne pouvait vivre ni avec les hommes ni seul. 'Le monde me fatigue les yeux et la tête,' disait-il. ... Et, le lendemain, il se rejetait dans le monde, où son orgueil, la sécheresse de son cœur et la délicatesse de son esprit lui préparaient de rares tortures. ... Joie, vertu, bonheur, fierté, contentement, tout se desséchait entre ses doigts arides. ... Quel enchantement ce désenchanté n'a-t-il pas revé? ... Aussi, comment se fier à un homme qui cherche éperdument la passion quand la passion le fuit, qui méprise les hommes et travaille à les rendre libres, et dont la parole n'est que le brillant cliquetis des contradictions acérées qui déchirent son intelligence et son cœur?   (62, 66-67, 71)

Here, I think, we feel ourselves to be particularly close to leading traits in Heyst—the man who inwardly suffers 'the shock of sharp contradictions that lacerate our intelligence and our feelings' (*V* 66-67), the 'enchanted' Heyst, the spiritually delicate observer who proclaims his independence from the world but cannot bear his isolation, the man of defective sensibility who despises men but, like Constant, is 'capable de sympathie et d'une sorte de pitié réfléchie' (69), and for whom the spectacle of suffering 'offensait la délicatesse de ses sens et la pureté de son intelligence' (70). Above all, Heyst shares with Constant the defects of temperament which prevent him from persisting in any emotion for very long and make of his inner history an unending conflict between potential selves: hence Heyst is by turns neurotically sensitive and insensitive to the point of brutality, possesses a fund of powerful emotion but also gives the impression of spiritual bankruptcy, and can be as dangerous in his unbalanced passivity as he is in his unnatural impetuousity.

Containing much of Constant's own life-history, *Adolphe* is a first-person narrative written by an older man, now dead to the world, looking back upon his early disastrous 'ties' with a life which he has always fundamentally distrusted. The tragedy linking Adolphe and Heyst is that they fully realize their emotional impotence and suffer from it—as do those with whom they come into contact—but are powerless to remedy it. Indeed their debilitating habit of reflective self-consciousness forms the basis of the cautionary moral offered by each story. *Victory* warns against the 'habit of profound reflection ... [which] is the most pernicious of all the habits formed by the civilized man'[11] and ends with Heyst's lament: 'Ah, Davidson, woe to the man whose heart has not learned while young to hope, to love—and to put its trust in life!' (410). The Preface to the second edition of *Adolphe* speaks of 'cette analyse perpétuelle, qui place une arrière-pensée à côté de tous les sentiments, et qui corrompt des leur naissance,'[12] a sentiment implicitly echoed later when Adolphe cries out: 'Malheur à l'homme qui, dans les premiers moments d'une liaison d'amour, ne croit pas cette liaison doit être éternelle!' (66).

Adolphe is the son of a father who, as 'un observateur froid et caustique,' is partly responsible for encouraging his son in 'impressions primitives et fougueuses qui jettent l'âme hors de la sphere commune, et lui inspirent le dédain de tous les objets qui l'environnent' (47). Adolphe's sense of rootless insecurity, timidity and fastidiousness lead him to seek protection by adopting the role of 'observateur froid et impartial' (56) and 'spectateur indifférent d'une existence à demi passée' (94). Like Heyst, he commits himself to a programme of looking on and making no sound. Impatient of all ties and fearful of making new ones, he schools himself into habits later to be associated with Heyst, the habit of 'une plaisanterie

---

[11] 'Author's Note,' *Victory*, x-xi.
[12] *Œuvres de Benjamin Constant*, ed. Alfred Roulin (Paris: Gallimard, 1957), 41. All further references to *Adolphe* are to this edition, hereafter cited as *O*.

94   OWEN KNOWLES

perpétuelle' which serves to hide his real thoughts (48), and the habit of
maintaining 'une taciturnité profonde' (50) as a protective refuge—both
symptoms of 'ce cœur étranger à tous les intérêts du monde, solitaire au
milieu des hommes, et qui souffre pourtant de l'isolement auquel il est
condamné' (61). In addition, these habits of mistrust have been encouraged
in Adolphe, as in Heyst, by long periods spent at the death-bed of an influential figure whose severely analytic mind drains all vitality from life and
strengthens sceptical mistrust 'par l'idée de la mort' (49). Elusive, wraith-
like, and shielded from the outside world by 'des mots vagues ou une
ironie plus ou moins amère' (48), Adolphe cannot deny the instinct which
demands some relief from an 'isolement effroyable' (66). Rationally committed to making his life a masterpiece of aloof detachment, he is to find
himself, like Heyst, 'irrationally moved by this sense of loneliness which
had come to him in the hour of renunciation' (V 66); as with Heyst, this
dreamy spectator cannot remain at ease within the limits he has erected for
himself, is fatally tempted into making a 'tie,' and must struggle with an
inner character which he is unable to dominate.

'Distrait, inattentif, ennuyé' (52), Adolphe becomes entangled in the
sentimental experiment of having an affair with the mistress of a Comte de
P—, a Polish woman ten years older than himself called Ellénore (the syl-
lables of whose name might easily be reshuffled to produce 'Lena'). With
little sustaining faith, he drifts into a 'tie' out of boredom, loneliness,
aroused sensuality, and a desperate need to fill an inner void. Like Heyst,
he allows a woman to 'infect' and break into his heart (V 84). The opening
stages of this relationship are remarkably similar to those between Heyst
and Lena. Primarily at work in Adolphe's first response to Ellénore is a
curious mixture of timidity, detached politeness, romantic enchantment, and
an inflamed imagination immediately aroused by her charm 'presque
magique' and 'une grace inexplicable' (56). Mistaking pity for love and
agitation for passion, Adolphe commits himself to being Ellénore's 'protec-
teur' (88) though he has little confidence in his ability or inclination to
meet the demands of his newly formed tie. On her part Ellénore, 'rêveuse
et taciturne' (55), unthinkingly sacrifices her future to Adolphe and, with
a submissive veneration similar to Lena's, finds her mission in self-
sacrifice. Initially she is attracted to him for the same reasons as Lena
finds Heyst attractive. The former reacts with astonished surprise to
Adolphe and 'un mélange particulier de mélancolie et de gaieté, de dé-
couragement et d'intérêt, d'enthousiasme et d'ironie' (55-56), while Lena
responds to the novelty of Heyst's 'delicate, polished playfulness' and the
mixture of melancholy, playfulness, and quiet irony in his manner (V 75).

Adolphe accepts responsibility for a woman who has unthinkingly sacrificed herself to him and incurred social calumny in doing so, but he is tragically incapable of fulfilling his obligations as a protector. On the contrary, an irony common to *Adolphe* and *Victory* is that both females become the protectors of the males who set out to protect them (*V* 309; *O* 88). The later part of *Adolphe* dramatizes the anguished sense of self-betrayal which Adolphe suffers, the inquiétude which gradually contaminates the relationship between man and woman, and 'le mal que font éprouver meme aux cœurs arides les souffrances qu'ils causent' (*O* 43). Adolphe can neither commit himself to Ellénore nor make up his mind to leave her. Fatally tempted into a world in which he places little trust, he finds himself burdened with a tie which has become a wearisome bond. The later Adolphe is most like Heyst in his alarming inaction (91), the hesitation and duplicity he attributes to delicacy (73), the artificial gaiety he practises to veil 'profonde tristesse' (82), and in his habit of placing responsibility on 'les difficultés de notre situation' (95-96). A crisis arrives with Ellénore's horrified discovery that Adolphe is plotting to abandon her. Her subsequent death allows him a vision of life he has missed, can never have, and what he must henceforth endure as an 'étranger pour tout le monde' (113): 'J'allais vivre sans elle dans ce désert du monde, que j'avais souhaité tant de fois de traverser indépendant. J'avais brisé l'être qui m'aimait' (110). He is condemned to a 'moral desert as arid as the sands of Sahara' which seems to be Heyst's natural habitat (*V* 80) and, like Heyst, he must suffer the anguish of awakening from a dream-plot which he himself has perversely shattered. Adolphe is a man 'accablé de peine, que le sommeil a consolé par un songe, et qui pressent que ce songe va finir' (93).

The study of literary debt and influence is always most valuable when it points to a significant pattern of affinities and allegiances which underlies particular borrowings. If the figures of Decoud and Heyst represent an important side of Conrad's own sensibility, as many critics believe, then early nineteenth-century French life and letters are, I would argue, an important and hitherto neglected part of his tradition as a novelist—a tradition partly clarified for him by Anatole France. Conrad's interest both in *homo duplex* whose predicament is complicated by the intellectual's distrust of the world of action to which he is drawn, and in the human character as an endlessly warring duality, seems inextricably linked with the spectacle of the agitated *désillusioné* suggested by Mérimée and Constant. The Constant material presented by France appears to provide him with a detailed model for a major figure, the pattern of whose entire life is determined by the conflict between a lawless imagination and a

fastidious scepticism. *Adolphe* seems to play its part by supplying hints for
a concrete plot, a patterned contrast between male apostate and female
devotee, and a type of diagnostic vocabulary for describing the splintered
sensibility with disconcertingly cool clarity. The result is that Conrad
manages to capture in *Victory* (and in parts of *Nostromo*) the quality of
human suffering which Martin Turnell associates with Constant: 'The
interior void, the feeling of life ebbing into the sand, which is at the heart
of *Adolphe*, is something new in European literature.'[13]

It is in the light of this debt that Conrad's fascination for France's *Le
Lys rouge* must be seen, for the latter novel variously continues and
extends the traditions established by Constant, Chateaubriand, and others.
This novel—from which Conrad could quote by heart, according to Jean-
Aubry[14]—has received surprisingly little attention from Conrad critics, yet
its influence upon *Victory* is at times remarkably specific. France's novel
centres on a romantic affair involving a Parisian woman with a 'past,'
Thérèse Martin-Bellème, who tries to escape a barren marriage and seek
fulfilment through a passionate, but finally unsuccessful affair with an
artist, Jacques Dechartre. While dramatizing the failure of their relationship
(which has much to do with Jacques's disordered sensibility), France is also
committed to exploring the 'carbon' of the male and female identity which,
as the novel progresses, largely takes the form of a patterned contrast
between the woman's semi-religious impulse towards sacrifice at the altar
of love and the male's more fastidious, earthbound egotism. In so far as
these contrasting 'faiths' are seen by the sceptical France as merely
different kinds of sustaining illusion in a cruelly obstructive world, they
can be embraced within a single, overriding myth central to 'l'éternelle
douleur humaine'[15] which crystallizes the timeless contradictions between

---

[13] Turnell, *The Novel in France*, 122.

[14] *Lettres françaises*, ed. G. Jean-Aubry (Paris: Gallimard, 1930), 12.

[15] *Le Lys rouge* (Paris: Calmann-Lévy, 1894), 259. Hereafter this volume is cited
as *LR*. Conrad seems generally to have been in the habit of transplanting some of
France's reflective wisdoms in *Le Lys rouge* into new and challenging dramatic contexts of his own. For example, an artist in France's novel is responsible for the
following comment on art: 'pour que la vie soit grande et pleine, il faut y mettre le
passé et l'avenir. Nos œuvres de poésie et d'art, il faut les accomplir en l'honneur des
morts, et dans la pensée de ceux qui naîtront' (157). Clearly this lies behind Mrs.
Gould's recognition in *Nostromo*: 'It had come into her mind that for life to be large
and full, it must contain the care of the past and of the future in every passing moment
of the present. Our daily work must be done to the glory of the dead, and for the good
of those who come after' (520-21). At another point France attributes to Napoleon the
words: 'Un trone, c'est quatre morceaux de bois recouverts de velours? Non! un trone,

human aspiration and consequence, ideal and practice, the promise of love and the actuality of death. *Le Lys rouge* is strongly reminiscent of *Victory* in the way in which it brings to bear upon a modern love story a sceptical revision of the Eden myth and presents human illusions, disappointment, and suffering as part of a remorselessly secular cycle of pointless ordeal ending in 'nothing.'[16] Yet the impulse in *Le Lys rouge* towards a sceptical re-working of traditional Eden mythology is complicated, and the pervasive irony checked by another factor: France's tendency to distinguish Thérèse's Christ-like sacrifice from the more 'modern' creedlessness of Jacques, and to contemplate her life as that of a latter-day St. Teresa yearning for nobility of vocation in cruelly alien conditions. Thus France's attitude becomes ambiguously divided—and here he seems close in spirit to the Janus-like author of *Victory*—at the point where his sceptical reading of Christian myth meets, and collides with, a more tangible record of Christ-like suffering in human life. The ending of *Le Lys rouge* is poised evenly

---

c'est un homme, et cet homme c'est moi!' (*LR* 45). This seems to occur to Conrad in *Under Western Eyes* when he has Razumov think: 'What is a throne? A few pieces of wood upholstered in velvet. But a throne is a seat of power too' (36).

[16] Both *Le Lys rouge* and *Victory* draw heavily upon Eden mythology, the first to express Thérèse's sense of transfigured individuality when she leaves a spiritually dead Paris and commits herself to Jacques in Italy, the second to intensify the temporary idyll which Heyst and Lena enjoy on the island of Samburan. Even so, for both Conrad and France this is a fragile earthly Eden, whatever momentary intimations it may yield of a higher spiritual order. When *Le Lys rouge* moves towards its crisis it accommodates suggestions of cataclysm and deluge, the Day of Judgment and the final hope of purification. Forebodings of the world annihilated are, in fact, a constant motif throughout *Le Lys rouge*, with Thérèse at one point discussing 'la fin du monde' with a friend (109) in a way strongly reminiscent of Lena and Heyst, who contemplate the 'vision of a world destroyed' (*V* 191). At moments of crisis, the two heroines react similarly: there is a common tone of resigned expectation in Lena's thought that 'the heart of hearts had ceased to beat and the end of all things had come' (373) and Thérèse's feeling that 'c'était le moment qu'elle vint finir le monde pour la tirer d'affaire' (*LR* 197). Interestingly, during one of these reveries Thérèse imagines herself to be where Heyst figuratively is—islanded 'sur un des sommets de l'Himalaya' (86). At the climax of *Le Lys rouge* Thérèse's forebodings of cataclysm are actualized in the background of a theatrical performance of Goethe's *Faust* and by the streets of a darkened Paris which was 'noir et mêlé à la terre dans un chaos de ténèbres épaisses' (392-93). These would seem to correspond to the gathering storm over Samburan, the erupting volcano and the 'shuddering universe' which Heyst sees (392). At the climax of this *Walpurgisnacht* both novels bifurcate into open-ended possibility— on the one hand, the hope of final purification (*LR* 409; *V* 410) and, on the other, a vision of human aspiration coming to 'nothing' (*LR* 409; *V* 412).

between Christian romance and secular distress: the possibility of spiritual victory for the elect through earthly mortification is juxtaposed finally with the disastrous wreckage of human hopes and illusions.

An important borrowing in *Victory* from *Le Lys rouge* leaves one in little doubt that Conrad conceives of Lena and Thérèse as belonging to a devout sisterhood with an ancestry stretching back to medieval saint's legend. In the following passages we find two minds with one thought: the first describes Lena's thoughts while waiting for her final momentous meeting with Ricardo; the second depicts France's heroine in San Marco in Florence where she anticipates a meeting with her lover:

> While lifting the curtain, she felt the *anguish* of her disobedience to her lover, *which was soothed by a feeling* she had known before—a gentle *flood of penetrating sweetness*. She was not automatically obeying a momentary suggestion; *she was under influences more deliberate, more vague, and of greater potency. She had been prompted, not by her will, but by a force that was* outside of her and *more worthy. She reckoned upon nothing definite; she had calculated nothing.* She saw only her purpose of capturing death—savage, sudden, irresponsible death, prowling round the man who possessed her; death embodied in the knife ready to strike into his heart. *No doubt it had been a sin to throw herself into his arms.* With that inspiration *that descends* at times from above for *the good or evil of our common mediocrity*, she had *a sense of having been for him only a violent and sincere choice* of curiosity and pity—*a thing that passes. She did not know him. If he were to go away from her and disappear, she would utter no reproach, she would not resent it; for she would hold in herself the impress of something most rare and precious*—his embraces made her own by her courage in saving his life.
>
> (*V* 394-95; my italics)

> Elle ressentait une *angoisse* qu'apaisait un sentiment inconnu, *d'une douceur profonde*. Elle ne retrouvait pas la stupeur de la premiere fois qu'elle s'était donnée par amour, la vision brusque de l'irréparable. *Elle était sous des influences plus lentes, plus vagues et plus puissantes.* Cette fois, une rêverie charmante trempait le souvenir des caresses reçues et baignait la brulure. Elle était abîmée de trouble et d'inquiétude, mais elle n'éprouvait ni honte ni regrets. *Elle avait agi moins par sa volonté que par une force qu'elle devinait meilleure.* Elle s'absolvait sur son désintéressement. *Elle ne comptait sur rien, n'ayant rien calculé. Sans doute, elle avait eu le tort de se donner quand elle n'était pas libre,* mais aussi n'avait-elle rien exigé. Peut-être *n'était-elle pour lui qu'une fantaisie violente et sincère. Elle ne le connaissait pas.* Elle n'avait pas fait l'épreuve de ces belles imaginations vives et flottantes, *qui passent de haut, pour le bien comme pour le mal, la médiocrité commune. S'il s'éloignait d'elle brusquement et disparaissait, elle ne le lui reprocherait*

pas, elle ne lui en voudrait pas;—du moins elle le croyait.—*Elle garderait en elle* le souvenir et *l'empreinte* de ce qu'on pouvait trouver au monde *de plus rare et de plus précieux.*   (*LR* 227-28; my italics)

For the details as well as the presiding logic of Lena's intimations of heroic sacrifice, Conrad is heavily dependent upon France's portrayal of the excited religious sensibility. One obvious reason for this extensive borrowing may be that Conrad, under pressure and over-tired at this late stage of the novel, decided to take the shortest and quickest route to his fnal destination. Yet the amazing ease with which France transfers so appropriately into the context of *Victory* at this point also suggests, I think, how generally dependent the latter may be upon *Le Lys rouge* for its conception of female 'dreamy innocence'[17] and for a kind of prose with which to describe religious imaginings.[18] In large part, Conrad's difficulties in *Victory* stem from the ambitious shift in his attention from the male *désillusioné* to the uncongenial area of female Christian martyrdom, and these difficulties cannot be totally solved without the aid—and sometimes direct intervention—of France. Such dependence is bound to create further problems, largely felt in the uneven prose style of *Victory* which oscillates awkwardly between the drab colloquial style appropriate to Lena's background and *la belle page* of more elevated French romance.

If Lena fails to carry conviction as a character with a distinctively felt life, it is mainly because Conrad remains content with the semi-idealized postures of womanhood and a sculptured, iconographic prose style which have a long history in nineteenth-century French fiction and which France picturesquely elaborates. The figure of Jacques, the *désillusioné*, presumably engaged Conrad's attention more fully, and here we find an interesting and suggestive parallel with Heyst. The differences between the two men—Jacques is younger than Heyst, a Parisian, and eventually a victim of corrosive sexual jealousy—are much less important than the common poisonous malady which they share. Jacques offers the following self-diagnosis:

---

[17] 'Author's Note,' *Victory*, xvii.

[18] Thérèse and Lena are remarkably alike in appearance, response and statuesque posture. Compare, for example, the account of Lena's death (*V* 405-7) with the following description of Thérèse (*LR* 254-55): 'Elle se jeta dans ses bras et s'y abandonna. Il la porta inerte, comme la dépouille précieuse de celle devant qui il avait pali et tremblé. Elle goûtait, les paupières mi-closes, l'humiliation superbe d'être une belle proie. Sa fatigue, sa tristesse, ses dégoûts de la journée, le souvenir de la violence, sa liberté reprise, le besoin d'oublier, un reste de peur, tout avivait, irritait sa tendresse. Renversée sur le lit, elle noua ses bras autour du cou de son ami.'

Je sais bien ce qu'il y a dans ma jalousie. Quand je l'examine, j'y trouve
préjugés héréditaires, un orgueil de sauvage, une sensibilité maladive, un
mélange de violence bête et de faiblesse cruelle, une révolte imbécile et
méchante contre les lois de la vie et du monde. Mais j'ai beau la con-
naître pour ce qu'elle est: elle est et me tourmente. Je suis le chimiste
qui, étudiant les propriétés de l'acide qu'il a avalé, sait avec quelles
bases il se combine et quels sels il forme. Cependant l'acide le brule et
le brulera jusqu'aux os.   (*LR* 276-77)

This might stand in essence as an accurate diagnosis of the self-divided
Heyst and of the 'nauseating and corrosive ... poison' (*V* 218) which proves
to be his fatal chemistry. Additionally Conrad seems drawn to the various
properties of the poison which make Jacques a tragically 'lost' modern
man. For one thing he labours, like Heyst, under the inherited weakness of
being 'un enfant gâté' (*LR* 97), and in one scene takes up a Heystian stance
before the portrait of the parent who has dominated his life: 'La chambre
de ma pauvre maman est comme moi ... elle le souvient' (305). As an artist
and dreamer partly at home with shadows, he has lost faith in the world of
substance and shrinkingly retreats into a kind of self-preoccupation which
allows him only to love 'généreusement lui-même dans tout ce qu'il
rencontre de beau au monde' (99). Afflicted by a manner continually
'nerveux, irritable, inquiet' (348) and a posture in life 'trop étranger, trop
lointain' (169), he has rarely moved beyond the cool politeness which
prompts him to cross the street and salute Thérèse in courtly fashion (81).
Unlike Jacques, Heyst is not basically a type of *fin de siècle* romantic
æsthete (though Conrad begins by suggesting that the latter, with his
portfolio of sketches, is an artist of sorts). What Jacques and Heyst do have
in common is a sensibility scarred by *fin de siècle* life-negation which,
rooted in adolescence and the habits of the dreamer, has become an
ingrained feature of the middle-aged mind. This is clear when one compares Heyst's feeling that 'the death of that bitter contemner of life did not
trouble the flow of life's stream, where men and women go by thick as
dust, revolving and jostling one another like figures cut out of cork' (*V*
175) with Jacques's lament that the individual counts for little in a world
'où les êtres, agités comme, dans le van, les grains et la balle, sont mêlés
et séparés par la secousse du rustre ou du dieu' (331).

Jacques's test comes in the tie he establishes with Thérèse, who
offers a challenge to his flagging faith and introduces this faltering
mother's boy to the world of adult passion and commitment. With a manner 'gauche et maladroit' (166) reminiscent of Heyst, he enters a new
territory open to mystery, complication, and surprising pressures. The lost
mental poise of two self-contained egotists who descend into the world's

arena suggests itself in their growing sense of absorption in a feminine dream-plot which is both fascinating and obnoxious (*V* 92; *LR* 318). In both men the undisciplined imagination attracts them to areas of instinctive passion which they later come to distrust. Like Heyst who inordinately drinks in Lena's charm (*V* 74), Jacques breathes the seductive grace of Thérèse (*LR* 207) and confesses: 'Oh! je n'ai jamais eu l'imagination discrète à votre égard' (231). As the imaginative Heyst feels himself to have been betrayed by the 'primeval ancestor' in him (*V* 173), so Jacques finds 'les instincts des hommes primitifs' aroused in his love for Thérèse: 'je sens que je vous aime avec une simplicité sauvage' (*LR* 206).

Jacques and Heyst are tested and fail differently of course, but the root causes for their failure are not essentially different. The two men are foredoomed, as both Conrad and France agree, because in their 'masculine fussing' (*V* 308) they are products of an age too old and wrinkled to come to terms with the female's child-like faith. Heyst confesses to being of a later date in the world's history than Lena, while Jacques feels—speaking of all men: 'Nous étions déjà si vieux quand nous sommes nés! ' (*LR* 276). But primarily both are victims of a flawed and splintered sensibility which is incurably aggravated by the world's testing conditions. Erratically susceptible to the charm of romantic love and idealistically inclined to project onto others the shape of their unrequited yearnings, both men are just as prone to lapse into gloomy despair when confronted by the call to action in a world which they persist in regarding as a 'filthy hole' (*V* 215). Habitual wanderers in a desert, they can only regard love as a pleasing, but temporary oasis. Their potentiality for passionate commitment is so vitiated by sceptical mistrust that both men become victims of an unbreachable division between the extremes of an utterly remote idealism and an ugly undercurrent of cynical disgust for naked passion, the effect of which is to make Heyst an expert in the 'mastery of despair' (*V* 196) and Jacques half in love with 'un désespoir délicieux' (*LR* 302). Such a crippling dual vision—of what Jacques calls 'les délices de la vie et les affres de la mort' (302)—transforms love into constant anguish, since all involvement with the world only offers evidence of the searing contradiction between ideal and real, storm and dust. Hence the 'acid' at work in both men manifests itself in a kind of gloomy sensual desire which demands not primarily sensual satisfaction but a total absorption of the female into itself. This, aggravated by self-distrust and the habit of reflection, leads both to a constant anguish at not being able to attain what they crave, and leaves them disarmed before the multiplying spectres of life—Heyst before the spectral Jones, Jacques before the phantoms of jealousy. The former does not know how to respond to Lena's appeal to love her 'simply' (*V* 221), while Jacques makes a bewildered acknowledgement of failure: 'Je devrais t'aimer naïvement, sans cette espece de métaphysique passionelle qui me rend absurde et méchant' (*LR* 303).

The perpetual fascination of Conrad's fiction is that it stands in suggestive relationship to so many European literary traditions—English, Polish, and French—without ultimately belonging to any single one. Yet some of its most important roots are undoubtedly in the unexplored territory of early nineteenth-century French fiction. The main theme of Constant's *Adolphe*—the unhappy progress of the timid, disaffected, and detached solitary towards spiritual sterility in what is felt to be a hostile world—together with the sophisticated vocabulary with which the hero's crisis is described, make this novel a seminal work in a tradition of French romantic-realists that includes Mérimée and Anatole France. It would appear that Conrad, attracted by the image of *homo duplex* which emerges from the life-histories of some of these writers and their fictional models, also found a congenial alphabet for describing the crises of the *désillusioné*—in terms of 'angoisse métaphysique,' 'besoin de sensibilité,' the man who is 'étranger pour tout le monde,' and a state of mind in which 'l'univers n'est qu'une suite d'images incompréhensibles.' Interestingly and perhaps characteristically, the roots Conrad discovers are in a tradition of writing which deals with rootless cosmopolitanism and dangerously unfettered isolation. This fact adds an interesting perspective to the characters of Decoud and Heyst. In them one can detect much of the anxious, even tormented private history of their creator as well as his obsession with men who are interesting by virtue of eccentric moral failures that are unknown to average men. Yet Conrad probably felt that such figures as Decoud and Heyst have an ancestry and belong to a brotherhood, albeit a tragic one. In early nineteenth-century French life and letters he seems to have found a strange family of solitaries whose common predicament forms a tragic inheritance appropriate to a distressed modern world, an inheritance which can still be expressed, if with considerable strain, as a bond connecting 'the dead to the living and the living to the unborn.'[19] Such a sense of fellowship in isolation allows Conrad to bring to his treatment of the lonely sceptic what is characteristically Conradian—that clear-sighted yet sympathetic feeling for the relationship between exceptional individualities and the 'general formula expressing the moral state of humanity' (*N* 246).

---

[19] 'Preface,' *The Nigger of the 'Narcissus,'* viii.

'One can learn something from Balzac':
Conrad and Balzac

J. H. Stape
Visiting Professor, Kyoto University

Conrad's awareness of Balzac's works has not gone entirely unnoted in Conrad criticism, but despite the intense interest in French influences on his writing, it has not been closely scrutinized. His friend and first biographer Jean-Aubry noted Conrad's 'étonnante connaissance des romans de Balzac' (Jean-Aubry 12), and Henry-D. Davray, one of his early French translators, recalled how Conrad, who had, it seemed to him, read everything, 'disséquait les personnages de Balzac' (Davray 34). Conrad himself refers to the ethos and concerns of *La Comédie humaine* in his 1905 essay 'Books' as 'the monstrous world created by Balzac' wherein 'the comical, appalling truth of human rapacity' is exposed (*NLL* 7), and in *The Mirror of the Sea* (1906), he describes his French shipmates as Balzacian characters, 'irresponsible young men ... who, as if drunk with the Provençal sunshine, frittered life away in joyous levity on the model of Balzac's *Histoire des Treize*' (*MS* 156), an allusion, seemingly, to the third episode of that work, 'La Fille aux yeux d'or,' and to Henri de Marsay and Paul de Manerville, whose wealth and social status allow them to spend their lives in the pursuit and seduction of attractive and exotic women.

Conrad's most extended comment, which hints at the range of his knowledge of Balzac's canon, occurs in 'Stephen Crane: A Reminiscence' (1923) in a flamboyantly dramatic and obviously highly self-conscious anecdote relating his first meeting with Crane:

> at ten o'clock in the evening he demanded insistently to be told in particular detail all about the 'Comédie Humaine,' its contents, its scope, its plan, and its general significance, together with a critical description of Balzac's style ... and I had no option but to hold forth over the remnants of a meal, in the rush of hundreds of waiters and the clatter of tons of crockery, caring not what I said (for what could Stephen want with Balzac?) ...   (*LE* 105)

His passing comments on Balzac in the more private context of letters to friends are brief but nonetheless revealing. Writing to John Galsworthy in the spring of 1906, he characterizes Ada Galsworthy's unequivocal antipathy to Balzac as 'shocking' (*CL3*, 327), and a letter of June 1918 to Hugh Walpole advises the younger writer, who later went on to achieve popular acceptance, that 'One can learn something from Balzac' (*Life and Letters* 2: 206). What that 'something' might be, however, Conrad left tantalizingly and suggestively unspecified.

In addition to these scattered references in essays, memoirs, and letters, there is at least one explicit reference to Balzac in Conrad's fiction. In 'An Outpost of Progress,' Kayerts and Carlier read *Le Père Goriot* (1835), a grimly ironic choice, not only because that novel's diverse metropolitan settings contrast, at least superficially, with the crudity and claustrophobia of their jungle outpost, but also because their own activities in the Congo echo *Le Père Goriot*'s sustained dissection of the primacy of the economic impulse in human relations, of the destructive power of sentimentalized greed and rapacity, and of unrelenting hypocrisy. In their patronizing and naïve attitudes to their human surroundings, Kayerts and Carlier affectionately dub Gobila, their kindly and sentimental African neighbour, 'Father Gobila,' in what is seemingly a tribute to Balzac's most famous character.[1]

Scholarly commentary has pursued the links between Conrad and Balzac with varying intensity. Jocelyn Baines, in the first scholarly biography of Conrad, suggested affinities between the time-shifts of *Almayer's Folly* and *Le Curé de Tours* (267). Paul Kirschner's pioneering study of Conrad's debts to French writers, *Conrad: The Psychologist as Artist* (1968), which itself makes no mention of Balzac, inspired further investigation into Conrad's reading in French literature and the extent of individual influences.[2] In this search Balzac has, however, figured much less prominently than might be expected, given the scope of his artistic achievement, his contributions to the handling of character and narrative, and his widespread popularity during the late nineteenth century, to say nothing of Conrad's expressed interest in, and occasional affinities with his writing. Even Yves Hervouet's exhaustive *The French Face of Joseph*

---

[1] Watts has pointed out Conrad's possible debt to H. M. Stanley's *The Congo and the Founding of its Free State* (1885) for this appellation (255-56), but an allusion to Balzac is also possible since Kayerts and Carlier's reading is mentioned prior to the reference to 'Father Gobila.'

[2] Knowles provides a selective listing of individual studies. For a general contextual discussion of these topics, see Watt.

Conrad (1990) devotes only a few pages to Balzac in a concluding survey of Conrad's knowledge of French writers. Hervouet suggests the nature of Conrad's general interest and offers one specific borrowing, convincingly demonstrating that the description of the decaying Robinson of *Lord Jim* is indebted to Balzac's portrayal of Poiret in *Le Père Goriot* (235).

For the most part, Balzac has been linked with Conrad only in occasional references,[3] but that such a lacuna exists is not altogether surprising. The affinities between the two writers are less immediately apparent than those between Conrad and Anatole France, Alphonse Daudet, and Guy de Maupassant, writers active during Conrad's lifetime, and on whom he commented in the essays he collected in *Notes on Life and Letters*. Moreover, the late-nineteenth-century attitudes and values of these three writers have a more direct resemblance, as a number of critics have argued, to Conrad's own, being nearer to the ethos of his own time.[4] Balzac's influence, on the other hand, tends to be general rather than local and is, on the whole, more a case of shared thematic concern than of verbal borrowings or stylistic echoes. The sheer size of Balzac's canon, which comprises no less than ninety-four novels (Adamson 7), is enough to daunt even the most intrepid researchers. To complicate matters further, hard evidence about what precisely Conrad read out of this immense body of writing amounts only to the handful of titles mentioned above. And Balzac's intense concentration on the realistic depiction of contemporary social particulars may also have played a part in discouraging comparative investigation. Lastly, Conrad's more obvious technical and thematic debts to Flaubert as well as his own stated, if qualified, admiration of Maupassant, France, and Daudet has, at least to some extent, determined the main lines of scholarly comment, as has the fact that scholarly interest in Conrad developed along with the emergence of New Criticism, which placed much emphasis on Flaubert and little on Balzac. The present essay makes no claim to comprehensiveness but aims, first, to outline some general aspects of Conrad's relationship with his great predecessor in the realistic tradition, and then to adduce intertextual parallels, suggesting in the specific cases of 'The End of the Tether' and 'The Duel' what Conrad himself, as a diligent student of a number of fictional traditions, might have 'learned' from Balzac.

---

[3] Exceptions are Henig and Talamantes's essay on 'The Sisters,' 'The *Tremolino*,' and *The Arrow of Gold* and three dissertations written during the 1980s on shared narrative patterns, especially the frame narrative (see Waggoner).

[4] In particular, see Hervouet on Conrad's interest in Maupassant and Anatole France.

Conrad and Balzac: General Connections

One of the strongest links between Conrad and Balzac is in a sense extra-literary, residing as it does in their common fascination with the major events, figures, and psychology of the French Revolution and the Napoleonic period and its immediate aftermath. The era, to which a good deal of Balzac's fiction looks back, offers a singularly rich and varied vein for the presentation of ideas, character traits, and behaviour during periods of extreme political and social stress. Indeed, both Balzac and Conrad pitilessly expose the selfishness, hypocrisy, corruption, ambition, and sentimental self-delusion that flourish when normal societal constraints dissolve and human institutions, ever fragile, collapse entirely. Conrad's notable hostility to the person of Napoleon himself, whom he presents as the archetype of the fanatical and ruthless egotist obsessed and ultimately destroyed by his obsession with power and grandeur, and to Napoleonism as a political creed is forthrightly stated in his 1905 essay 'Autocracy and War.' Its fictional expression is found in his works set during the Napoleonic period—'The Duel,' *The Rover*, and *Suspense*—and his view of the age significantly influences his treatment of political ideologies and moral situations in *Nostromo* and *Under Western Eyes.*

While the influence of Stendhal, whose *Le Rouge et le noir* and *La Chartreuse de Parme* Conrad admired, can be clearly discerned in his Napoleonic fictions, the example of Balzac is arguably more central and more intense. Conrad shares with Balzac a conception of social groups organized less on the basis of shifting political allegiances than on an adherence to certain core values, which, although primitive and unconscious (or only partly conscious), determine the well-being of both the group and the individual. The essential force governing human activity in Balzac is almost Darwinian in its simplicity and direction: blind self-love and unrelenting self-interest are the main pivots on which his plots turn. He asserts the existence of these forces as natural phenomena, immune to alteration and forever reproducing themselves. While Balzac's searingly realistic, even clinical and scientific, analysis of the construction of the individual and society often appears straightforwardly descriptive, like a mere given that is simply put on display in various altering situations, Conrad's depiction of motive is, on the contrary, morally charged and overtly judgemental, and it is hence, as some readers have complained, often bleakly pessimistic in the absence of any appeal to transcendent values. His is not, however, a world devoid of the heroic impulse, as Balzac's largely appears to be because of the more severely restricted lines on which it is constructed.

On the other hand, although it may lack heroes, Balzac's world is peopled by villains who are presented primarily as spectacle, the most notorious case being perhaps that of Vautrin, the homosexual villain first introduced in *Le Père Goriot*, whose elegant demeanour, linguistic sophistication, and ostentatious gynophobia make him a precursor and likely part-model for *Victory*'s self-dramatizing Mr Jones. The notion of villainy as self-conscious spectacle also partly accounts for the occasionally stagy and completely 'unrealistic' length of Vautrin's monologues. In the case of Balzac generally, a marked tendency towards lengthy and rhetorically sophisticated monologue functions as a sign of obsessional self-concern, and while Conrad's thematic intentions may differ, his own manipulation of the monologue form may be indebted to his predecessor's practice. The over-extended monologue, most notably found in the case of Conrad in *Lord Jim*, is an obvious transgression of the dominant conventions of realistic speech, a point at which the 'realist' novel deliberately turns towards stylization and theatricality.

In addition to providing Conrad with certain technical possibilities, Balzac's *œuvre*, the sheer size of his historical canvas with its recurring characters, may have served as a model for the epic scale of *Nostromo*, which shares not only a characteristically Balzacian scepticism about political change and social institutions but also deals centrally with the corrupting influence of money, and in particular with its commodification of emotion, in nearly all the main aspects of individual and societal life. The simple and faithful Nostromo, the pawn of class and political forces of which he is never fully aware, may be indebted more specifically to the rough-hewn Michu of *Une ténébreuse affaire* (1841), whose unwavering and unexamined fidelity to the system of values embodied by his aristocratic masters makes him the hapless victim of the larger and subtly manipulative political intrigues that enmesh him and eventually cost him his life or to Marche-à-Terre of *Les Chouans* (1829), with his similar dogged fidelity to the waning and ultimately doomed royalist cause.

The intersection of political and intensely domestic spheres is even more clearly evident in *The Secret Agent* with its ironic backdrop of the ruthlessly impersonal, all-devouring city, usually seen by critics as indebted heavily to Dickens generally, and more specifically to *Bleak House*.[5] But Conrad's vision of London at least partly echoes Balzac's conception and portrayal of Paris, which is envisaged as a sinister modern Babylon

---

[5] See Epstein, pp. 121-42 below, for an extended discussion of Conrad's interest in *Bleak House*, as well as the essays on *The Secret Agent* in *Conrad's Cities*, ed. Moore.

vampiristically draining its inhabitants of their energies and lives. This idea, which evolves and gains force throughout the Parisian novels of *La Comédie humaine*, is presented in summary form in the famous opening paragraphs of 'La Fille aux yeux d'or' (which Conrad possibly echoes at the conclusion of 'Karain'):

> Un des spectacles où se rencontre le plus d'épouvantement est certes l'aspect général de la population parisienne, peuple horrible à voir, hâve, jaune, tanné. Paris n'est-il pas un vaste champ incessament remué par une tempête d'intérêts sous laquelle tourbillonne une moisson d'hommes que la mort fauche plus souvent qu'ailleurs ...   (209)

Indeed, although Balzac often depicted the *mores* of his native Touraine in his large *œuvre*, he is no less than Dickens the novelist of the faceless, cannibalizing modern city, itself the physical expression of the primacy of the economic impulse that gives it not only its existence but also its corrosive force and amoral anonymity. Balzac anticipates both Dickens and Conrad in his presentation of the city as a fertile spawning ground for various kinds of criminal activity that reach their true apogee in violence, whether inspired by anarchism, as is at least potentially the case in *The Secret Agent*, or fuelled by the revolutionary fevers for reform that cyclically destroy and then reconstruct Paris. (In this light, too, the imaginary Sulaco of *Nostromo* has more in common with the political construction of Balzac's Paris than with Dickens's London.[6])

The Devouring Father:
Conrad's 'The End of the Tether' and Balzac's Le Père Goriot

Balzac's most sustained influence on Conrad is arguably to be found in the plotting, characterization, and thematics of 'The End of the Tether,' a short story focusing on the destructive aspects of a number of fixations and illusions including, centrally, that of paternal love. The presence of Balzac may similarly be detected in 'To-morrow,' which, even darker in tone, traverses much the same thematic territory as 'The End of the Tether' and, moreover, employs the symbol of physical blindness as a metaphor for paternal selfishness and egotism. *Le Père Goriot* and *Eugénie Grandet* (1833), two of Balzac's best known novels, and *Le Cousin Pons* (1847), his last novel, provide models for Conrad's nuanced reshaping and highly

---

[6] For a nuanced discussion of the ideological underpinnings of Conrad's attitudes towards revolution, see Hay.

condensed treatment of the theme of paternal egotism masquerading as self-sacrificing love.

Le Père Goriot and 'The End of the Tether' are similarly structured in that the father-figure ultimately exerts a destructive impulse in his attempt to dominate and control his own fate through the 'love' he expresses towards his offspring. This love itself, highly exaggerated in its manifestations and histrionically expressed in emotional outbursts, is played out for the benefit of callously 'indifferent' (and hence, at least on the surface, morally culpable) children, who are seemingly 'unnatural' in their lack of responsiveness. Balzac's scrupulous avoidance of sentimentality in his distanced treatment of his subject matter represents a technical challenge that may directly influence Conrad's own presentation and exploration of this theme, one that even *Almayer's Folly*, his first novel, is devoted to exploring. While the tangled skeins of Balzac's thematic ideas extend as far back as the *senex iratus of* Greek and Roman comedy and have numerous literary precedents, one might note that Conrad's fascination with this idea is also at least partly personal, being rooted in the psychological history of his own troubled, often anxiety-ridden, relationship with his father, whose amply documented obsessive character, self-sacrificing temperament, tendency towards morbid possessiveness, and histrionic displays marked Conrad's formative years.[7]

The presentation of Captain Whalley appears to owe not only its general outline but a number of specific debts to Balzac's portrayal of Goriot and Cousin Pons, elderly men who, like Whalley, suffer intensely from a fundamental and naïvely preserved unworldliness that causes their undoing. Goriot and Whalley see themselves as sacrificing themselves for the benefit of children whom they insistently, despite evidence to the contrary, idealize and sentimentalize. The two characters thus remain tragically unaware, even in the final moments of their lives, of their complicitous responsibility for neglecting to oppose the cynical machinations that have led to their downfall. Pons similarly provides a model for the tragically naïve old man beset by self-seeking intriguers and caught up in a complicated web of worldly snares. Indeed, the great themes of *La Comédie humaine*—unbridled egotism, lack of self-awareness, obsession of various kinds but especially with economic advancement and social advantage, and an abiding interest in family drama—are all to be found in

---

[7] For a full-length, if highly speculative, psycho-critical analysis of Conrad's relationship to his father, see Dobrinsky. Najder's more even-handed portrayal of Korzeniowski is balanced by Bross's carefully argued dissent from it.

Conrad's story and influence his shaping of Whalley's character and
destiny.

Conrad most particularly follows Balzac in his clear-sighted dissection of the pernicious effects and underlying motivations of Whalley's self-
sacrificing 'love' for his daughter, which is exposed as nothing more than
a pernicious and deeply rooted self-love. Goriot's rending deathbed
agonies, punctuated by his repeated lamentations over his daughters'
deliberate absence and his futile invocation of their names, culminates in
his unmasking when in his possessive hysteria he cries out 'Je veux mes
filles! je les ai faites! elles sont à moi!' (*PG* 347). The words un-self-
consciously reveal the actual foundations of his earlier nearly superhuman
generosity and extreme indulgence: the supposedly selfless love that Goriot
has relentlessly averred is based upon a profound self-regard, a form of
egotism ultimately no less monstrous than the 'unnatural' apathy of his
estranged daughters towards him, and, in some measure at least, the cause
of their indifferent rejection of him. In terms of his aberrant psychology,
they exist only so far as his imaginative apprehension of them allows them
to, having become for him a reified form of his wealth and the surrogates
of a frustrated social ambition that he himself has failed to realize. Captain
Whalley, no less obsessed by Ivy's social status, and especially anxious
about the degradation of the Whalley name by her running of a common
boarding-house, similarly replaces his daughter's individuality by a concern
with her socio-economic circumstances. As Robert Kimbrough has noted,
Conrad's narrative strategies collaborate to make the reader hear 'the "I"
in Ivy' (xxiv).

On a psychological level, Goriot ingests his daughters as a kind of
obverse—because eagerly willing—Ugolino, feeding off their social success
and elevation in class status as a means of sustaining his illusions about
himself. Whalley creates a no less fantasized Ivy out of his imagination,
replacing a real woman by an obsession that he habitually resorts to in
order to justify his suspect behaviour to himself. As a corollary, and
perhaps as an act of self-protection or even of revenge, the daughters of
such fathers fail to develop what would be considered a normal emotional
receptivity to others. Goriot's spoiled daughters live only to experience
pleasure and the power of beauty aligned with wealth, having too well
learned the lesson that their father's emotional dependency has taught them.
Whalley's Ivy has been so ground down by circumstance that she likewise
becomes emotionally estranged from herself, and in direct parallel to
Balzac's Delphine and Anastasie, is unable to react to the news of her
father's death with much more than dismissal, as Conrad's ironic borrowing from Flaubert makes clear (see Hervouet, 80).

As Balzac demonstrates, Goriot's 'love,' which in the end has helped to render his daughters soulless, is essentially a form of exploitation and an attempt to assert ownership. Balzac treats this topic with equal intensity in *Eugénie Grandet*, in which the title-character's father, in professing a right to ownership over the course of his daughter's feelings (a typical motif of patriarchal domination and control), literally imprisons her in their home for her contravention of his will. In 'The End of the Tether' and *Père Goriot*, the offspring effect an escape into non-feeling, and in this respect Ivy's physically handicapped husband trenchantly symbolizes her atrophied emotional capacities that in the face of over-demand have lost their ability to respond.

Conrad's reliance on the symbol of blindness to explore these quint-essentially Balzacian themes in 'The End of the Tether' and 'To-morrow' gives singular force to the fatal unawareness that in the end undermines Whalley's very existence and creates the tragic conditions in which Bessie Carvil is fated to live out a life entirely lacking in emotional satisfaction. Neither Whalley nor Goriot is capable of 'seeing' or perceiving, let alone coming to terms with, the fundamentally self-seeking character of his pro-fessed 'love' for his children, while for the blind Josiah Carvil no universe outside his own immediate needs even exists, his daughter being for him only a means by which he fulfils his wants. These tyrannical fathers remain, then, not only 'blind' to their motivations but self-deluded about the nature of their feelings.

Although some critics have failed to appreciate the bitter and distan-cing ironies through which Conrad presents Captain Whalley, neither in the case of Goriot nor of Whalley is the reader invited to sympathize with the 'abused and neglected' father.[8] In 'The End of the Tether,' another strategy by which Conrad ironically undermines Whalley's self-appraisal is the mirror character of Mr Massy, an uncontrollable gambler who like-wise expresses an unconscious (and equally futile) desire to assert control over randomness and flux, and who acts as a further exploration of the nature of obsession and blind self-love. Although Whalley's sentimen-talization has obscured for him a realization that money 'counts' even in the world of feeling, Massy cynically recognizes no other basis for social life than the economic imperative. His means of coming to terms with this insight are, however, ultimately grimly comic: he leaves for Manila to lose not only his money in the lottery but also, it seems, his increasingly precarious hold on his sanity. He functions in ways parallel to Rastignac,

---

[8] For a general overview of the contemporary and more recent critical fortunes of 'The End of the Tether,' see Stape.

the would-be creator of his own destiny in *Le Père Goriot*, as an out-rageously clear-sighted analyst of bourgeois illusions and sentimental hypocrisy who ambitiously attempts to leap over the boundaries set by fate and circumstance.

The Braggart Soldier and the Gambler:
Conrad's 'The Duel' and Balzac's La Rabouilleuse

The conflation of callous self-interest, the emotional neglect of a loving, over-indulgent parent, and the motif of compulsive gambling in *La Rabouilleuse* (1842) offer yet further variations on Balzacian interests that recur in Conrad's writings. In particular, Conrad appears to have drawn upon this novel while composing both 'The End of the Tether' and 'The Duel.' Although the immediate plot sources of 'The Duel' were identified long ago,[9] the significance of Balzac's *La Rabouilleuse* for the presentation and development of its themes has gone unnoticed, and the story's general ambience and, in particular, Conrad's conception and elaboration of Feraud appear to be indebted to Balzac.

Set mainly at the close of the Napoleonic period and in the early years of the Bourbon Restoration, *La Rabouilleuse* depicts the opposed fortunes and sharply contrasting personalities of two antagonistic brothers. As in Conrad, the mythological sources of Balzac's story of *les frères ennemis* are, of course, biblical and classical, but they are particularized by the historical setting and the close observation of social realities. Joseph Bridau, a shy painter whose laboured struggle for artistic achievement and public recognition is eventually crowned with success, is set against the failure of the world's favourite, Philippe, a ne'er-do-well soldier and the self-styled victim of political and historical circumstance, whose un-restrained selfishness remains unrecognized by—and ultimately causes the death of—his blindly adoring mother. Philippe's braggart self-confidence (as a type he, like Feraud, can be traced to the *miles gloriosus* of Roman comedy) is bolstered by his fanatical support of, and identification with the exiled Napoleon. This is patterned after his late father's fidelity, the grandiose identification of a minor functionary in the Ministry of the Interior, to the Emperor's person and cause:

> Bridau s'attacha fanatiquement à Napoléon ... il accepta les plus lourds
> fardeaux, tant il était heureux de seconder l'Empereur; il l'aimait comme

---

[9] For a summary of the story's sources, based, in part, on unpublished research by Hans van Marle, see Desforges, pp. 133-35.

homme, il l'adorait comme souverain et ne souffrait pas la moindre
critique sur ses actes ni sur ses projets.   (*Rabouilleuse* 32-33)

Philippe's sentimental championship of the Napoleonic cause
becomes increasingly exaggerated after the Emperor's final exile to St.
Helena and serves, as far as he himself is concerned, to excuse his
subsequent failure in the new world order in which he degenerates into a
social malcontent, becoming a reckless and inveterate gambler, a drunkard
who ends up as an emotional and economic parasite living off the meagre
income and generous sympathies of his increasingly impoverished mother
and long-suffering brother:

> Philippe fut un des bonapartistes les plus assidus du Café Lembelin ... il
> y prit ses habitudes, les manières, le style et la vie des officiers à demi-
> solde; et, comme eût fait tout jeune homme de vingt et un ans, il les
> outra, voua sérieusement une haine mortelle aux Bourbons, ne se rallia
> point, il refusa même les occasions qui se présentèrent d'être employé
> dans la Ligne.   (57)

Philippe Bridau is a direct literary model for Conrad's Feraud, who
so 'loved the Emperor' (231) that his existence after Napoleon's exile to
St. Helena becomes a mere half-life bereft of purpose and governed by a
fixed idea. As a consequence, like Bridau, Feraud steadfastly refuses to
adapt to the new age that has dawned, and, like the duel that obsesses his
imagination and emotions, he is locked into a pattern of obsessive repeti-
tion that is rooted in the past.

The novel is another rearrangement of a limited number of Balzacian
motifs and character types. Philippe, the consummate egotist and monstrous
son, sustains himself by cynically preying upon, and actually stealing from,
his family and their immediate circle. An obvious re-working of the character of Goriot, Madame Bridau blindly maintains her maternal illusions
about her favourite and heartless son despite accumulating and incontro-
vertible evidence against him, and even prefers him to her talented and
gentle-natured Joseph. No less than Goriot or Whalley, she thus becomes
a parent whose emotional blindness is both culpable and eventually self-
defeating.

The Napoleonic backdrop of *La Rabouilleuse*, its central contrast
between two brothers of differing inclinations and temperaments, and the
ardent Bonapartism of its villain, all suggest a more than casual or simply
coincidental relationship between it and 'The Duel.' Conrad's Feraud and
Balzac's Philippe are cut from the same sizable block of material: both are
outsiders who play up an ardent and showy patriotism, that famous 'last

refuge of a scoundrel,' to excuse a lack of worldly success; both have reputations as womanizers; and both in the end depend economically on self-sacrificing counterparts whom they hold in open contempt.

The motif of gambling, which occurs repeatedly in Balzac as a symbol of the inherent instability of social and economic position (most notably, perhaps, in *La Peau de chagrin*, where the wager is for life itself), plays an especially important role in this novel, not only with respect to Philippe but also as the central force in the life of Madame Descoings, Madame Bridau's live-in friend and Philippe's indulgent patroness. Madame Descoings' obsession with the near-impossible chance of winning the national lottery ironically mirrors Philippe's fluctuating insouciance about money, and has the double role of playing up the theme of self-concern.[10]

Madame Descoings' fanatical devotion to the lottery, especially to a particular set of numbers, suggests that in addition to finding materials for 'The Duel' in this novel Conrad may have drawn on it to delineate Massey's obsession with the Manila lottery in 'The End of the Tether.' The old woman, like Massey, is dominated by a fixed obsession with chance that has become the ruling passion of her life:

> Cette joueuse obstinée ne manquait jamais un tirage: elle poursuivait son terne, qui n'était pas encore sorti. Ce terne allait avoir vingt et un ans, il atteignait à sa majorité. ... Elle voulait, au dernier tirage de Paris, risquer toutes ses économies sur les combinaisons de son terne chéri. Cette passion, si universellement condamnée, n'a jamais été étudiée. Personne n'y a vu l'opium de la misère.   (90-91)

Her cabbalistic dreams and those about lottery numbers, tantamount to a kind of religious faith, are echoed in Massey's belief that what merely appears to be random chance has a discernible order that is subject to discovery:

> He nourished a conviction that there must be some logic lurking some-where in the results of chance. He thought he had seen its very form. His head swam; his limbs ached; he puffed at his pipe mechanically; a contemplative stupor would soothe the fretfulness of his temper, like the passive bodily quietude procured by a drug, while the intellect remains tensely on the stretch. Nine, nine, nought, four, two. He made a note.
> (266)

---

[10] For Conrad's own interest in the French national lottery, see *CL*4, 8, 22, 56, 60f., 72.

Like Madame Descoings, who literally dies when she learns of a stroke of bad luck (her number does come up, but she has been unable to afford a ticket, Philippe having purloined her hidden nest egg), Massey is physically affected by his monomania, another point at which Conrad's nuanced psychological presentation resembles Balzac's depiction of the nature and effects of obsessional behaviour.

Conrad's indebtedness to Balzac may be variously calculated: there are both specific instances of influence on narrative strategy and the presentation of character, and the more general confluence of theme and *Weltanschauung* that unites writers otherwise individual in their fictional practice and interests. Whatever Crane may have 'wanted with' Balzac, the rhetorical formulation of this question makes it abundantly clear that Conrad himself wanted rather a good deal from a writer whom many have considered the progenitor of the realistic novel. Like all good students, however, he moved on, having assimilated the lessons learned from a predecessor to whom Henry James also paid tribute, averring that 'Balzac stands signally apart ... he is the first and foremost member of his craft' (90).

WORKS CITED

Adamson, Donald. Introduction. Honoré de Balzac, *The Black Sheep*. Harmondsworth: Penguin, 1970. 7-20.

Baines, Jocelyn. *Joseph Conrad: A Critical Biography*. London: Weidenfeld & Nicolson; New York: McGraw-Hill, 1960.

Balzac, Honoré de. *The Black Sheep*. Tr. Donald Adamson. Harmondsworth: Penguin, 1970.

————. *Le Cousin Pons*. 1847. Intro. Maurice Maurier. Paris: Pocket, 1994.

————. *Eugénie Grandet*. 1833. Intro. Samuel S. de Sacy. Paris: Gallimard, 1972.

————. 'The Girl with Golden Eyes.' Tr. Jno. Rudd. In *Compendium / Scenes from The Comédie Humaine*. Philadelphia: Gebbie Publishing, 1900. 61-145.

————. *Histoire des Treize. Premier et troisième épisode: Ferragus / La Fille aux yeux d'or*. 1834. Ed. Michel Lichtlé. Paris: Garnier Flammarion, 1988.

————. *La Peau de chagrin*. 1831. Paris: Garnier Flammarion, 1971.

————. *Le Père Goriot*. 1835. Intro. Félicien Marceau. Paris: Gallimard, 1971.

————. *La Rabouilleuse*. 1842. Intro. René Guise. Paris: Gallimard, 1972.

————. *Une Ténébreuse Affaire*. 1841. Intro. René Guise. Paris: Gallimard, 1973.

Bross, Addison. 'Apollo Korzeniowski's Mythic Vision: *Poland and Muscovy*, "Note A."' *The Conradian* 20 (1995), 77-102.

Conrad, Joseph. 'Books.' 1905. *Notes on Life and Letters*. London: Dent, 1921. 3-12.

————. *The Collected Letters of Joseph Conrad*. Vols. 3 (1903-7) and 4 (1908-11). Ed. Frederick R. Karl and Laurence Davies. Cambridge: Cambridge University Press, 1988 and 1990.

————. 'The Duel.' 1908. *A Set of Six*. London: Dent, 1923; rpt. 1954. 165-266.

————. 'The End of the Tether.' 1902. In *Youth / Heart of Darkness / The End of the Tether*. Ed. Robert Kimbrough. Oxford: Oxford University Press, 1984. 163-339.

———. *Joseph Conrad: Life and Letters*. Ed. G. Jean-Aubry. 2 vols. New York: Doubleday, Page; London: Heinemann, 1927.

———. *Lord Jim*. 1900. Ed. John Batchelor. Oxford: Oxford University Press, 1983.

———. *The Mirror of the Sea* and *A Personal Record*. 1906 and 1912. Ed. Zdzisław Najder. Oxford: Oxford University Press, 1988.

———. 'An Outpost of Progress.' In *Heart of Darkness and Other Tales*. Ed. Cedric Watts. Oxford: Oxford University Press, 1990. 3-34.

———. 'Stephen Crane: A Reminiscence.' *Last Essays*. Ed. Richard Curle. London: Dent, 1926. 93-118.

Davray, Henry-D. 'Joseph Conrad.' *Mercure de France*, 175 (1 October 1924), 32-55.

Desforges, Michel. 'Postface.' *Joseph Conrad: Le Duel*. Tr. Michel Desforges. Toulouse: Éditions Ombres, 1991. 127-38.

Dobrinsky, Joseph. *The Artist in Conrad's Fiction: A Psychocritical Study*. Ann Arbor: UMI Research Press, 1989.

Hay, Eloise Knapp. '*Nostromo*.' In *The Cambridge Companion to Joseph Conrad*. Ed. J. H. Stape. Cambridge: Cambridge University Press, 1996. 81-99.

Henig, Suzanne, and Florence W. Talamantes. 'Conrad and Balzac: A Trio of Balzacian Interrelationships—'The Sisters,' 'The *Tremolino*,' and *The Arrow of Gold*.' *The Polish Review* 20:2-3 (1975), 58-70.

Hervouet, Yves. *The French Face of Joseph Conrad*. Cambridge: Cambridge University Press, 1990.

James, Henry. 'Honoré de Balzac, 1902.' *Literary Criticism: French Writers, Other European Writers, The Prefaces to the New York Edition*. New York: Library of America, 1984. 90-115.

Jean-Aubry, G. Introduction. *Lettres françaises de Joseph Conrad*. Ed. G. Jean-Aubry. Paris: Gallimard, [1929]. 7-23.

Kimbrough, Robert. Introduction. *Youth / Heart of Darkness / The End of the Tether*. Ed. Robert Kimbrough. Oxford: Oxford University Press, 1984. vii-xxvi.

Kirschner, Paul. *Conrad: The Psychologist as Artist*. Edinburgh: Oliver & Boyd, 1968.

Knowles, Owen. *An Annotated Critical Bibliography of Joseph Conrad*. Hemel Hempstead: Harvester/Wheatsheaf, 1992.

118 J. H. STAPE

Moore, Gene M., ed. *Conrad's Cities: Essays for Hans van Marle*. Amsterdam and Atlanta, GA: Rodopi, 1992.

Najder, Zdzisław. *Joseph Conrad: A Chronicle*. Tr. Halina Carroll-Najder. New Brunswick, NJ: Rutgers University Press; Cambridge University Press, 1983.

Stape, J. H. 'Conrad's "Unreal City": Singapore in "The End of the Tether."' In *Conrad's Cities: Essays for Hans van Marle*. Ed. Gene M. Moore. Amsterdam and Atlanta, GA: Rodopi, 1992. 85-96.

Waggoner, Mark W. *Bibliography of Balzac Criticism 1930-1990*. Encintas, CA: French Research Publications, 1990.

Watt, Ian. *Conrad in the Nineteenth Century*. Berkeley: University of California Press, 1979.

Watts, Cedric. Explanatory Notes. *'Heart of Darkness' and Other Tales*. Oxford: Oxford University Press, 1990. 253-77.

Bleak House and Conrad:
The Presence of Dickens in Conrad's Writing

Hugh Epstein
London

Conrad's writing is permeated by his lifelong experience of reading Dickens. The contention of this preliminary and purely descriptive excursion into the large territory that could be surveyed by considering the relationship between these two writers, is that Dickens's habitually grotesque satire and his predilection for the incongruous and the bizarre inform Conrad's composing mind, not so much with precise examples, lessons, and locutions, as with starting-points for Conrad's own, and even more visionary, distortions and manipulations of narrative style into an arrestingly original mode that carries his own signature, authorized, as it were, by his predecessor. *Bleak House* was Conrad's favourite novel. I will try to imagine the importance for Conrad's writing of only *Bleak House* amongst Dickens's works, and in so doing aim to highlight the way in which much of what is so vivid and original in Conrad is characteristically collaborative in its production. Whilst Conrad reworked passages of Flaubert, Maupassant, and Anatole France into English, his creative encounter with Dickens is less amenable to detection and generally more diffuse. The French authors provided him with solutions to problems of expression and even of psychology, but Dickens seems to be, rather, a verbal medium through whose agency Conrad re-imagined aspects of his own experience or conceived artistic forms for his own visions.

There is an extraordinary moment in *Bleak House* in which an unforgettable gesture lights briefly the configuration of an unpenetrating narrator observing an inscrutable intention. Esther has just watched Lady Dedlock's pointed preference for her new favourite Rosa extend to taking the girl up into her carriage, leaving her maid Hortense disregarded and abandoned at the edge of the park: 'Her retaliation was the most singular I could have imagined. She remained perfectly still until the carriage had turned into the drive, and then, without the least discomposure of countenance, slipped off her shoes, left them on the ground, and walked deliberately in the same direction, through the wettest of the wet grass'

(312).[1] Mademoiselle Hortense's cool repudiation of Lady Dedlock's disregard by her own gesture of disregard is allowed to mask another drama that is closer to Esther yet also hidden from her understanding. As she contemplates the peaceful sight of Chesney Wold now with 'everything refreshed by the late rain,' Esther fails to perceive the transforming effect of her preceding encounter with Lady Dedlock that her own narrative conveys. The closing words of the chapter present 'the little carriage shining at the doorway like a fairy carriage made of silver. Still, very steadfastly and quietly walking towards it, a peaceful figure too in the landscape, went Mademoiselle Hortense, shoeless, through the wet grass' (312). Syntactically, this superbly extended sentence is rather different from most of Conrad, but it is difficult not to think that features of this evocation such as 'without ... discomposure,' 'deliberately,' 'steadfastly and quietly' would not have remained with him, so strikingly consonant are they with his own concern to depict the declaration made by human action before the uncomprehending gaze of indifference.

We can, of course, only conjecture what Conrad made of this moment from the novel that he saw as 'a work of the master for which I have such an admiration, or rather such an intense and unreasoning affection ... I have read it innumerable times both in Polish and in English; I have read it only the other day ...' (PR 124). Whether the equally arresting image of repudiation that figures as the climactic moment of his first novel, Almayer's Folly, was fashioned from a recollection of Mademoiselle Hortense's footsteps through wet English grass is a question impossible to answer; however, it can be perceived as fitting a pattern of Conrad's compositional method, which is to work up a literary borrowing by intensifying its sensational qualities and finding a larger scope for the resonances implicit in its configuration. It is the powerful difference between the two scenes that is likely to strike the reader first. As Nina leaves her father, walking across the beach with Dain, Conrad represents Almayer's sense of abandonment through six consecutive sentences that insist upon the scene as seen items more systematically than Esther's contemplations, in the deliberate and repetitive style that belongs more to Dickens's satire than to his descriptions (the staring Marseilles sun at the opening of Little Dorrit

---

[1] All references to Conrad's works follow the pagination of Dent's Collected Edition (London: Dent, 1947-54), apart from The Secret Agent and Almayer's Folly, where reference is to the Cambridge Edition. References to Conrad's letters are to The Collected Letters of Joseph Conrad, ed. Frederick R. Karl and Laurence Davies (Cambridge: Cambridge University Press, 1983-) cited as CL. All references to Bleak House are to the Penguin Classics edition (Harmondsworth: Penguin Books, 1971).

perhaps comes nearest to it). Two of these run: 'He looked at the line of their footsteps marked in the sand. He followed their figures moving in the crude blaze of the vertical sun, in that light violent and vibrating, like a triumphal flourish of brazen trumpets' (*AF* 146). The distinctively Conradian concern with the impact upon the senses, the impression as received, creates the swift violence of the image of sunlight, which is extended much more insistently by the inverted word order ('that light violent and vibrating') than it would have been in more idiomatic English; then, by a kind of synæsthesia, the effect upon Almayer of what he sees swells with an irony that becomes harsher as we dwell upon 'brazen' and recall the reveries that open the novel. However, like Hortense, Almayer is quite impassive in the face of abandonment until, with a gesture of much greater imaginative scope than that given to Hortense and conceived, perhaps, in opposition to it, he wipes out the footsteps that have taken Nina to a life that denies the heritage he would have liked to bequeathe to her, as if it were his own to give:

> To Ali's great dismay he fell on his hands and knees and creeping along the sand erased carefully with his hand all traces of Nina's footsteps. He piled up small heaps of sand leaving behind him a line of miniature graves right down to the water. After burying the last slight imprint of Nina's slippers he stood up and turning his face towards the headland, where he had last seen the prau, he made an effort to shout out loud again his firm resolve to never forgive.   (*AF* 147)

This is, in a sense, the reverse of the passage from *Bleak House* in which, in practice, Esther has unknowingly found her mother. In losing his daughter, Almayer can only attempt to reassert the identity that has been constructed upon fantastic notions of a European life, by turning the gesture of repudiation into one of complete abolition. The burial would seem to comprehend both his daughter and himself, the far-reaching penetration of the image of the 'miniature graves' foreshadowing Almayer's inability to forget Nina, and his own sense of degradation, by turning each one of her abandoning steps into a small monument. This great Conradian moment is only questionably a violent transportation of a Dickensian glimpse to the full glare of a climax under very different skies, but the trace that it bears conveys the suggestive presence with which Dickens, uniquely I think, inhabited Conrad's imagination.

Conrad used other writers more deliberately as prompts and guides. For instance, Conrad's most Dickensian creation, the London setting of *The Secret Agent*, in fact owes a more specific debt to Ford Madox Ford than it does to Dickens; and the fantastic invasion of the grotesque trio of

Victory owes a direct and formative literary origin to Stevenson, though the delight with which it is carried off is certainly impelled by Conrad's love of the ghastly-comic effects to be found everywhere in Dickens.[2] Whilst Conrad readily used other writers to the point of imitation, it is the imagined life itself depicted in Dickens's novels that seems to have dwelt in his mind with a vivacity that did not admit of direct translation into his own work. Donald C. Yelton, in his acute consideration of the linguistic affinities between Dickens and Conrad, goes as far as to claim that Conrad 'gave himself up to his [Dickens's] enchantment in entire surrender, with incalculable effect upon his imaginative development.'[3] While the calculation is certainly difficult to make, Conrad's letters reveal the way in which Dickens provided an outlet for self-expression and also a world whose imagined reality could be shared with his correspondents without preliminaries. His amused reference to himself seen 'as a kind of "hinfant phenomenon"' by his publishers (*CL*1, 313); his desire for 'a quiet half-hour' with Ford Madox Ford lent a little spice by the assurance 'Codlin's your friend—not Short' (*CL*2, 111), and his enjoyment of the reception of *Romance*—'Even The Times is as friendly as Short and Codlin rolled into one' (*CL*3, 71); deriding the Censor of Plays as 'provided by the state with the immortal Mr Stiggins's plug hat and umbrella' (*CL*3, 494); his regret that he is 'not like Mr Peter Magnus—I afford no entertainement [*sic*] to my friends' because of gout (*CL*4, 8); complaining that the language for talking about books 'not to put (in the words of the immortal Snagsby) too fine a point on it stinks in my nostrils' (*CL*4, 274); having Podsnap judge 'Freya of the Seven Isles' as '"no blush to the cheek of the young person" sort of thing' (*CL*4, 413); expressing his hope to Pinker for magazine publication of whole works by slightly misquoting *The Pickwick Papers*: '"Don't presume dictate" (as Mr Jingle said about the dinner)' (*CL*5, 311); and slipping into Mr Jingle's mode of speech directly when promising Violet Hunt that he will present himself in her drawing-room, writing 'Never happened to me before. Didn't think could be. Smacks of fairy-tale' (*CL*5, 23); and welcoming a letter of praise from Gissing as 'a Christmas gift in my hands as no lavishness of Dickens' imagination could have

---

[2] See Hugh Epstein, 'A Pier-Glass in the Cavern: The Construction of London in *The Secret Agent*,' in *Conrad's Cities*, ed. Gene M. Moore (Amsterdam and Atlanta, GA: Rodopi, 1992), especially 176-89; and '*Victory*'s Marionettes: Conrad's Revisitation of Stevenson,' forthcoming in a volume in the series *Joseph Conrad: Eastern and Western Perspectives*.

[3] *Mimesis and Metaphor: An Enquiry into the Genesis and Scope of Conrad's Symbolic Imagery* (The Hague: Mouton, 1967), 86.

contrived for the felicity of a poor devil in a Christmas Tale' (*CL2*, 464)—
the last apart, these all have an unpremeditated air, as if such characters
and the words associated with them had permeated Conrad's internal verbal
life and taken up residence.

No other writers are accorded this sort of inwardness in Conrad's
correspondence. He certainly refers more often, and always more respect-
fully, to both Flaubert and Maupassant. His well-known statement to
Marguerite Poradowska about Flaubert is what we might have expected
him to say about Dickens, but it has a certain distance and the air of a
pronouncement about it: 'Few authors could be as much a creator as he.
One never questions for a moment either his characters or his incidents:
one would rather doubt one's own existence' (*CL1*, 111). His equally
famous exclamation about Maupassant ('Studied *Pierre et Jean*—thought,
method and all—with the profoundest despair' [*CL1*, 185]), and his
frequent and precise quotation from both authors, suggest a relationship
belonging to a fellow-practitioner, in which Conrad is much more
consciously engaged in thinking about their art than he is with Dickens. We
set foot on personal territory of a different sort when we read this, for
instance, in a letter to Norman Douglas thanking him for providing some
brown sauce for a meal at Capel House:

> 'Sir! you are a nobleman: you are a baron of the land' as Mr Crook [*sic*]
> said to Mr Guppy when Mr Guppy presented him with a bottle of
> eighteen-penny gin out of Sol's Arms at the corner of Chancery Lane.
> I bet you don't know who and what I am talking about.
>
> (*CL5*, 162)

The intimacy that marks his relation with Dickens even makes a
uniquely explicit appearance in the fiction: Mrs. Fyne's remembrance of
'de Barral clinging to the child at the side of his wife's grave' is given the
coda, 'Figures from Dickens—pregnant with pathos' (*C* 162). Is this a sign
of Marlow's portentousness or an unguarded voice nearer Conrad's own?
A comment by Frederick R. Karl provides us with a way of reading the
recurrence of these figures from Dickens which links a note struck in the
letters to this sudden surfacing in *Chance*, and which will take us back to
the deep appeal that *Bleak House* held for Conrad: 'Like a Dickens character or Dickens himself, he was an orphan even before his parents died.'[4]
Perhaps the 'unreasoning' aspect of Conrad's affection for Dickens, and for
Bleak House in particular, arises from Dickens's multiple exploration of

---

[4] *Joseph Conrad: The Three Lives* (New York: Farrar, Straus & Giroux, 1979), 16.

orphanage, recalling Conrad's statement about writing in English in the
'Author's Note' to *A Personal Record*: 'well, yes, there was adoption; but
it was I who was adopted by the genius of the language' (*PR* v), which can
be read as covert testimony of his feelings towards Dickens himself. We
could hazard that a buried reference to a figure from Dickens is what
touches the thirty-four-year-old aspiring writer into visualizing himself as
the simultaneously loved and disregarded plaything of a lonely child. Of
'the Punch of my childhood' he writes to Marguerite Poradowska in 1891:
'He was a faithful friend ... He was a gentleman ... This evening I seem to
be in a corner, spine cracked, nose in the dust. Would you kindly scrape
together the poor devil, put him tenderly in your apron, introduce him to
your dolls, make him join the dinner party with the others' (*CL1*, 98).
Mark Wollaeger finds here a representation of the blocked writer 'guiltily
haunting the world as a writer who is not writing';[5] and it is only a short
imaginative journey (considering Conrad's reading) back to Esther Sum-
merson and her doll, another incipient narrator trying to find a means of
expression:

> My dear old doll! I was such a shy little thing that I seldom dared to
> open my lips, and never dared to open my heart, to anybody else. It
> almost makes me cry to think what a relief it used to be to me, when I
> came home from school of a day, to run upstairs to my room, and say,
> 'O you dear faithful Dolly, I knew you would be expecting me!' and
> then to sit down on the floor, leaning on the elbow of her great chair,
> and tell her all I had noticed since we parted.   (62)

Though in a personal letter, Conrad's patterned drawing out of the
image strikes a more formal and literary note than Esther's coy disclosure,
and points to the literariness involved in finding what might be taken to be
his own voice. Whilst fidelity is the shared value of the Polish gentleman
and Dickens's fictional surrogate, the shared action envisaged by both
pieces of writing is the restoration of the absent mother, in Esther's case
through the knowingly sad irony of the 'elbow of her great chair,' and in
Conrad's case through Poradowska herself. In fact, Lady Dedlock seems
to have played a significant role in Conrad's imagination, living with sufficient vividness for him to write in *A Personal Record* how in Marseilles
the 'ineffable' Madame Delestang used to remind him of her, to the point
of deliberate simulated confusion in the account: 'And it was generally on

---

[5] *Joseph Conrad and the Fictions of Skepticism* (Stanford: Stanford University
Press, 1990), 41.

these occasions that under the great carriage gateway Lady Ded—I mean Madame Delestang, catching sight of my raised hat ...' (*PR* 125). Madame Delestang's sad motherly advice that 'one must, after all, take care not to spoil one's life' (*PR* 126) is exactly what Dickens explores through the alienated figure of Lady Dedlock to whom Conrad is so drawn, albeit with the fear that he expresses in so many letters to Poradowska and others. Conrad's complex relation with Dickens, then, involves him not only as a professional writer but is also a means by which he finds a verbal bridge into some of the painful areas of his own experience.

A result of Dickens's influence far more pervasive than these rare retrievals from the depths is, however, Conrad's adoption of a comic tone of sardonic irony derived from his reading of such depictions as this of the Smallweeds:

> There has been only one child in the Smallweed family for several generations. Little old men and women there have been, but no child, until Mr Smallweed's grandmother, now living, became weak in her intellect, and fell (for the first time) into a childish state. With such infantine graces as a total want of observation, memory, understanding and interest and an eternal disposition to fall asleep over the fire and into it, Mr Smallweed's grandmother has undoubtedly brightened the family.
> (341)

This sort of broadly comic satire whose irony borders on invective often makes the characters seem mere victims of the narrator's delight in scorn. This is exactly Martin Price's objection to Conrad's treatment of his subject(s) in 'An Outpost of Progress' and *The Secret Agent*.[6] It is not difficult, for instance, to see the features of Grandmother Smallweed (and the Smallweeds generally) resolving themselves into the portrait of Karl Yundt:

> On the other side of the fire-place, in the horsehair armchair where Mrs Verloc's mother was generally privileged to sit, Karl Yundt giggled grimly, with a faint black grimace of a toothless mouth. The terrorist, as he called himself, was old and bald, with a narrow, snow white wisp of a goatee hanging limply from his chin. An extraordinary expression of underhand malevolence survived in his extinguished eyes. When he rose painfully the thrusting forward of a skinny groping hand deformed by gouty swellings suggested the effort of a moribund murderer summoning all his remaining strength for a last stab. (*SA* 37-38)

---

[6] 'Conrad: Satire and Fiction,' *Yearbook of English Studies* 14 (1984), 226-42.

Characteristically, Conrad is less funny than Dickens but even more grotesque. The moral commentary is less explicit but Conrad heightens a different sort of parade in the writing by staging Yundt's posturing hypocrisy in a series of incongruous pairs ('giggled grimly,' 'survived ... extinguished,' 'thrusting ... groping,' 'moribund murderer') that are as much a representation of the effort to receive adequately the impression of the awful old man as they are a recognizable picture. This sort of distortion of realistic representation, so that the reader *sees* more completely, is of course a mark of Conrad's Modernism and his difference from Dickens, but it has roots in Dickens's own grotesque visualization.[7] Perhaps all ages are ages of uncertainty, but the reader surely feels that Grandmother Smallweed is packaged up and bundled off more securely and completely than Karl Yundt. Conrad's last sentence here is not entirely dismissive, for Yundt's derided rhetoric still retains a frightening and destructive force when apprehended by Stevie: 'Stevie swallowed the terrifying statement with an audible gulp, and at once, as though it had been swift poison, sank limply in a sitting posture on the steps of the kitchen door' (*SA* 44). When Dickens wishes to condemn, he is more forthright, and the operative image he typically chooses is really more conceptual in its effect than attached to sense impressions. We are happy to learn that Grandfather Smallweed's 'mind is unimpaired. It holds, as well as it ever held, the first rules of arithmetic, and a certain small collection of the hardest facts. In respect of ideality, reverence, wonder, and other such phrenological attributes, it is no worse off than it used to be. Everything that Mr Smallweed's grandfather ever put away in his mind was a grub at first, and is a grub at last. In all his life he has never bred a single butterfly' (342). Let me state emphatically that this passage does *not* offer a precursor to Stein, though we might wonder about Conrad's amusement on reading *Bleak House* again after writing *Lord Jim*.

Dickens does, of course, possess an enormous power of comic visualization, and other pictures of Grandfather Smallweed in the novel surely *do* provide a literary stimulus that helps Conrad transform the brilliant scene in Stevenson's *The Ebb Tide* of the trio's arrival at Attwater's island into

---

[7] For this aspect of Conrad's writing, see Werner Senn, *Conrad's Narrative Voice* (Bern: Francke, 1980). Senn's very detailed study builds upon Edward Said's observation that 'the author himself appears to be participating in the tale as an audience, or more precisely in Conrad's case, as the dramatized *recipient* of impressions' ('Conrad: The Presentation of Narrative,' *Novel* 7 [1973-74], 125). On Conrad's Modernism, see Kenneth Graham in *The Cambridge Companion to Joseph Conrad*, ed. J. H. Stape (Cambridge: Cambridge University Press, 1996), 203-22.

the peculiar and different brilliance of the scene in *Victory* in which his own trio arrives on Heyst's island. The incongruity of the Smallweed party's invasion of Sir Leicester Dedlock's town-house carries with it the visual memory of Grandfather Smallweed as a collapsed marionette after his 'act of jaculation' of throwing the cushion at his wife leaves him 'a broken puppet. The excellent old gentleman being, at these times, a mere clothes-bag with a black skull-cap on top of it, does not present a very animated appearance until he has undergone the two operations at the hands of his granddaughter, of being shaken up like a great bottle, and poked and punched like a great bolster' (343). The alarming comedy of Mr. Jones seen as 'the thin back of a man doubled up over the tiller in a queer, uncomfortable attitude of drooping sorrow' (*V* 237) and the disconcerting violence that accompanies the arrival of the three strange desperadoes is located at the point on the globe furthest removed from the London homes of the Smallweeds and the Dedlocks, but Conrad not only transports Dickens's delight in portraying the deformities men inflict upon themselves and each other to the antipodes, but also uses it as a means of heightening the unease in a scene where the outcome is much more uncertain. In *Bleak House* we have the reassurance of Detective Inspector Bucket's control of the scene in Sir Leicester Dedlock's drawing-room; Conrad, on the other hand, writes a scene exhibiting the incomprehension of all parties concerned deliberately to exploit the conflict between the reader's thirst for comic effect and his presentiment of tragedy. The insistence upon how the whole implausible scene is received by the senses is Conrad's; the zany exuberance of the display is the trace of Conrad's continuing delight in reading Dickens:

> As soon as the first man had recovered the breath knocked out of him by the irresistible charge, a scream of mad cursing issued from the stern-sheets. With a rigid, angular crooking of the elbow, the man at the tiller put his hand back to his hip.
> 'Don't shoot him, sir!' yelled the first man. 'Wait! Let me have that tiller. I will teach him to shovè himself in front of a *caballero!*'
> Martin Ricardo flourished the heavy piece of wood, leaped forward with an astonishing vigour, and brought it down on Pedro's head with a crash that resounded all over the quiet sweep of Black Diamond Bay. A crimson patch appeared on the matted hair; red veins appeared in the water flowing all over his face, and it dripped in rosy drops off his head. But the man hung on. Not till a second furious blow descended did the hairy paws let go their grip and the squirming body sink limply. Before it could touch the bottom-boards, a tremendous kick in the ribs from Ricardo's foot shifted it forward out of sight, whence came the

noise of a heavy thud, a clatter of spars, and a pitiful grunt. Ricardo
stooped to look under the jetty.

'Aha, dog! This will teach you to keep back where you belong,
you murdering brute, you slaughtering savage, you! You infidel, you
robber of churches! Next time I will rip you open from neck to heel, you
carrion-eater! *Esclavo!*'

He backed a little and straightened himself up.

'I don't mean it really,' he remarked to Heyst, whose steady eyes
met his from above. He ran aft briskly.

'Come along, sir. It's your turn. I oughtn't to have drunk first. 'S
truth, I forgot myself! A gentleman like you will overlook that, I know.'
As he made these apologies, Ricardo extended his hand. 'Let me steady
you, sir.'

Slowly Mr. Jones unfolded himself in all his slenderness, rocked,
staggered, and caught Ricardo's shoulder. His henchman assisted him to
the pipe, which went on gushing a clear stream of water, sparkling exceedingly against the black piles and the gloom under the jetty.

(*V* 230-31)

Conrad's highly wrought recollection in 'Poland Revisited' (1915) of
his first visit to London in September 1878 suggests, although it does not
confirm, the importance for him of his reading of Dickens in enabling a
fictional construction of London to arise from the crowding impressions of
his first-hand experience. He was in search of what he calls 'a Dickensian
nook of London, that wonder city, the growth of which bears no sign of
intelligent design, but many traces of freakishly sombre phantasy the Great
Master knew so well how to bring out by the magic of his understanding
love. And the office I entered was Dickensian too ...' (*NLL* 152).

Conrad's own 'freakishly sombre phantasy' of London, though
everywhere informed by Dickens (and, as many critics have claimed, by
Bleak House in particular) is in significant ways distinct from Dickens's
creation and also fashioned from other influences. The more precise
confirmation of the creative presence of *Bleak House* in the writing of *The
Secret Agent* lies in the phantasmagoria of Esther's account of the desperate
pursuit of Lady Dedlock:

I was far from sure that I was not in a dream. We rattled with great
rapidity through such a labyrinth of streets, that I soon lost all idea where
we were; except that we had crossed and re-crossed the river, and still
seemed to be traversing a low-lying, waterside, dense neighbourhood of
narrow thoroughfares, chequered by docks and basins, high piles of
warehouses, swing-bridges, and masts of ships.   (827)

As the narrator is Esther, the reader is offered glimpsed sense-impressions rather than a detailed evocation of the localities so well known to Dickens. This method of rendition is close to Verloc's apprehension of 'the enormity of cold, black, wet, muddy, inhospitable accumulation of bricks, slates, and stones, things in themselves unlovely and unfriendly to man' (*SA* 48), or Comrade Ossipon's 'diminishing in the interminable straight perspectives of shadowy houses bordering empty roadways lined by strings of gas lamps' (*SA* 224). The suggestion for Winnie's 'resolution to go at once and throw herself into the river off one of the bridges' (*SA* 201), and her inability to do so, also finds an origin in Esther's recollections, where it is envisioned much more fully:

> The river had a fearful look, so overcast and secret, creeping away so fast between the low flat lines of shore: so heavy with indistinct and awful shapes, both of substance and shadow: so death-like and mysterious. I have seen it many times since then, by sunlight and by moonlight, but never free from the impression of that journey. In my memory, the lights upon the bridge are always burning dim; the cutting wind is eddying around the homeless woman whom we pass; the monotonous wheels are whirling on; and the light of the carriage-lamps reflected back, looks palely in upon me—a face, rising out of the dreaded water. (828)

With its attention to recollecting and seeing (the 'look' transferred from river to narrator to reflected light), this *tour de force* might almost be Conradian, except that, in keeping with her systematically incurious nature, Conrad does not allow Winnie either such a collected series of impressions or such a self-conscious reflection that arrives, in Esther's typical fashion, in that last delayed clause raising, and not laying to rest, the spectre of her half-conscious identification. However, Conrad's brilliant compression of this 'fearful look' is both more sensational and remarkable in its own way in finally conjuring a more extensive resonance in fewer words: 'She floundered over the doorstep head forward, arms thrown out, like a person falling over the parapet of a bridge. This entrance into the open air had a foretaste of drowning; a slimy dampness enveloped her, entered her nostrils, clung to her hair' (*SA* 202).

This foretaste bears comparison with Esther's haunted aftertaste. Despite the intensity he summons so swiftly, Conrad always maintains the reader at a slight and comic distance from Winnie's sense of things, as when 'perceiving the utter impossibility of walking as far as the nearest bridge, Mrs Verloc thought of a flight abroad' (*SA* 203). Her final sense of herself, which surely achieves a grandeur that exceeds her own consciousness, offers not Esther's psychological reflection but a visionary

apprehension of a dark metropolis that is more inertly grim than any of the
Great Master's sombre fantasies: 'She was alone in London: and the whole
town of marvels and mud, with its maze of streets and its mass of lights,
was sunk in a hopeless night, rested at the bottom of a black abyss from
which no unaided woman could hope to scramble out' (*SA* 203).

The powerfully rendered scene of Esther crossing the Thames surely
remained with Conrad beyond the composition of *The Secret Agent* to
reappear in *Under Western Eyes* as Razumov stares out from the bridge in
Geneva: 'He hung well over the parapet, as if captivated by the smooth
rush of the blue water under the arch. The current there is swift, extremely
swift; it makes some people dizzy ...' (*UWE* 197). Typically, Conrad has
made explicit Esther's implied captivation by the symbolic items of her
vision—the beckoningly dark waters of her mysterious journey, the home-
less woman, her own face emerging from this darkness—and hardened this
suggestiveness into a physical sensation of the 'vertiginous rapidity' and
'terrible force' of the current that yields a picture of Razumov imprisoned
by the forces that have led him to this spot: 'The water under the bridge
ran violent and deep. Its slightly undulating rush seemed capable of
scouring out a channel for itself through solid granite while you looked.
But had it flowed through Razumov's breast, it could not have washed
away the accumulated bitterness the wrecking of his life had deposited
there' (*UWE* 198).

In like manner, the presence of the London of *Bleak House* is not
confined to *The Secret Agent*. When Esther is taken to meet Mrs Jellyby,
the house is found in 'a narrow street of high houses, like an oblong cistern
to hold the fog' (83). At the end of 'Karain' the narrator and Jackson meet
in London: 'The whole length of the street, deep as a well and narrow like
a corridor, was full of a sombre and ceaseless stir' (*TU* 55). Yet again,
however, while Dickens's London is animated by the intersection of the
diverse lives lived there, and, in the end, by the course of their narratives,
Conrad's London in the manner of Modernism is animated by the fragmen-
tary impressions that become almost the lyric expression of the alienated
observer: 'Innumerable eyes stared straight in front, feet moved hurriedly,
blank faces flowed, arms swung. Over all, a narrow ragged strip of smoky
sky wound about between high roofs, extended and motionless, like a
soiled streamer flying above the rout of a mob' (*TU* 55). The 'still uproar'
of this suddenly vivid tableau looks forward to Eliot as much as it looks
back to Dickens.

Whilst in Conrad's work 'London' might almost seem to stand for
a condition (a role it plays in *Little Dorrit*), in *Bleak House* it functions
more realistically as one of the two sites in which Dickens locates one of

his abiding concerns as an artist and one of his greatest gifts to Conrad as his successor—the representation of the interface between private life and the life of public institutions. *The Secret Agent* in particular draws upon Dickens's characters to throw into relief a vision of individuals trapped by the public face required of them by the institutions they serve, and *Nostromo* exhibits how Conrad found some of his political education and the means for its literary expression in *Bleak House*.

Children are used to show the cruel absurdity of how society works. Jo the crossings sweeper, who in his innocence knows nothing except that Captain Hawdon 'wos wery good to me, he wos' (687), can be seen as a formative literary antecedent to the equally innocent Stevie, wanting to know what the police are for, secure in nothing except Winnie's love and in the unshakeable conviction that 'Mr Verloc was obviously yet mysteriously *good*' (*SA* 135). At the other end of the spectrum are those who seem, initially at any rate, empowered by their public personæ. Leading Esther in her search for Lady Dedlock is Detective Inspector Bucket, who can plausibly be seen as the literary forbear to both Chief Inspector Heat and the Assistant Commissioner. Like Heat he is a type of the self-regarding professional, proud of knowing and being known. His bullying and confident 'That's what you are' to all and sundry arises from the same sources as Heat's public statement, 'There isn't one of them, sir, that we couldn't lay our hands on at any time of night and day' (*SA* 69), and his private reflection about the Assistant Commissioner: 'you, my boy, you don't know your place, and your place won't know you very long either, I bet' (*SA* 97). Dickens, however, holds Bucket in much higher esteem than Conrad does Heat. Like the Assistant Commissioner, Bucket is alert, persistent, and successful in tracking the crime to its source, even though he is too late to save Lady Dedlock. Chief Inspector Heat, on the other hand, is concerned with departmental convenience and wishes to shunt the Greenwich bomb affair 'into a quiet (and lawful) siding called Michaelis' (*SA* 96). The criticism of Bucket and the Assistant Commissioner is more oblique and implicit, suggesting a comparable authorial ambivalence towards them. In reporting Bucket's prattle to the Bagnet children—'These blandishments have entirely won the family heart' (728)—the narrator allows the reader to feel that Bucket's cheerful disingenuousness in his arrest of Mr George actually trespasses upon and against the values that the novel endorses; and when Mrs Bagnet, watching Bucket and George going off down the street arm in arm, remarks that Buckekt 'almost clings to George like, and seems to be really fond of him' (733) we can hear a prefiguring of another parody of family relationships—'Might be father and son' (*SA* 142). The Assistant Commissioner certainly performs a public

service in exposing Mr Vladimir, but the gloss on the 'real work' he
undertakes to achieve this aim becomes a little tarnished when we learn
that his private motive for opposing Heat over Michaelis is 'extremely
unbecoming his official position ... The instinct of self preservation' (*SA*
89): a fear that his wife will never forgive him if Michaelis returns to
prison, and that his domestic arrangements will be upset. The entanglement
of public duty with private need is given an ironic reading in both novels.

    This portrayal of the limits of professionalism extends also to Mr
Vholes—sleek, self-satisfied, and self-interested—who finds a later incar-
nation as a miracle whose 'starched collars and got-up shirt-fronts were
achievements of character ... he was devoted to his books which were in
apple-pie order' (*HD* 158). Amid the human desolation of Chancery and
the Grove of Death, two men make a living and keep up proper appearances while doing so. Dickens and Conrad continually exploit and expose
the linguistic dress worn in public life. Jeremy Hawthorn, in calling *The
Secret Agent* an investigation into 'the symbiotic relation between the
domestic and the public,' goes so far as to say that Conrad's investigation
was 'made possible by his great literary predecessor.'[8] While Sir Ethelred
and Toodles clearly derive from the portrayal of the Tite-Barnacles and the
Circumlocution Office, the section devoted to the use made of Mr Vholes's
reputed 'respectability' to impede any changes in the conduct of public life
provides the sort of insight into the procedures of governments and com-
mittees that underlies much of the narrative of *Nostromo*: "'Question. Mr
Vholes is considered, in the profession, a respectable man? Answer"—
which proved fatal to the enquiry (into restrictive practices) for ten years—
"Mr Vholes is considered, in the profession, a *most* respectable man"'
(604).

    The attitude of the implied author here is not far from Martin
Decoud's professed view that 'Of course, government in general, any
government anywhere, is a thing of exquisite comicality to a discerning
mind' (*N* 152). In Chapter 40 of *Bleak House*, 'National and Domestic,' we
learn that 'England has been in a dreadful state for some weeks. Lord
Coodle would go out, Sir Thomas Doodle wouldn't come in, and there
being nobody in Great Britain (to speak of) except Coodle and Doodle,
there has been no Government' (619). The farce of Costaguana is more
macabre, as Decoud would have it, but parliamentary system and revolutionary upheaval are both treated with comparably swift and broad satire.
A little more subtly, the discerning Mrs Gould ironically assures the

---

    [8] *Joseph Conrad: Narrative Technique and Ideological Commitment* (London:
Edward Arnold, 1990), 135.

chairman of the railway that 'nothing ever happened in Sulaco. Even the revolutions, of which there had been two in her time, had respected the repose of the place. Their course ran in the more populous southern parts of the Republic, and in the great valley of Santa Marta, which was like one great battlefield of the parties, with the possession of the capital for a prize and an outlet to another ocean. They were more advanced over there' (*N* 36). The slight thread of mournfulness that runs through the irony here will of course thicken with the deepening of Mrs Gould's apprehension of the failure of material interests to effect the social amelioration she so desires, and the deepening of her feelings of personal isolation. Whether it is Decoud's intelligence, or Mrs Gould's capacity for feeling, that is closer to the heart of the novel's vision is a much debated and disputed point. It has to be said, however, that the note struck by Mrs Gould is alien to *Bleak House*, in which Dickens conducts his satire on the comic-opera lines espoused by Decoud:

> Doodle has found that he must throw himself upon the country—chiefly in the form of sovereigns and beer. In this metamorphosed state he is available in a good many places simultaneously, and can throw himself upon a considerable portion of the country at one time. Britannia being much occupied in pocketing Doodle in the form of sovereigns, and swallowing Doodle in the form of beer, and in swearing herself black in the face that she does neither—plainly to the advancement of her glory and morality—the London season comes to a sudden end, through all the Doodleites and Coodleites dispersing to assist Britannia in those religious exercises. (619-20)

Conrad, of course, did not adopt this sort of bravura set-piece as part of his narrative strategy in *Nostromo*, in which 'national and domestic' are entangled more intricately in the portrayal of the fortunes of all of the major characters. However, his delight in Dickens's depiction of the incongruities of public professions and actions can be read everywhere in his account of national politics, though its ironies are apparently restrained, unlike those of Dickens, by an imperturbable narrative voice. If we take an unremarkable and typical moment in the history of Costaguana, what *is* remarkable is the witty agility contained within this voice: the ear that produces this voice could surely hear the same wit in the more facetious tones of Dickens's satire:

> Less than six months after the President-Dictator's visit, Sulaco learned with stupefaction of the military revolt in the name of national honour. The Minister of War, in a barrack-square allocution to the artillery

regiment he had been inspecting, had declared the national honour sold
to foreigners. The Dictator, by his weak compliance with the demands
of the European powers—for the settlement of long outstanding money
claims—had shown himself unfit to rule.   (*N* 145)

The interweaving here into the neutral narrative language of another discourse that is almost the free indirect speech of national institutions, is a
technique Conrad developed from the more jocular mixing of terms that we
can see in Dickens's use of 'throw himself upon the country,' 'advancement,' 'glory and morality,' 'religious exercises.' Conrad's 'in the name of
the national honour,' 'sold to foreigners,' 'weak compliance,' and 'unfit to
rule' are given their unstable comic edge through the contrasts supplied by
'stupefaction,' 'allocution,' and the parenthesis about outstanding debts in
a more subdued and subtle manner than Dickens, but one that can be maintained for lengthy stretches of narration in a way that the satire of *Bleak
House* cannot.

This destabilizing effect is at work in *Nostromo* and *The Secret Agent*
wherever any sort of public declaration is concerned. The portrayal of Don
José Avellanos, for instance, is sympathetic, but from the outset the reader
is made aware that honourable intentions are evacuated of their substance
by the hollow language of their profession: 'The second Sulaco regiment,
to whom he was presenting this flag, was going to show its valour in a
contest for order, peace, progress; for the establishment of a national self-
respect without which—he declared with energy—"we are a reproach and
a byword amongst the powers of the world"' (*N* 137).

It is easy to show that in practice—or in print, at least—Dickens
professed a faith close to that which Conrad parodies. In 'The Poetry of
Fact,' published in *All The Year Round* for 14 September 1867, Dickens
celebrates the fact that what

> were, and are, really products of the poetic imagination, have been in the
> present, and will be in the future, actualised by the ingenuity of science,
> or the progress of society ... the proper sympathy between classes will be
> promoted, by their better acquaintance with each other; and the mists of
> ignorance being dispelled from the popular mind, the human objects of
> admiration will be seen in their natural proportions ...

This reads like something from Comrade Ossipon's 'good sized rosy sheet,
as if flushed by the warmth of its own convictions, which were optimistic'
(*SA* 58-59). In *Bleak House*, however, the clichés of political oratory are
the targets of Dickens's amusement (as if he were innocent of manufac-
turing them himself), as when Mr Rouncewell's questioning of the feudal

mentality leads, by 'the swift progress of the Dedlock mind,' to 'the obliteration of landmarks, and opening of floodgates, and cracking of the framework of society' (456). Conrad's amusement at such imbecile mouth-ings is hardened by a scorn greater than that of Dickens for the press, which was, after all, Dickens's primary means of earning a living, but which Conrad saw as the disseminator of a language that creates facile popular notions and destroys apprehension and thought. In this respect *Nostromo* develops a critique of public institutions beyond the scope of that offered in *Bleak House*:

> Even a Monterist press had come into existence, speaking oracularly of the secret promises of support given by 'our great sister Republic of the North' against the sinister land grabbing designs of European powers, cursing in every issue the 'miserable Ribiera,' who had plotted to deliver his country, bound hand and foot, for a prey to foreign speculators.
> (*N* 145-46)

The play back and forth between speech that is directly attributed and phrases that have indirectly found their way into the narrative brilliantly enacts the slippage of language into a compromised conceptual currency. Whilst the equivalent satire in *Bleak House* remains a flourish upon the portrayal of the doomed Dedlocks, in *Nostromo* the examination of lan-guage is ceaseless and central, yet the incipient comic extravagance ('sinister,' 'bound hand and foot') reads like ebullient Dickensian licence just kept on the leash.

Bleak House extends its exposure of the fraudulence of public professions to include the crew of self-promoting philanthropists that comprise the Chadbands and their followers, and Mrs Jellyby and Mrs Pardiggle, of whom, perhaps, Marlow offers us chauvinistically a late excrescence in Mrs Fyne, writing her 'sort of handbook for women with grievances' (*C* 65), and who had an 'aspect breathing a readiness to assume any responsibility under Heaven' (*C* 137). The Dickensian shaping spirit in *Chance* is, of course, *Little Dorrit*; *Bleak House* is present more explicitly in *The Secret Agent*: just as Mrs Pardiggle 'seemed to come in like cold weather, and to make the little Pardiggles blue as they followed' (151), so Mr Verloc 'generally arrived in London (like the influenza) from the Continent, only he arrived unheralded by the Press; and his visitations set in with great severity' (*SA* 11). Like many other novelists, but in a shared manner of extreme stylization as these examples show, Conrad and Dickens explore how the construction of a public persona destroys personal relationships; and in the pursuit of this theme Conrad's 'verbal vision' (the way in which he apprehends his fictional world through a language known to be already inhabited by other writing) is permeated by *Bleak House* in particular.

So far, the discussion has been shaped by a consideration of linguistic affinities arising from aspects of temperament and outlook that Conrad found congenial in Dickens. In conclusion, the issue of form requires some comment. What must, above all, strike a reader of *Bleak House* is the manner in which Dickens starts his story from so many different points on the social spectrum, and impels his subjects to a meeting point in which they are all comprehended—the mystery of Esther's relationship to her mother. Whilst the fortunes of the Jarndyces and the Dedlocks take precedence as parallel main plots, the Jellybys, the Smallweeds, Miss Flite and Krook, Jo and Alan Woodcourt, George and the Bagnets, Tulkinghorn (in no particular order and to name but a few) start so many sub-plots, and draw in so many other characters, that the form of the novel alone provides a social and moral commentary. Dickens's web of interconnecting sub-plots provided Conrad with a formal example of how to achieve the panoramic quality he sought in *Nostromo*. The separate yet contingent stories of the Violas, Nostromo, the Goulds, the Avellanoses and Martin Decoud, Dr Monygham, and Captain Mitchell all command the point of view or colour the narrative at points in the novel, acting almost as competing plots, and thus enacting in their collisions and elisions the novel's analysis of politics and the composition of History.

Whilst *Victory* provides the most obvious example of a Dickensian management of a main plot in which the characters are handled with comparative naturalism (Heyst and Lena) while being assailed, as it were, by a sub-plot inhabited by grotesques (the trio of desperadoes), *The Secret Agent* shows Conrad's very deliberate use of competing sub-plots as a tool for social analysis in the manner of *Bleak House*. Whilst from the outset the reader has the sense that the central focalizing agent is Verloc, we are also entertained by the question of whose plot is he caught up in? Which of the sub-plots in fact drives the action? Is it that of the Professor in his scorn for the other anarchists? Heat and the Assistant Commisioner? the Assistant Commissioner and Vladimir? the Assistant Commissioner and the Lady Patroness? Vladimir and Sir Ethelred? Mrs Verloc's mother and Winnie? Winnie and Ossipon? None of these suggestions is more fantastic than any other; but Conrad uses the Dickensian device of interconnecting sub-plots not to show the human connections hidden by social hierarchy, but to show precisely the opposite, the almost total insulation of all these lives despite the interconnections of their worlds.

The most extreme examples of this vision of life, and the most striking single imaginative contribution of *Bleak House* to the form of Conrad's
works, derive from Dickens's grotesque conception of the spontaneous
combustion of Krook. Of course, Conrad did not need Dickens's fictional
episode in order to conceive of the blowing up of Stevie: newspapers
carried the story of Bourdin's attempt on the Greenwich Observatory, one
under the sensational heading 'Blown To Pieces!' However, by placing the
mysterious and inexplicable death of Krook right at the centre of his novel,
Dickens provided Conrad with a provocative example of a novel with a
centre of darkness, if not exactly to emulate, at least to harbour as an
imaginative strategy that perhaps issued in a metamorphosed form in the
vividly imagined night episode in the Golfo Placido and, more definitely,
in the later scene where Nostromo sees but does not comprehend the
hanging body of Hirsch and confides to Monygham, in a clear echo of
Dickens's narrator (see below), 'I was running away from his shadow when
we met' (*N* 425). In *The Secret Agent* Dickens's great invention leads
initially to Greenwich Park but finds its true home in Brett Street. Krook's
death is like a black hole at the centre of *Bleak House*, swallowing up
reason and intelligibility in symbolic implosion, a metaphor that Conrad
almost literalizes, first in reverse, in Ossipon's imagination of the exploded
Silenus as 'a dreadful black hole belching horrible fumes choked with
ghastly rubbish of smashed brickwork and mutilated corpses' (*SA* 56), and,
second, directly, in Winnie's eyes which 'seemed like two black holes' (*SA*
159). The stretched-out time sequence between the first imagination of the
blast and the eventual registration of its meaning in the only organ that can
feel it, Winnie's 'moral nature,' is Conrad's bold manipulation of what had
been suggested by Dickens's brilliantly extended sequence of delay in
Chapter 32, 'The Appointed Time.'

From the facetiously grandiloquent opening—'It is night in Lincoln's
Inn—perplexed and troublous valley of the shadow of the law, whose
suitors generally find but little day—' (498) to the resounding conclusion
addressed to 'Your Highness,' '—Spontaneous Combustion, and none other
of all the deaths that can be died' (512), the journey that Dickens takes the
reader involves so many tones derived from comic observation and the
manipulations of irony, suspense, and horror that it can be said to suffuse
its own melodramatic quality with the 'atmospheric symbolism,' 'evocative
metaphor,' and 'atmospheric density' that Donald C. Yelton perceives as
the most salient common feature of the art of Conrad and Dickens.[9] Mr

---

[9] *Mimesis and Metaphor*, 87.

Weevle (Tony Jobling) first remarks upon 'a queer kind of flavour in the place tonight. I suppose it's chops at the Sol's Arms' (500). Mr Snagsby having sniffed and tasted this suggestion replies, 'I don't think—not to put too fine a point on it—that they were quite fresh, when they were shown the gridiron' (500). This leisurely, partly deceptive, partly revelatory approach to the truth is compounded later by Mr Guppy's more tactile encounter when 'he happens to look at his coat-sleeve. It takes his attention. He stares at it, aghast ... "See here, on my arm! See again, on the table here! Confound the stuff, it won't blow off—smears, like black fat!"' (505). Four pages later he draws back his hand from the windowsill, staring in horror at his fingers: 'A thick, yellow liquor defiles them, which is offensive to the touch and sight and more offensive to the smell. A stagnant, sickening oil, with some repulsion in it that makes them both shudder' (509).

Dickens paces these gradations towards the 'crumbled black thing ... upon the floor ... seeming to be steeped in something' (511) with the eleven o'clock and twelve o'clock striking of the bell of St Paul's that brings no news of redemption:

> 'Listen (says Tony) and you'll hear all the bells in the city jangling.'
> Both sit silent, listening to the metal voices, near and distant, resounding from towers of various heights, in tones more various than their situations.   (507)

The various voices and tones are, of course, gathered into that of an authorial voice pronouncing a single doom: 'The Lord Chancellor of that Court, true to his title in his last act, has died the death of all Lord Chancellors in all Courts, and of all authorities in all places under all names soever, where false pretences are made, and where injustice is done' (511).

Whilst Conrad resists the plangency of this moralizing conclusion, he does not recoil from either the macabre or melodramatic tendencies of Dickens's great chapter. The suggestion of human flesh as tainted meat, passed idly between two rather innocuous men who have become more involved than either of them wished, persists comically yet more unpleasantly in Heat's 'slightly anxious attention of an indigent customer bending over what may be called the by-products of a butcher's shop with a view to an inexpensive Sunday dinner' (*SA* 71). However, as Conrad locates the narration of events in the consciousness of 'Chief Inspector Heat, an efficient officer of his department' (*SA* 70), he achieves ironies that are different from what is primarily a simple dramatic irony enacted between

Weevle and Snagsby. Heat contemplates 'a heap of rags, scorched and blood stained, half concealing what might have been an accumulation of raw material for a cannibal feast' (*SA* 70). In as much as he is an efficient officer of his department who understands and plays by the rules of 'the game,' Heat fails to understand the resonance of the image attributed to him here. It is, perhaps, more far-reaching than the trumpet of Dickens's rhetoric that envisages retribution for wrong-doing, as Stevie is a victim of *all* the processes inherent in the conduct of public and private life as depicted in the novel, right or wrong. When Mr Verloc partakes 'ravenously, without restraint and decency,' of 'The piece of roast beef, laid out in the likeness of funereal baked meats for Stevie's obsequies' (*SA* 190), the irony offers a disturbance that Dickens's more emotive satire actually tries to lay to rest in a vision of a Last Judgement.

What preoccupies Heat with a far more acute intensity than the professionally hardened humour of his jest is the feeling upon which Conrad structures more than sixty pages of his novel: 'he evolved a horrible notion that ages of atrocious pain and mental torture could be contained between two successive winks of an eye' (*SA* 71). Conrad extends Dickens's Faustian attention to time as recorded by the bells of St Paul's to his whole management of the *durée* of Winnie's response to Heat's arrival in the shop with the triangular name tag. To recall Dickens's chapter, with its intense but conventionally achieved sense of suspense, is to see vividly the audaciousness of Conrad's art in his application of this suffocating atmosphere to the one-sided exchanges in Brett Street under the eye of the apparently stopped and unticking clock. Whilst the chapter in *Bleak House* slowly gathers momentum towards an identifiable climax—which is the discovery of an absence, a nothing 'from which we run away' (511)—Chapter XI of *The Secret Agent* is almost unbearably uncomfortable to read, conducted as it is at a constant level of climax and of stoppage. The grotesque invention of Dickens—the spontaneous combustion of Krook—is replaced by the grotesque imagination of Conrad in portraying Winnie's mind receiving the impression of Stevie's combustion 'pictorially.' There is, then, not an absent centre to the chapter, but, rather, an inconceivable one, that can only be conveyed, perhaps, to a reader who knows he is being anæsthetized by the humorous distancing tone of the narrative voice. This is the calculated risk that irony takes. The humour seems almost callous, but the shockingly comic detachment of the words renders the distance between our comfort as readers and the fictional agony that we are reading about:

> A park—smashed branches, torn leaves, gravel, bits of brotherly flesh
> and bone, all spouting up together in the manner of a firework. ... Mrs
> Verloc closed her eyes desperately, throwing upon that vision the night
> of her eyelids, where after a rainlike fall of mangled limbs the decapi-
> tated head of Stevie lingered suspended alone, and fading out slowly like
> the last star of a pyrotechnic display.   (*SA* 195-96)

The Conradian grotesque exceeds the Dickensian grotesque here
because, finally, Dickens's relationship with his readership is very much
more confident and direct. We can be asked to participate almost as a
pantomime audience in the dramatic steps that lead Guppy and Tony to
Krook's remains, and we can be summoned as both orator and addressee
simultaneously in the chapter's resounding finale. Conrad never feels that
sort of intimacy with the audience to be able to step forward as a conductor
in the Dickens manner; so he is not as spectacular as the predecessor of
whom he is always conscious, but his artistic risks are sometimes, as here,
necessarily more extreme. This is typical of what we have seen throughout
this investigation: that Dickens is the great inventor for Conrad —to the
point, even, in inventing for literature so much of the genius and idiom of
the English language that adopted Conrad, that he plays a major role in
inventing Conrad as an author. Dickens licenses and authorizes Conrad's
negotiation of the limits of literary English. Conrad absorbs Dickens's
inventive power and subjects it sometimes to sensational fancy and
sometimes to a severer discipline, often turning comfort to discomfort in
his attempts to touch his readers in a comparable but different manner. He
rarely borrows directly; like that of a child, it is a deeper yet more troubled
affinity than a set of borrowed mannerisms that characterizes this least
professional and most personal of Conrad's literary relationships.

The Sources of Conrad's *Suspense*

Hans van Marle and Gene M. Moore
Amsterdam

When a literary work lapses into obscurity and neglect, the various contexts which lent it meaning also fade from view. Although it may prove to be greater than the sum of its parts, every literary text serves as an interface between the various pre-textual sources that went into its composition and the post-textual discussion it generates in reviews and critical commentaries. By its focus on 'texts,' academic criticism in recent years has made it difficult for scholars to appreciate the importance of non-textual sources and influences. Conrad's 'borrowings' have usually been understood textually and literally, but his work also incorporates other sources that are not necessarily verbal. For example, *Suspense* 'borrows' the entire city of Genoa as it was in early 1815 for use in a variety of contexts that are not merely topographical, but also political and social. The novel opens with a panoramic view of the harbour, and a number of streets and architectural features are described in the course of the novel, although Conrad's known textual sources had little to say about the townscape itself (and critics of the novel have disagreed about the real-world referents of specific locations, like Cosmo's hotel). The vivid memory of recent historical events shared by all the characters, and especially the atmosphere of 'suspense' generated by Napoleon's precarious presence on Elba, provides a corresponding 'mental geography' borrowed from history, which is ready-made to find expression in conversations that need not be borrowed from earlier texts. In ways that have as much to do with personal experience as they do with specific texts, the origins of *Suspense* (and *The Rover*) can be traced not only to Conrad's penchant for Napoleonic memoirs, but also to his youthful admiration for the novels of Captain Marryat and to his own personal memories of the turbulent years he spent along the Mediterranean coast in the 1870s. These influences can help us to account for Conrad's choice of the Mediterranean coast in the days of Napoleon as the place and time in which to dwell in imagination during the last years of his creative life. The people Conrad met and the conversations in which he took part during those years may also have provided him with sources for the names of the fictional characters with which he peopled *Suspense*.

Madame de Villeparisis and the Countess de Montevesso

The primary textual source for *Suspense* has long been recognized as the *Memoirs* of Adèle d'Osmond, Comtesse de Boigne (1781-1866), whose *Récits d'une tante* provide a vivid and detailed record of more than half a century of French aristocratic life from the reign of Louis XVI to 1848. Ostensibly written for her grand-nephew, these memoirs were first published in Paris in 1907, more than forty years after her death.[1]

They were reviewed for *Le Figaro* by Marcel Proust, who is generally thought to have used the Comtesse de Boigne as a model for the character of Madame de Villeparisis, the intellectual 'aunt' of both Robert de Saint-Loup and the Baron de Charlus in *A la recherche du temps perdu*.[2] Relatively few scholars are aware of the fact that at roughly the same time, a younger Adèle d'Osmond was also serving Conrad as the model for the unhappy heroine of *Suspense*, Adèle d'Armand.[3] While the propriety of Proust's social or historical 'borrowings' has not been challenged (and scholars like Hannah Arendt have even cited Proust's novel as a source of historical information on the Dreyfus Affair), Conrad's 'borrowings' from the Comtesse de Boigne have generally been regarded not as an exercise in intertextuality worthy of closer scrutiny, but as a deplorable form of laziness symptomatic of the exhaustion of an aging writer at the end of his creative tether.

Conrad made no secret of his interest in the Boigne *Memoirs*. Had he lived to see *Suspense* published, he might well have acknowledged his debt

---

[1] *Récits d'une tante: Mémoires de la Comtesse de Boigne, née d'Osmond*, ed. Charles Nicoullaud (Paris: Plon, 1907), 4 vols. An English translation of Nicoullaud's edition, entitled *Memoirs of the Comtesse de Boigne*, was published in two volumes later the same year by Heinemann in London and by Scribner's in New York. The printed catalogue of the holdings of the London Library (1912), of which Conrad was a member, lists copies of both the French original and its English translation. References in the text are to the Heinemann edition.

[2] 'Journées de lecture,' originally published in *Le Figaro* for 20 March 1907, rpt. in *Contre Sainte-Beuve, précédé de Pastiches et mélanges et suivi de Essais et articles*, ed. Pierre Clarac and Yves Sandre (Paris: Bibliothèque de la Pléiade, 1971), 527-33. By a curious coincidence, Conrad, who had been living with his family in Montpellier since December, was in Paris the following day to put Miss Wright (his wife's cousin, who had been helping them as a nurse and typist) and a servant on a train back to England; see his letter to Pinker of 13 March 1907 (*CL3*, 419-22).

[3] The role of the Comtesse and her husband in *Suspense* is not mentioned in Desmond Young's biography of General de Boigne, *The Fountain of the Elephants* (London: Collins, 1959), nor by Jean-Claude Berchet, the editor of the most recent reprint of the *Mémoires* (Paris: Mercure de France, 1971).

in an 'Author's Note' as he had done in the cases of *Nostromo* and *The Secret Agent*. In any event, there is little doubt that he found the situation of the Comtesse and her father in Genoa at the moment of Napoleon's return from Elba useful as a historical pivot for the 'Mediterranean novel' that had preoccupied him for almost twenty years before he finally began to write it in June 1920.

Borrowing and Creative Bankruptcy

At least two of Conrad's friends were aware of the importance of the *Memoirs* as a source for *Suspense*. On 10 October 1925, less than a month after the novel was published, Edward Garnett responded to an unfavourable review by P. C. Kennedy in *The New Statesman* with a defence of Conrad published in the *The Weekly Westminster*.[4] Garnett, who had been among the very first 'discoverers' of Conrad and was by this time the dean of publisher's readers in England, declared *Suspense* the 'most mature' of all Conrad's works, 'almost faultless' in its construction, 'a pure work of art': '*Suspense* is a masterpiece, richly mellow in its philosophy of life, with scenes flowing naturally out of one another, a natural drama, stirring, actual and complex.' Garnett found only one flaw: 'There is one chapter he would probably have rewritten, as it follows too closely the Memoirs of a French lady ...' He may have been thinking of Chapter II, which paraphrases the situation of the Comtesse and her parents who, as refugees from the French Revolution, found shelter in England as the guests of Sir John Legard; but the influence of the *Memoirs* cannot be confined to a single chapter of *Suspense*. Garnett's defence of the novel was challenged by Gerald Gould in the London *Saturday Review* in an article entitled 'The Danger of Idols.' In a prompt reply to Gould, Garnett recalled that Conrad had asked him to read the first three chapters of the novel in typescript.[5] 'I criticized Chapter I severely,' Garnett wrote, and 'Conrad endeavoured to meet my criticisms.' The surviving letters from Garnett to Conrad in 1921 support Garnett's recollection: he told Conrad that 'Chapter I is

---

[4] Kennedy reviewed *Suspense* together with H. G. Wells's novel *Christina Alberta's Father* in the rubric 'Current Literature' in *The New Statesman*, 26 September 1925, 665-66. Garnett replied in 'The World of Books,' *The Weekly Westminster*, 10 October 1925, 614. Garnett's rejoinder was soon reprinted in *Sphere* 103 (31 October 1925), 157. Both reviews are included in Norman Sherry, ed., *Conrad: The Critical Heritage* (London and Boston: Routledge & Kegan Paul, 1973), 369-71.

[5] Gould, in 'The Danger of Idols,' *Saturday Review* (London) 140, no. 3652 (24 October 1925), 471-72. Garnett's reply was printed a week later, under the same title, in no. 3653 (31 October 1925), 505.

undoubtedly weak as it stands,' but he made only minor comments to Conrad about Chapters II and III.[6] Although Garnett was the first to suggest that Conrad had followed the *Memoirs* 'too closely,' he had made no mention of the Comtesse de Boigne in 1921. The solution he proposed in 1925, the rewriting of a single chapter, signals a lack of close familiarity either with the novel beyond the first few chapters, or (more likely) with the *Memoirs* themselves.

Garnett may have first learned of the Boigne borrowings in October 1925 from a scholarly essay by G. Jean-Aubry entitled 'The Inner History of Conrad's *SUSPENSE*.' Citing documents and letters, Jean-Aubry traced the history of the development of the novel since 1907. He was also the first critic to apply the term 'borrowing' to Conrad's intertextual appropriations:

> Even if I had not myself had the assurance of these facts in the course of several conversations with Joseph Conrad himself, it would be easy to determine by the precision ⁿf the details for whom these two personages [Adèle and her father] as well as the Count of Montevesso stand. The novelist obviously borrowed them from the *Mémoires de la Comtesse de Boigne* ...[7]

Unlike Garnett, Jean-Aubry had not the slightest doubt that Conrad's use of the *Memoirs* was thoroughly legitimate, and he registered his surprise at discovering how much Conrad had elaborated on the details she mentioned, as in the case of Doctor Martel:

> This character of a mysterious courier in touch with the principal personages of the period, and of whom we only get a glimpse in Madame de Boigne's Memoirs, had particularly struck Conrad. I remember one evening when he spoke to me about it at great length, and I was surprised to find afterwards how little Madame de Boigne says about it.   (7-8)

---

[6] Letter to Conrad of 31 August 1921, *A Portrait in Letters: Correspondence to and about Conrad*, ed. J. H. Stape and Owen Knowles (Amsterdam and Atlanta, GA: Rodopi, 1996), 183. Garnett faulted Conrad for using language too modern for 1815, as can be seen from two comments pencilled in the margins of Chapter III, and still just barely visible under deletion on the typescript now held at the Berg Collection, New York Public Library.

[7] 'The Inner History of Conrad's *SUSPENSE*: Notes & Extracts from Letters,' *The Bookman's Journal* 13:49 (October 1925), 7.

Jean-Aubry advised Conrad about books on Napoleonic history, and even prepared in advance a set of twenty-one application slips for Conrad to use when he visited the British Museum on 7 June 1920 for a day of research in the library. As it happened, Conrad submitted only three slips, all for books concerning Napoleon's stay on Elba: Marcellin Pellet, *Napoléon à l'île d'Elbe* (Paris: Charpentier, 1888); André de Pons (de l'Hérault), *Souvenirs et anecdotes de l'île d'Elbe* (Paris: Plon, Nourrit, 1897); and Neil Campbell, *Napoleon at Fontainebleau and Elba ...* (London: Murray, 1896). Conrad also borrowed several Napoleonic books from the Ajaccio library during his visit to Corsica in 1921. Jean-Aubry was thus fully aware that the Comtesse de Boigne was by no means the only source of Conrad's inspiration.[8]

In January 1926, Conrad's 'borrowings' from the Comtesse de Boigne were again signalled by Léonie Villard, who was apparently unaware of the recent publications of Garnett and Jean-Aubry. She sketched the life of the Comtesse in an article which appeared first in London and then in Boston, and she discussed Conrad's use of the *Memoirs* at greater length in an article published in April in the *Revue Anglo-Américaine.*[9] In February of the same year, equally unaware of her predecessors, Mildred Atkinson called attention to these 'borrowings' in a letter to the *The Times Literary Supplement* that was reprinted in *The Saturday Review of Literature.*[10] Both Villard and Atkinson saw the connection with the *Memoirs* as an interesting example of intertextuality (though the term had still to be

---

[8] Conrad's notebook and the application slips are now in the collection of the Beinecke Rare Book and Manuscript Library, Yale University. The notes Conrad took were transcribed and annotated by Jean-Aubry in his *Bookman* article; in his 'Nachwort' to the German translation of *Suspense* (as *Spannung*, Berlin: S. Fischer, 1936), 319-21; and in the 'Appendice' to his own French translation as *Angoisse* (Paris: Gallimard, 1956), 348-53.

[9] Léonie Villard, 'A Conrad Heroine in Real Life: Countess de Boigne the Original of "Suspense,"' *T.P.'s & Cassell's Weekly* (London), vol. 5, no. 118 n.s. (23 January 1926), 476; reprinted as 'A Conrad Heroine in Real Life' in *The Living Age* (Boston), vol. 328, no. 4263 (20 March 1926), 637-39; followed by 'Joseph Conrad et les mémorialistes (A propos de SUSPENSE),' *Revue Anglo-Américaine* (Paris) 3:4 (April 1926), 313-21.

[10] Mildred Atkinson, 'Conrad's "Suspense"' ('Correspondence'), *The Times Literary Supplement* 25:1258 (25 February 1926), 142; rpt. in *The Saturday Review of Literature*, 27 March 1926, 666. Wilfred Partington, the editor of *The Bookman's Journal*, responded to Atkinson's letter with a note reminding readers that the 'discovery' of the Boigne connection had already been announced by Jean-Aubry in his own journal (*TLS* 25:1259 [4 March 1926], 163) .

coined) and as a demonstration of Conrad's masterful use of historical material. The same 'discovery' was made once again, independently but somewhat belatedly, by Miriam Hatheway Wood in 1935.[11] 'What incentive for research!' wrote Wood (391); but the past sixty years have produced no detailed research into Conrad's use of historical sources in *Suspense*.

Jean-Aubry was not only the first to record Conrad's debt to the Comtesse de Boigne, but he also enjoys the distinction of being the first scholar to have noticed that Conrad's textual borrowings from the Comtesse de Boigne were apparently taken not from the original 1907 French text of the *Memoirs*, but from the English translation published that same year in New York and London.[12] In occupied Paris during the Second World War, Jean-Aubry set about translating *Suspense* into French. One can easily imagine how his need to *re*-translate passages taken directly from the Comtesse de Boigne back into French would have led him to consult both the French and English editions of her *Memoirs*. He would have found that in many instances Conrad followed the exact wording of the 1907 English translation, which often renders the Comtesse's French in ways that are not immediately obvious (see the Appendix to this essay).

Although it has been included in all the collected editions of Conrad's works published since 1925, *Suspense* has long been neglected by critics as an unfinished and unduly derivative work. No one put this position more strongly than Thomas C. Moser in *Joseph Conrad: Achievement and Decline* (Cambridge, MA: Harvard University Press, 1957), an influential study that established Conrad's canon for a generation or more. Moser considered both the early and the late works as vastly inferior to the great literary monuments of the middle period. He condemned *Suspense* with unprecedented severity in the final chapter of his book, entitled 'The Exhaustion of Creative Energy.' Moser's dismissive judgement was tantamount to an obituary notice relegating *Suspense* to critical oblivion for more than thirty years. He questioned Conrad's ability to write historical fiction at all, and argued paradoxically that 'The *Memoirs*, in fact, supply practically all that is new in *Suspense*.' He concluded that Conrad at this

---

[11] 'A Source of Conrad's *Suspense*,' *Modern Language Notes* 50:6 (June 1935), 390-94.

[12] This discovery was recorded in Jean-Aubry's Appendix to *Angoisse*: 'ce n'est pas dans l'édition française que l'écrivain en prit connaissance, mais dans la traduction anglaise' (p. 339). In the 1936 'Nachwort' (n. 8 above) Jean-Aubry still referred his readers to the original French edition of the *Memoirs*.

final period in his career was using history in general, and the *Memoirs* in articular, 'as a crutch for exhausted creativity' (203).

The Historical Background of Suspense

Moser claimed that the novel 'gives us little sense of the past'; yet much of the difficulty of appreciating *Suspense* lies precisely in the nature of the demands it makes on the historical imagination of the reader, who needs ideally to possess a detailed familiarity not only with the Congress of Vienna and the events leading up to the Hundred Days, but also a knowledge of Italian politics in the time of Napoleon, whose conquests in the north supplied the forerunners of irredentism with a perspective of liberation from Habsburg and Bourbon domination. A comparison of Conrad's fiction with the (relatively) factual accounts recorded by the Comtesse de Boigne and other witnesses of these momentous events provides a unique opportunity to understand how Conrad put these historical materials to fictional use, and reveals that Conrad's creative energy was by no means exhausted towards the end of his career.

The 'borrowings' from the Comtesse de Boigne are essential in establishing the basic structure of *Suspense*, but Conrad often changed dates and locations as necessary for his own dramatic purposes, and many scenes and sub-plots in the novel are entirely independent of her account. The scenes set in the Palazzo Rosso and in Cantelucci's inn make use of a number of characters and situations mentioned in the *Memoirs*, but the opening and closing scenes in the harbour and at sea with Attilio have nothing to do with them. Adèle's family situation and background are modelled on those of the historical Comtesse, but the protagonist Cosmo Latham, his sister Henrietta, and many other characters, including Attilio, Cantelucci, Spire, Clelia, and Father Carpi, are Conrad's own creations. Conrad's Doctor Martel is based on a Dr Marshall described in the *Memoirs*, but his abrupt visit to inform Adèle's father of Napoleon's preparations to leave Elba actually occurred not in Genoa in late February 1815, but in Turin the previous month (II, 27).

A brief survey of the life of the Comtesse de Boigne can help us to identify those points at which Conrad alters or departs from his main source. Her father, René-Eustache d'Osmond (1751-1838), was a French officer and diplomat whose inherited wealth came from estates in Santo Domingo in the Caribbean. In 1778 he married Éléonore Dillon (1753-1831) from a wealthy Irish family, and their only child, Charlotte-Éléonore-Louise-Adélaïde, was born in Versailles on 20 February 1781. After ten years of service as an infantry officer, Adèle's father entered the diplomatic service and was named minister to The Hague in 1789. Adèle's mother served as lady-in-waiting to Madame Adélaïde, one of Louis XV's spinster daughters. Adèle's father was named ambassador to Saint Petersburg in 1790, but the revolution intervened and the family sought refuge in England. They stayed first in Brighton, in the vicinity of the Prince of Wales (the future George IV) and the Irish widow Maria Fitzherbert, whom he had secretly married in 1785, and who was a cousin of Adèle's mother. (The marriage was not considered valid, and the Prince married Caroline of Brunswick in 1795.) During a brief return to Versailles, young Adèle remembered weeping at the sight of Queen Marie-Antoinette, who was by that time a virtual prisoner under guard in her own palace. The Osmond family spent ten months in Italy in 1792, at the court of the Queen of Naples, a sister of Marie-Antoinette. In Rome they met Sir John Legard and his wife, Molly Aston, who was likewise a cousin-german of Adèle's mother. Sir John Legard offered them the hospitality of his country seat in Yorkshire, and thus provided Conrad with the figure of Sir Charles Latham, Cosmo's father, although the historical Sir John Legard was childless.[13]

The duties of Adèle's father required the family to leave the countryside to settle in the London suburb of Brompton. At the age of sixteen, Adèle accepted a marriage proposal from the much older General de Boigne in order to guarantee the financial security of her parents. Like Adèle's husband in *Suspense*, the Count de Montevesso, the real General de Boigne was an 'upstart' who had grown wealthy in the service of various princes in India. Unlike Conrad's character, the original Benoît Le Borgne de Boigne (1751-1830) came from Chambéry, in the Alps of Savoy, and not from Piedmont on the eastern side of the Alps.

By the time Napoleon's army had been decimated by the Russian campaign of 1812, Adèle was living separately from her husband, who had retired to his property near Chambéry. Her father, the Marquis d'Osmond, had declined an ambassadorship to Vienna offered by Louis XVIII, the returned Bourbon King of France, but he accepted the ambassadorship to the Kingdom of Sardinia, and he and Adèle moved to Turin.

In December 1814 the Congress of Vienna, redrawing the map of post-Napoleonic Europe, decided to award Liguria and the Republic of Genoa to the King of Sardinia, Victor-Emmanuel I. The King had already

---

[13] Villard hinted that Cosmo's strange vision of a woman with a dagger in her breast may owe something to Adèle d'Osmond's participation in the famous *tableaux vivants* staged by Lady Hamilton in Naples, which were painted by George Romney.

arrived in Turin on 20 May 1814, but the Queen remained behind in Sardinia until February 1815. The court travelled from Turin to Genoa to welcome her, and the diplomatic corps followed in its wake. Thus it was that Adèle and her father arrived in Genoa on 26 February 1815, only two days before Napoleon set sail from Elba for the south coast of France. The action of *Suspense* takes place during three days immediately prior to Napoleon's return, but Adèle, her husband, and her father show no sign of having just arrived in Genoa. Even before he left England to begin his journey, Cosmo was told by his father that he would find the Marquis 'either in Turin or Genoa.'[14] Adèle tells Cosmo that they are in Genoa to await the arrival of the Queen of Sardinia, 'who may or may not come within the next month or so' (90). The elderly relative of the Count who lives on an upstairs floor arrived in the Palazzo Rosso 'just five weeks ago' (158).

When scrutinized closely, the major chronological details also bear witness to Conrad's unfettered imagination. Adèle d'Armand was twenty-six in early 1815 and had been married 'nearly ten years' (91), which dates her birth in 1788 and her marriage in 1805, whereas her real-world counterpart Adèle d'Osmond was born in 1781 and became Madame de Boigne in 1798. Conrad had a fairly precise chronology in mind while composing *Suspense*, as can be shown by examining his revisions to the typescripts, which often serve to correct implications that could call into question the dates of the major events in Adèle's life. One such example involves the Peace of Amiens (24), which came to replace a reference to the Battle of Austerlitz in earlier typescripts: the peace was concluded in 1802, and the battle was fought in the next Napoleonic war in 1805. Not all of the ambiguities or chronological inconsistencies had been clarified in the text that remained when Conrad died. He would perhaps have realized that the Duke of Wellington (17) did not receive his dukedom until after the Peninsular campaign, and that the Comte de Boigne received his title only in 1816, while Montevesso is already a count by 1805 (32).

Such temporal indications can also be used to challenge certain long-standing critical assumptions about *Suspense*. Critics from Ford to Moser have found suggestions in the text to the effect that Sir Charles Latham was actually Adèle's biological father, thereby making her Cosmo's half-sister. The received text states explicitly that the Marquis and Marquise d'Armand were the best friends Sir Charles had made in France in 'those

---

[14] Joseph Conrad, *Suspense: A Napoleonic Novel* (London: Dent's Collected Edition, 1954), 40. Page references in the text are to this edition.

last days before the Revolution' and that he later heard while in Italy that a daughter had been born to them (18). Yet at the time of the novel's main action in early 1815, Spire, Cosmo's valet, twice refers to his travels with Sir Charles in France and Italy as having taken place 'thirty years ago' (47, 52), thus in 1785. The co-presence in Paris of the Marquise d'Armand and Sir Charles in or shortly before 1785 would evidently preclude the possibility of his being the father of a daughter born in 1788.

What's in a Name?

The proper names in *Suspense* can also shed some light on Conrad's use of his sources and the workings of his imagination. Nearly all of the geographical names found in the novel belong to the real world and have not been changed, with only three exceptions: Westmoreland is replaced with Yorkshire (17, 24); Brompton with Chiswick (34); and Savoy with Piedmont (32, 146). Details of the townscape of Genoa may well derive from Conrad's visits to the city, the first of which occurred in 1879 when he was a sailor plying the Mediterranean on board the *Europa*, the second in 1889 when he returned from Australia to England in the *Nürnberg*, and the third in 1914 when he and his family were making their way back to England from a visit to Poland that was rudely interrupted by the guns of August heralding the First World War. These occasions may also have acquainted Conrad with the somewhat pejorative slang term *sbirri* ('cops') that is used regularly to identify policemen in *Suspense*.

Members of ruling families have kept their names and ranks in the novel, as have other major figures from the political, military, and naval history of the period: not only Napoleon, 'the Man of Destiny' (145), but also Lord William Bentinck (109, misprinted as 'Bentick'[15]), Count Bubna and his wife (113-14), Louise Durazzo (110), Monsieur de Jaucourt (211), Admiral Keith (4, 66), Montrond (193-94), Lord Nelson (59), Pitt (20), Pozzo di Borgo (180), Sir Charles Stewart (101), Talleyrand (106), and Wellington (17, 64). The name Wycherley (107) does not appear in the Boigne *Memoirs*, but Conrad could have come upon it in other memoirs of the years around 1815, along with that of Fazackerly, as Wycherley was called in the first typescripts of the novel.[16] Several other names were

---

[15] All printed versions of *Suspense* also give the name of the renowned Fieschi family as 'Pieschi' (256), although the typescripts have the correct spelling.

[16] These typescripts are surveyed in our article, 'The Crying of Lot 16: The Drafts and Typescripts of Joseph Conrad's *Suspense*,' *Papers of the Bibliographical Society of America* 88:2 (June 1994), 217-26.

also borrowed from the Comtesse de Boigne, but removed from the type-scripts in the course of revision: Blacas, Burghersh, and Calonne. The same fate befell the Duchess of Albany, the German-born widow of Bonnie Prince Charlie, the Jacobite Young Pretender to the thrones of England and Scotland, and her companion, the Italian poet Vittorio Alfieri.

The more prominent members of the cast of *Suspense* owe their names to the Boigne volumes. Adèle d'Osmond herself has retained her given name but acquired the slightly modified surname of d'Armand. Sir John Legard eventually becomes Sir Charles Latham—a late afterthought, since he was still Sir John in typescript versions of the beginnings of Part III of the text on which Conrad was working in December 1922.[17] Lady Legard *née* Aston (no given name mentioned, from London) appears in *Suspense* as Molly Aston, the girl from Florence that Sir Charles married. Rather minor changes in names are not unusual in Conrad's novel: Bermont became Bernard, Marshall was renamed Martel, and Madame Sappio entered the world of letters with a vowel change as Seppio (132); but all three keep the professions they exercised in the *Memoirs*. Aglae, the Negro maid, was nameless in the Boigne volumes (in which she was ultimately abandoned by Bermont to die of starvation in Dôle, in the Jura mountains, after placing her children in an orphanage). Father Carpi, the savage Clelia, and the trusted Spire owe their fictional names and perhaps also their fictional existence entirely to Conrad's imagination.

The major *dramatis personæ* not provided by the Comtesse de Boigne are Attilio and Cosmo. The former (named Luigi in the early typescripts of Part III) is usually identified by his strange cap with a tassel, and Cosmo does not learn his name until very near the end of the novel (234). Several explanations are possible for Conrad's choice of this name for his romantic revolutionary. *Marco Attilio Regolo* (1719) is the title of one of the many operas by Alessandro Scarlatti, the father of the more famous Domenico. Pietro Metastasio's drama *Attilio* (1740) was translated into English during his lifetime. The opera *Attilio Regolo* (1797) by the Neapolitan composer Domenico Cimarosa concerns the fate of the same early Roman consul who honoured a solemn promise to his Carthaginian captors and was then cruelly put to death by them. Attilio is also the given name of the young patriot Bandiera (1810-1844), who was executed by the

---

[17] The real-world Sir John Legard, sixth baronet (d. 1807) married in 1782 Jane Aston (d. 1833) from Cheshire. See Bernard Burke, *Dictionary of the Peerage and Baronetage* ..., 104th ed. (London, 1967), *s.v.* Legard. Will Conrad also have known that Thomas Paul Latham, of a Manchester family, was made a baronet on 24 May 1919? See *Burke's Peerage, Baronetage and Knightage* (1967), 1147.

Neapolitan authorities for his efforts to unite all of Italy into the Italia Una cherished by Giorgio Viola in *Nostromo*. Unfortunately, there is no evidence to show that Conrad was familiar with the lives of either the Italian patriot or the Roman consul, or with any of the works devoted to the latter's memory; but it can scarcely be doubted that Regulus's concept of honour and Bandiera's dedication to his divided fatherland would have appealed to Conrad.

In *Suspense* Lady Latham is said to have 'insisted on calling [her son] Cosmo' because she had an ancestress 'supposed to have been a connection of the Medici family' (19). Conrad, who knew at least one living person in England called Cosmo (*CL5*, 605), may not have been aware that the second Duke of Gordon (ca. 1721-1752) was also named Cosmo, 'in honour of the Grand Duke of Tuscany [a scion of the Medici family], with whom ... his father was very intimate.'[18] A number of the duke's descendants, in several aristocratic families, have been and perhaps are still being given this shortened form of the name of Cosimo il Magnifico. Conrad seems to have wanted to stress the partly Italian roots of Lady Latham, which may also help to explain Cosmo's apparent fluency in Italian.

Adèle's husband, Count Helion de Montevesso, is Italianized in *Suspense*, but his names are not simply Italian variants of those of his counterpart in the *Memoirs*. It may be possible to account for Conrad's choice of these names, but the story is rather long and complicated. In the summer of 1978, during a Conrad conference at Amiens in Picardy, the late Professor Jean Deurbergue and the elder of the present authors sat down in the wings for a discussion. In its course we questioned each other about the identity of Roger P. de la S——, who figures in the *Tremolino* section of *The Mirror of the Sea* as one of the four partners in the 'international and astonishing syndicate' (*MS* 157) that used a balancelle to deliver guns to the Carlist Legitimists in Spain. P. de la S——, the only Frenchman among the four partners, was described as 'the most Scandinavian-looking of Provençal squires ... a descendant of sea-roving Northmen' (*MS* 159), and his given name Roger may have pointed to a Norman king of Sicily in the early Middle Ages. Much to our mutual surprise, both of us came up with the same solution: the squire could have been a Sabran-Pontevès, since we had been unable to find other young French aristocrats living in Marseilles around 1875 whose initials somehow fitted those given by

---

[18] G. E. Cokayne, *The Complete Peerage ... of the United Kingdom*, new edition, *s.v.* Gordon.

Conrad, and who were actively involved with the Carlist cause.[19] Moreover, P. de la S—, when pronounced, sounds close to Pontevès.

This hypothetical identity finds a measure of confirmation from Ford Madox Ford, who remembered Conrad's accounts of how 'with the Sabran-Penthièvre and other Macmahonists he painted red the port of Marseilles [and] intrigued for Napoleon III ...'[20] These words contain more than one anomaly, not unusual for Ford, who, as Wells put it, displayed a copious carelessness of reminiscence. The combination Sabran-Penthièvre is utterly impossible: Duc de Penthièvre was the title borne by one of Louis XIV's illegitimate descendants whose branch soon died out. But Ford's remark does suggest that Conrad had told Ford of his connection with Marseilles members of the Sabran family in the 1870s.

The Mirror of the Sea also mentions that P. de la S— took the syndicate to lunch at the house of 'his beautiful cousin, married to a wealthy hide and tallow merchant' (*MS* 159). In social terms this marriage is, to say the least, highly unlikely: a wife of the bluest French blood and a husband who deals in hides. A booklet on Conrad's life and works issued by Doubleday situates these lunches in a different venue, at the residence of the mother of P. de la S—.[21]

The most easily accessible tables with genealogical information on the Sabran-Pontevès family show that two twin brothers Pontevès were adopted in 1834 by the childless Duc de Sabran.[22] Both brothers had children born in Marseilles and both became widowers in the 1850s, but both were still alive during Conrad's years in Marseilles. Of the surviving sons in the two families, all but one had married before May 1873, and the unmarried son was the only one still in his mid-twenties. According to

---

[19] René Borricand, in *Nobiliaire de Provence* (Aix-en-Provence, [1975]) lists the following: de Paul de Sausses, de Paul de Lamanon, de Payan de la Garde, de Pelissier de la Coste, Pelletier de la Garde, Pene de la Borde, Pin de la Roche, de Pisani de la Gaude, and de Poulhariez la Réole, none of which meet all the requirements of the initials. The *Répertoire de généalogies françaises imprimées* by Étienne Arnaud (Paris: Berger-Levrault, [1982]) comes closer, with Paris de Sampigny, Pascalis de La Sestrière, Passana de Labusquière, Péres de Lagesse, Perrigault de La Saudrais, Perrotin de La Serre (de la Serrée), de Perthuis de La Salle, Poignand de la Salinière, de Pouzols de La Salce, and Prévost de La Saulaye; but with the sole exception of Pascalis, all these names are from other regions of France.

[20] *Joseph Conrad: A Personal Remembrance* (London: Duckworth, 1924), 71.

[21] *Joseph Conrad: A Sketch* (Garden City, NY: Doubleday, Page, 1924), 15.

[22] Detlev Schweinicke, ed., *Europäische Stammtafeln: Stammtafeln zur Geschichte der europäischen Staaten*, vol. 14, *Les Familles féodales de France, II* (Marburg: Stargardt, 1991), tables 21 and 22.

Conrad's text, P. de la S— had a 'heart blighted by a hopeless passion for his beautiful cousin'; and the North Carolinian member of the syndicate is described as 'the oldest of us ... nearly thirty years old' (*MS* 159, 157). Although the evidence is only circumstantial, the best candidate for a model for P. de la S— is therefore Jean, comte de Sabran-Pontevès (1851-1912). There can be little doubt about the family's traditionalist allegiance: one of Jean's brothers had served in the papal zouaves as a lieutenant,[23] and police documents show that he was a member of the legitimist Société de Saint-Louis, roi de France.[24] When a daughter was born to Jean's eldest brother in 1878, the Bourbon pretender to the throne of France stood as her godfather. The beloved cousin was most likely not the one mentioned by Conrad: the alleged hostess of the syndicate was almost seventeen years older than Jean.

The sisters of Jean de Sabran-Pontevès had both contracted suitable marriages with French noblemen, as had the three daughters of his uncle. There is absolutely no trace of a rich dealer in hides, but the name of the husband of one of Jean's cousins rings a familiar bell: Comte Paul de Boigne, whose residence was the Château de Buissonrond in Chambéry described in the *Memoirs*.

The marriage of Adèle d'Osmond and Benoît de Boigne had remained childless, but the mystery is easily solved. While in India, Boigne had fathered a son with Helen Bennett Begum, and this Charles-Alexandre de Boigne succeeded his father as owner of Buissonrond. He was in turn the father of Paul de Boigne, who in 1852 married a cousin of Jean de Sabran-Pontevès. Paul de Boigne was rich, but he was by no means a dealer in hides. Yet the Provençal squire may have voiced his disapproval of the marriage to Conrad using the term hide merchant, thus visiting his aristocratic disdain upon the children unto the third and fourth generation: a footnote in the *Memoirs* reveals that Adèle d'Osmond's husband was the son of a 'furrier' (I, 113n2). Another piece in our puzzle seems to fit.

The genealogical tables also provide the information that the adoptive father of the twin Pontevès brothers belonged to a branch of the Sabran family that used to own the castle on the Giens Peninsula near Hyères that was bombarded into ruins by a British man-of-war in 1793. The peninsula, the setting of most of Conrad's *The Rover*, was already known to young Korzeniowski in his Marseilles days—perhaps from a visit in the company

---

[23] *Almanach de Gotha*, 1876, p. 242.
[24] From a list in the Archives départementales des Bouches-du-Rhône, M6-3381, 1880.

of Jean de Sabran-Pontevès? The peninsula may also have been used as a base for the gun-running activities in which Conrad was involved.

This is not yet the end of our series of associations. The genealogical tables contain another surprise. When in 1873 a son was born to one of Jean de Sabran-Pontevès' male cousins, the little boy was given the highly unusual name of Hélion. If Conrad was familiar with the family, he may well have heard the name and remembered it precisely because of its extreme rarity. If so, he was indebted to P. de la S— for his choice of both the given name and the surname of Count Helion de Montevesso.[25]

When Conrad sat exploring the Boigne volumes for what was to become his last novel, his memory of the Provençal member of the *Tremolino* syndicate may well have been recalled from the past as he encountered references to the Sabran family.[26] Context can thus inspire the author's creative imagination in ways that leave readers in suspense.

Appropriations and Intertexts

While critics were prompt, as we have seen, to recognize the indebtedness of *Suspense* to the Comtesse de Boigne, this particular case of textual appropriation has been understood not as an interesting and natural phenomenon typical all historical fictions, but chiefly as evidence of an aging author's creative exhaustion. The theory of Conrad's final 'decline' has made it difficult to appreciate the resourcefulness and ingenuity with which Conrad seized the chance offered by the Comtesse. As the title of the book indicates, Conrad was seeking, in *Suspense*, to dramatize an atmosphere, to make the reader see and feel the tensions of a war-weary world poised unwittingly on the brink of Napoleon's fateful Hundred Days. He chose for this purpose to invent a naive protagonist, a young man preoccupied neither with politics nor with personal ties, and then to plunge him into a complex world of domestic unhappiness and political intrigue. Cosmo Latham's entry into the world of Adèle de Montevesso can thus be seen as a dramatic rendering of Conrad's own entry into the historical world of the Comtesse de Boigne. *Suspense* is not primarily the story of

---

[25] Conrad may also have been aware that in 1821 Marie-Louise, the estranged wife of Napoleon I, had given birth to a son who received the title of Prince of Montenuovo from the Austrian Emperor, a nephew of his mother. Montenuovo clearly alludes to the name of the boy's natural father (and later husband of his mother), Count Neipperg, which suggests Neuberg—New Mountain. One Monte- association could easily have led to another.

[26] *Memoirs*, vol. I, pp. 133, 184, 188. The name of de Barral, one of the protagonists of Conrad's *Chance*, also occurs in the *Memoirs* (vol. I, pp. 140, 212-13).

Adèle de Montevesso, but of Cosmo Latham, and the domestic plot which takes place within the confines of the Palazzo Rosso is framed with a second, more dynamic and political set of adventures with Attilio that have nothing to do with the social world of the Comtesse de Boigne. The main interest of *Suspense* lies not in what Conrad has taken from the *Memoirs* of the Comtesse, but in what he has added to them.

The Boigne *Memoirs* are, after all, only one of many sources for the characters and events which come together in Conrad's novel, and these appropriations are by no means exclusively textual. The evocation of Genoa in the troubled days immediately prior to Napoleon's return from Elba is based on a wide assortment of historical and topographical information, the result of Conrad's lifelong fascination with the Napoleonic Era. It is surely no accident that all of Conrad's late novels return to the 'center of the earth,' the Mediterranean shores of Captain Marryat and of his own first maritime adventures.

There can be little doubt that the remarkable talent of Yves Hervouet for recognizing and identifying passages from nineteenth-century French classics in Conrad's works has laid a firm foundation for future studies of Conrad's intertextual and translinguistic appropriations. The phenomenon of Conrad's 'borrowings' continues to raise questions that cannot readily be answered. Yet we would hardly expect the 'French face' of such a cosmopolitan author to display simple traits: indeed, in the last of his novels, it appears that Conrad's 'French face' was wearing an English mask.

APPENDIX: THE BOIGNE *MEMOIRS* AND *SUSPENSE*

In the following columns, passages from the 1907 French and English versions of the Memoirs *of the Comtesse de Boigne are juxtaposed with equivalent passages from* Suspense. *The patient reader will soon see from this sample (which is by no means complete) that Conrad's 'borrowings' from the* Memoirs *are drawn not from the original French text, but from the English translation, since Conrad's choice of wording is all too often identical with the choices made by the anonymous translator. This comparison extends only to samples from the published version of Conrad's novel; earlier typescripts reveal that Conrad's 'borrowings' from the* Memoirs *were initially more extensive, and that some passages were later deleted in revision.*

from *Récits d'une tante: Mémoires de la Comtesse de Boigne*, 4 vols. (Paris: Plon-Nourrit, 1907):	from *Memoirs of the Comtesse de Boigne*, 2 vols. (London: William Heinemann, 1907):	from *Suspense* (London: Dent's Collected Edition, 1954):
Né avec l'esprit le plus fin, le goût le plus délicat, l'imagination la plus vive, le besoin de toutes les communications intellectuelles, il avait passé, par goût, toute sa jeunesse dans la retraite d'une gentilhommière de Yorkshire avec les associés les plus vulgaires. (I, 120)	Endowed with a brilliant intellect, the most delicate taste, the most lively imagination, with a supreme desire for intellectual intercourse, he had spent the whole of his youth in the country society of Yorkshire with associates entirely vulgar. (I, 89)	Born endowed with a good intellect, a lively imagination, and a capacity for social intercourse, it had been his fate ... to spend his early youth in the depths of Yorkshire in surroundings not at all congenial to his tastes. (17-18)
... l'aînée se tenait pour engagée avec lui. (I, 121)	... the elder regarded herself as engaged to him. (I, 89)	... she regarded herself in some way as being engaged to him ... (19)

Elle n'aurait pas osé demander des chevaux pour aller se promener, encore moins pour faire une visite; mais lorsque son mari lui disait d'une voix bien solennelle: «Milady, il est convenable que vous alliez à tel château des environs», son cœur bondissait de joie. «Certainement, sir John, bien volontiers», et elle allait préparer ses atours. (I, 122)

She would never have dared to ask for a horse to go for a ride, much less to pay a call, but if her husband said to her in a solemn voice, 'My lady, it would be advisable for you to call at such and such a house,' her heart would leap for joy. 'Certainly, Sir John, most certainly,' and off she went to get out her finery. (I, 90)

She would never have dreamed of asking for horses for a visit in the neighbourhood, but when her husband remarked, 'I think it would be advisable for you, my lady, to call at such and such a house,' her face would light up, she would answer with alacrity, 'Certainly, Sir Charles,' and go off to array herself magnificently indeed ... (20)

Il était très *Pitt* plutôt que *Tory*. ... Il n'aimait pas beaucoup la noblesse, méprisait les gens à la mode, détestait les parvenus. Il était passionnément attaché à son pays, et avait tous les préjugés et les prétentions des Anglais sur leur suprématie audessus de toutes les autres nations. (I, 125)

He belonged to the party of Pitt rather than to the Tory faction ... He had no great love for the nobility, despised the fashionable world, and detested upstarts. He was passionately attached to his country, and entertained all the prejudices and claims of the English as to their supremacy over all other nations. (I, 92)

In politics he was a partisan of Mr. Pitt rather than a downright Tory. He loved his country, believed in its greatness, in its superior virtue, in its irresistible power. Nothing could shake his fidelity to national prejudices of every sort. He had no great liking for grandees and mere aristocrats, despised the fashionable world, and would have nothing whatever to do with any kind of 'upstart.' (20)

Ce Marshall avait en 1799 porté la vaccine en Italie: (II, 34)

In 1799 this Marshall had brought vaccine to Italy ... (II, 27)

'In '99, you know. ... I am the man who brought vaccine to Italy, first.' (61)

Mes recréations étaient de jouer aux échecs avec un vieux médecin, ou d'entendre causer quelques hommes que venaient voir mon père. (I, 135)	My amusements were to play chess with an old doctor, or to listen to the conversation of men who came to see my father. (I, 100)	'My only amusement was to play a game of chess now and then with an old doctor ... or listen to the conversation of the people who came to see us.' (130-1)
Des dames de la plus haute volée travaillaient dix heurs de la journée pour donner du pain à leurs enfants. ... elles se faisaient des nourceurs, se dénigrant sur leur travail, se plaignant que l'une eût plus de débit que l'autre, en véritables ouvrières. ... Les mœurs étaient encore beaucoup plus relâchées qu'avant la Révolution ... (I, 137-38)	Women of the highest rank worked for ten hours a day to get bread for their children ... they slandered one another, told falsehoods about their work, and complained if one was more successful in her business than another, in the style of ordinary work-women. Morals were even looser than before Revolution ... (I, 102-3).	'I have seen women of the highest rank work ten hours a day to get bread for their children, but they also slandered one another, told falsehoods about their conduct and their work, and quarrelled among themselves in the style of washerwomen. Morals were even looser than in the times before the Revolution.' (131)
Et là je fit la faute insigne, quoique généreuse, de lui dire que je n'avais aucun goût pour lui, que probablement je n'en aurais jamais, mais que s'il voulait assurer le sort et l'indépendance de mes parents, j'aurais une si grande reconnaissance que je l'épouserais sans répugnance. ... Il m'assura ne point se flatter d'en inspirer un plus vif [sentiment]. (I, 151)	I then committed the grave though generous mistake of telling him that I did not care for him in the least, and probably never should, but that if he were willing to secure my parents' future independence, my gratitude would be so great that I could marry him without reluctance. ... He assured me that he did not flatter himself with the possibility of inspiring any deeper feeling. (I,113)	'I could not appreciate what a fatal mistake I was committing by telling him that I didn't care for him in the least and probably never should; but that if he would secure my parents' future comfort my gratitude would be so great that I could marry him, without reluctance and be his loyal friend and wife for life. He ... told me that he didn't flatter himself with the possibility of inspiring any deeper feeling.' (134)

Il voulut prouver à la dédaigneuse beauté qu'une plus jeune, plus jolie, mieux élevée, autrement née, pouvait accepter sa main. (I, 154)	He wished to prove to the disdainful beauty that another girl, younger, prettier, better educated, and of higher birth would accept him. (I, 114)	'... he proposed to me simply to show her that he could find a girl prettier, of higher rank, and in every way more distinguished that would consent to be his wife.' (135)
Très probablement, à vingt ans, je n'aurais pas eu ce courage, mais à seize ans on ne sait pas encore qu'on met en jeu le reste de sa vie. Douze jours après, j'étais mariée. (I, 152)	Probably at the age of twenty I should have been less courageous, but at sixteen one does not know that the rest of one's life is at stake. Twelve days later I was married. (I, 113)	'Probably if I had been twenty or more I would have been less confident; perhaps I wouldn't have had the courage! But at that age I didn't know that my whole life was at stake. Three weeks afterwards I was married.' (136)
Nous avions un assez grand état, des dîners très bons et fréquents, de magnifiques concerts où je chantais. Monsieur de Boigne était ... bien aise de montrer qu'il avait fait l'acquisition d'une jolie machine bien harmonisée. Puis la jalousie orientale le reprenant, il était furieux que j'eusse été regardée, écoutée, surtout admirée ou applaudie, et il me le disait en termes de corps de garde. (116)	We lived in great state, constantly giving fine dinners and magnificent concerts, at which I sang. M. de Boigne was glad ... to exhibit the beautiful and well-articulated machine that he had acquired. Then his Eastern jealousy resumed the upper hand; he was furious because I had been seen or heard, and especially if I had been admired or applauded, and told me so in the language of the guardroom. (I, 116)	'Meantime we lived in great style—dinner parties, concerts. I had a very good voice. I daresay he was anxious enough to show off his latest acquisition, but at the same time he could not bear me being looked at or even spoken to. A fit of oriental jealousy would come over him, especially when I had been much applauded. He would express his feelings to me in barrack-room language.' (137)

Un long séjour dans l'Inde lui avait fait ajouter toutes les jalousies orientales à celles qui se seraient naturellement formées dans l'esprit d'un homme de son âge; mais, pardessus tout, il était doué du caractère le plus complètement désobligeant que Dieu ait jamais accordé à un mortel. ... Il voulait faire sentir la suprématie qu'il attachait à sa grande fortune, et il ne pensait jamais l'exercer que lorsqu'il trouvait le moyen de blesser quelqu'un. Il insultait ses valets; il offensait ses convives; à plus forte raison sa femme était-elle victime ...

... Je crois qu'une femme plus âgée, plus habile ... mettant un grand prix aux jouissances que donne l'argent ... aurait pu tirer beaucoup meilleur parti pour elle et pour lui de la situation où j'étais. (I, 155-56)

Years of life in India had added the full force of Oriental jealousy to that which would naturally arise in the mind of a man of his age; in addition to this, he was endowed with the most disagreeable character that Providence ever granted to man. He was anxious to make every one feel the domination of his great wealth, and he thought that the only mode of making an impression was to hurt the feelings of other people. He insulted his servants, he offended his guests, and his wife was, *a fortiori*, a victim to this grievous fault of character.

... I think that an older and cleverer woman, with greater powers of dissimulation, and attaching greater value to the pleasures which money gives ... would have been able to do better both for herself and him in my situation. (I, 115-16)

'His long life in India added the force of oriental jealousy to that which would be in a sense natural to a man of his age. Moreover, his character was naturally disagreeable. The only way he could make the power of his great fortune felt was by hurting the feelings of other people, of his servants, of his dependents, of his friends. His wife came in for her share. An older and cleverer woman with a certain power of deception and caring for the material pleasures of life could have done better for herself and for him in the situation in which I was placed ...' (137)

Après avoir regardé danser une espèce de ballet, l'Empereur en descendit seul et fit la tournée de la salle, s'adressant exclusivement aux femmes. Il portait son costume impérial ... la culotte en satin blanc ... un habit de velours rouge ... brodé en or sur toutes les coutures, le glaive, éclatant de diamants, par-dessus l'habit. Des ordres, des plaques, aussi en diamants, et une toque avec des plumes tout autour relevée par une ganse de diamants. Ce costume pouvait être beau dessiné, mais pour lui, qui était petit, gros et emprunté dans ses mouvements, il était disgracieux. ...

Je me trouvais placée entre deux femmes que je ne connaissais pas. ...

Selon son usage, il me demandait aussi mon nom; je le lui dis:

« Vous habitez à Beauregard?

— Oui, Sire.

— ... [V]otre mari y fait beaucoup travailler, c'est un service qu'il rend au pays et je lui en sais gré; j'ai de la reconnaissance pour tous les gens qui emploient les ouvriers. Il a été au service anglais?

After watching the performance of a kind of ballet, the Emperor came down alone and went round the room, speaking exclusively to the ladies. He wore his imperial dress ... the waistcoat and white satin knee breeches, the white shoes with gold rosettes, a coat of red velvet ... with gold embroidery upon all the seams ... The costume was well designed, but was utterly unsuited for him on account of his small size, his corpulence, and clumsiness of movement. ... the Emperor seemed to me frightful ... I was standing between two women unknown to me. ... [H]e also asked my name, which I told him.

'You live at Beauregard?'

'Yes, Sire.'

' ... [Y]our husband employs much labour there; I am grateful to him for the service he does to the country, as I am to all who employ workmen. He has been in the English army? ... He is a Savoyard, is he not?'

'Yes, Sire.'

'But you are French, entirely French, and we therefore claim you ... How old are you?'

'I found myself standing in the front row in the Galerie de Diane between two women who were perfect strangers to me. ... the Emperor came down alone, speaking only to the women. He wore his imperial dress of red velvet, laced in all the seams, with white satin breeches, with diamonds on the hilt of his sword and the buckles of his shoes and on his cap with white plumes. It was a well-designed costume but with his short thick figure and the clumsiness of his movements he looked to me frightful ... he asked me my name. I told him.

'"Your husband lives in his province?"

'"Yes, sire."

'"Your husband employs much labour, I hear. I am grateful to him for giving work to the people. This is the proper use of wealth. Hasn't he served in the English army in India?

' ... He is a native of Piedmont, is he not?"

'"Yes, sire."

'"But you are French, entirely French. We have a claim on you. How old are you?"'

... Il est savoyard, n'est-ce pas?»
— Oui, Sire.
— Mais vous, vous êtes Française, tout à fait Française; nous vous réclamons ... Quel âge avez-vous? »
Je le lui dis.
« ... [V]ous avez l'air bien plus jeune. »
... [P]uis revenant à moi, parlant plus bas et d'un ton de confidence:
« Vous n'avez pas d'enfants? Je sais bien que ce n'est pas votre faute, mais arrangez-vous pour en avoir, croyez-moi, pensez-y, je vous donne un bon conseil. »
Je restai confondue, il me regarda un instant, en souriant assez gracieusement, et passa à ma voisine. (I, 273-75)

I told him.
' ... You look much younger.'
... He stepped back half a pace, and then came up to me, speaking lower in a confidential tone:
'You have no children? I know that is not your fault, but you should make better arrangements. Believe me, I am giving you good advice.'
I remained stupefied; he looked at me for a moment with a gracious smile, and went on to my neighbour. (I, 204-5)

'I told him. He said, "You look younger."
Then he came nearer to me and, speaking in a confidential tone, said: "You have no children. I know. I know. It isn't your fault, but you should try to make some other arrangement. Believe me, I am giving you good advice."
'I was dumb with astonishment. He gave me again a very gracious smile and went on.' (146-47)